This edition published by SelectBooks, Inc.
For information address SelectBooks, Inc., New York, New York.

First Edition

ISBN 978-1-59079-286-5

Library of Congress Cataloging-in-Publication Data
Maalouf, Elza S.
 Emerge! : the rise of functional democracy and the future of the Middle East / Elza S. Maalouf.
    pages cm
 Includes bibliographical references and index.
 Summary: "Founder of Center for Human Emergence-Middle East presents a framework for conflict resolution during political polarization based on concepts of Large-Scale Psychology and theories of Levels of Existence, Social Judgment, and Spiral Dynamics. Examines democracy in an evolutionary, value-systems context, focusing on the critical role of Indigenous Intelligence to create functional democracies in the Middle East"-- Provided by publisher.
 ISBN 978-1-59079-286-5 (hardbound book : alk. paper)
 1. Democracy--Social aspects--Middle East. 2. Political culture--Middle East. 3. Political socialization--Middle East. 4. Conflict management--Middle East. 5. Social psychology--Middle East. 6. Social values. 7. Values. 8. Middle East--Social conditions. 9. Middle East--Politics and government. I. Title.
 JQ1758.A91.M33 2014
 320.956--dc23
                    2014016339

Interior book design and production by Janice Benight

Manufactured in the United States of America
10 9 8 7 6 5 4 3 2 1

TO MY DAUGHTER GHINWA
WHO I HAVEN'T SEEN
SINCE SHE WAS THE AGE OF FOUR
AND
TO ALL ARAB MOTHERS AND DAUGHTERS
MAY YOU EMERGE!

CONTENTS

Foreword

by Don Edward Beck, PhD

NEVER BEFORE HAS OUR WORLD carried such a rich tapestry of human diversity in the form of individuals, groups, and nations. Deep ethnic cores and beliefs that have long been repressed or hidden in every part of the world have now become visible. The oppressed and the marginalized are having their voices heard with the help of instant communications, social media, and the Internet. While the West has redefined politics through trade agreements and commerce, the Russians seem to be returning to policies of the Cold War. Everywhere we look dictators are being toppled, corrupt politicians are being exposed, and entire political systems are becoming ever more polarized. Add to that the decades of deconstructionism and egalitarianism in academia and popular culture, and one can see that the traditional model for democracy and its hierarchies of power and control can no longer serve the needs of a complex new world.

This is the chaotic reality we face today, and the tired and outdated tools of the old system can no longer manage the global intricacies shaped by seven billion voices. To understand the emerging trends and govern the future effectively, we need to embrace complexity models that see beyond the stereotypes of ethnicity, religion, culture, nationality, and even business interest and focus on the deeper codes and belief structures that cut across all these categories and identities.

A model that provides some of the answers for much of this emerging complexity is beautifully shown in this book written by my friend and colleague Elza Maalouf. I would first like to say a few words about Elza. After the events of 9/11, I was searching for a professional colleague who understood the value systems of the Middle East and with whom I can make an attempt to influence the course of the Arab-Israeli conflict. From the moment I met Elza, I was struck by her brilliance. It is as if she came prepared to grasp not only the complexities, but the nuances, both in English and Arabic. That simply amazed me. It was clear to me that my goal had been her top priority since she was a law student. No doubt her experiences in working in so many different cultures, including the Middle East, have enabled her to get to the core of any given issue in a microsecond.

With a degree in law from Lebanon coupled with her unchallenged background in spiritual practices, and a keen and experienced business mind, we teamed up to form the Center for Human Emergence Middle East.

Emerge; The Rise of Functional Democracy and the Future of the Middle East is a brilliant synthesis of the work of my late colleague Clare W. Graves, my own fieldwork in many hot spots around the world, including South Africa, and Elza's first-hand experience in our decade-long collaboration in the Middle East. I discovered Graves' work in the mid 1970s while doing academic research on 42 different psychological models. I was looking for a unifying theory that made sense of them all when I discovered his emergent, cyclical, double-helix model of bio-psycho-social development. Nothing else compared to its scholarly background, the painstaking research, and to the basic integrity of the man himself. Over our many years of collaboration, he challenged me to expand the theory by finding difficult places to field-test it, and make the changes that appear to be necessary as existential realities evolve and new and more sophisticated assessment systems become available. I followed Graves' instructions to not simply be the "keeper of his orthodoxy" and expanded the reach of his research with a worldwide constellation of practitioners just as brilliant as Elza. We were life-long friends and colleagues until his passing in 1986.

A considerable part of my post academic career has been focused on the development of Grave's research into models that help with large-scale systems change. From South Africa to the Middle East, and from The Netherlands to Iceland, this model has shown resilience when stakeholders and policy makers embrace a more complex view that is adaptive to change. The world cannot rely on solutions derived from the simple fixed ideologies of the past when we are heading into a future full of complexity and rapid change.

Graves' work identified eight distinct worldviews, or what he called value systems. My 1996 book *Spiral Dynamics* introduced much of Graves' research to the world. In it, I fused the Graves theoretical framework with the fledgling science of memetics, noting that each of the worldviews is in fact a values-MEME, a coding mechanism that inculcates every aspect of society. These worldviews or value systems are now commonly referred to as ᵛMEMES. The central thesis behind this framework, whether it is being used in the Middle East or in the West, is that external approaches designed to improve the human condition are faulted unless they include the essential steps and stages in interior social development. In short, economic, political, and technological innovations must correlate with the levels of complexity of thinking within individuals and entire cultures. Unless the external efforts match, in their respective operating codes, the existing capacities within leaders and the general population in specific countries, they will make things worse, not better.

By its very nature, our model is an open-ended system that sees no final state, no ultimate destination, and no utopian paradise. These cultural stages, much like the Russian dolls, have formed over time into unique mixtures and blends of instructional and survival codes, myths of origin, artistic forms, lifestyles, and sense of community. While they are all legitimate expressions of the human experience, they are not "equal" in their capacities to deal with complex problems in society, and herein lay the global crisis with political leadership today.

There is an old adage that says the safest place in a crisis is the hard truth. Although much of the work we undertook in the Middle East is the subject of this book, it is never enough to try to capture the historic underpinnings of the Middle Eastern conflict from this new and pioneering narrative. Before we began our initiative in Israel and Palestine I had outlined the value-systems nature of this historic conflict in a white paper in 2002. Much progress was made under the leadership of the Palestinian Prime Minister Fayyad, but it seems the historic narrative has returned and has taken a hard grip on the conflict again.

Here are the political realities that existed on the ground that have defined the conflict and patterns of negotiations for peace. On both the Israeli and the Palestinian sides there are distorted recriminations about the past and naïve idealism about the future that can be just as blinding as the tear gas. Alas, we often refuse to deal with the hard truths until all sides lie bloody, exhausted, and vanquished—having jointly destroyed the relationships and physical resources necessary to invent a better future. The mythical phoenix that rises from the ashes is too often a vengeful vulture. But, what if we can find the courageous hearts and shape the visionary minds who can address these core realities differently?

It makes no difference how often the Israelis and the Palestinians are brought to the negotiations table. As long as there exists an asymmetry between the value system structures in both cultures one cannot build a bridge across these very unequal and shaky social and political platforms. Neither the Oslo Accords nor the Camp David Accords had a prayer of being successful because of clear developmental gaps. Too often negotiators are seen as backing one side over the other or placing total blame in one camp. We knew the representatives to these accords are all trapped in highly emotive and historic cul-de-sacs and they were all vulnerable to life and death pressures within their own social groupings. As is most often the case, there is guilt enough to go around.

As you will read on the pages of this book, when our partners in both Israel and Palestine were doing the work on the ground, we sought to create a critical mass for the support of a comprehensive "solution." The focus was primarily on leveling the asymmetry that existed in order for negotiations to be more balanced. It had to have a wider arc of support and deeper levels of sophistication than what the traditional peace process had produced. The goal was to understand the needs of all the mindsets and to begin to craft "full spectrum" solutions, which are fundamentally different from those that a single perspective would offer. To us, the issues were less about democracy, than the question of how to design the best structures for meeting the needs of the people as they develop through the stages that are most natural to them: open, adaptive systems appropriate to their existential realities.

Had the funding mechanism for our work remained in place, the nature of the debate, indeed the very nature of conflict resolution, would have been viewed differently. This is the power of the value-systems approach that provides sophisticated answers to an increasingly complex world. Today, in spite of the conflict being overshadowed by events in the rest of the Middle East, the Israeli–Palestinian crisis remains critical to an overall peace in the region.

Emerge not only represents an accurate and analytical account of a whole systems approach to the Israeli and Palestinian conflict, it offers a platform for political leadership that is evolutionary. It takes into account the complexity of human nature and leaves behind the linearity of the old models. Today, books on the subject of politics rarely address issues of leadership and the design of political systems from a value-systems perspective.

While many so called political experts provide solutions that skim over the surface, in this groundbreaking work, Elza provides a blueprint for the deep change that political systems need. This book is written with a profound understanding of value structures that are at the core of political, economic, social, and religious models. Through her values-systems based analysis of the problems facing the Middle East and other parts of the world, Elza redesigns democracy through what she calls *Functional Democracy* that brings resilience to any given political system. Through rigorous field applications, the *Functional Democracy* model verifies an earlier model I introduced in 2001 entitled *Stratified Democracy*. Elza has injected the 2001 model with colorful real-life examples and identified many new and resilient elements that are being published here for the first time. This book is the definitive authority not only on the political future of the Middle East, but also on the evolution of democracy itself.

Graves would have been delighted with Elza's work and the depth of her perception. In language appropriate to his generation, she would have been "his kinda gal." I don't know how to define a modern feminist who has it all together, but it must be close to someone like Elza Maalouf. I have no doubt that in the history of the Middle East, Elza will be recognized as a person who shifted the culture profoundly, and found ways to do what no other person has been able to accomplish. Read what she says carefully. It is all authentic, well-researched, disciplined, and truly "holistic"—far beyond what others have discovered. She is surrounded by a highly-supportive cast that includes her husband, Said, and her noble puppy, li'l Buddha. I am honored to be called her friend, colleague, and associate.

—Don E. Beck, PhD
Founder, Global Centers for Human Emergence
Coauthor of *Spiral Dynamics: Mastering Values, Leadership, and Change*
Denton, Texas

Introduction

The date of February 2, 2008, holds no particular significance in recent Middle Eastern history. Countless members of NGOs roamed Palestine, going about their daily routine, unaware of an impending global financial crisis that would soon hamper their ability to continue their work. The Arab Spring was as intangible as a permanent peace between the Arabs and the Israelis. Oil prices were reaching record highs and Dubai was adding yet another skyscraper—the tallest building in the world—to its already crowded skyline. It was a Saturday, the Jewish Sabbath, and Israelis who had time off from practical obligations packed their favorite beaches in Tel Aviv or floated on the holy waters of the Dead Sea, their faces baked in therapeutic mud blessed by ancient prophets. At Checkpoint No. 300, Palestinians waited long hours in line to cross the few hundred feet from the West Bank into Israel. The young and the old, the healthy and the frail, all waited patiently to get to work, visit family members, or to receive medical care.

On that morning in February, I was holed up in my hotel room at the American Colony in Jerusalem going over final notes to a speech I was to deliver later that afternoon. The conference for the Build Palestine Initiative where I was speaking represented the culmination of more than three years of work aimed at providing the Palestinians with a new framework for peace. Our work up until that day was a grassroots effort designed to empower community leaders with a new understanding of the nature of change. Over the past three years, news of our work had spread. For weeks prior to the conference the word on the streets of the West Bank was that the "spiral people" were up to something big.

We were filled with anticipation as we left the relative safety of our hotel. In what seemed to be a blink of an eye, our taxi driver, Abu Nidal, drove my partner, Dr. Don Beck, and me through the Israeli checkpoints to our destination in Bethlehem. When we arrived at the Shepherd Hotel, we met our Palestinian colleague, Nafiz, who was in charge of the day's events. We immediately noticed the look of worry on his face as he announced that he expected as many as 1,200 people to attend the event.

We were elated, but Nafiz had only made plans for five hundred attendees. Among the people that were rumored to attend were high ranking Fatah party leaders, dignitaries, and government ministers. We made our way through the boisterous bustle of organizers and table setters. A vision began to crystallize. Could what we were doing here become some kind of a model that helps a uniquely Arab democracy emerge in the region?

Our plans have come a long way from where they started in 2005. Our approach was far different from anything the Palestinians had ever seen. We had gone against the tide of what everyone else was doing. From day one, we had faith in the collective intelligence of the Palestinian people to do the right thing if they were shown sophisticated tools that were more congruent with their culture. In our very first visit I explained to a television producer why members of our organization would not follow the herds of Westerners posing for a photo opportunity at the wall of separation between the West Bank and Israel. I don't see victims here, I explained. I see brilliant people who, if given the right chance, can control their own destiny.

From the beginning, we were asked by the Palestinians not to make them the subject of yet another experiment that deals with the desperate plight of people that Westerners know very little about. We sat and listened to an endless number of stories describing how Western aid organizations were unable to facilitate the creation of a sustainable, thriving habitat. Lost in Western process was a "Memetic" interpretation of what the Palestinian people needed, an understanding of their life conditions and value systems. We understood their plight first-hand and implored them to give our approach a chance.

Like the Palestinians, I was an Arab who fought against tyranny my whole life. I could relate to their struggles. When they inquired about my partner, who spoke with the same Texas twang as George W. Bush, I explained his work in South Africa—how he became one of the main pillars behind that nation's transition from apartheid. I pleaded with them to work with us to learn of a different paradigm, one that will result in meaningful change. They understood that neither my partner nor I were employees of an NGO or the United Nations. We weren't there to feed them for a day, comfort their misery for a fleeting hour, and then leave them on their own.

From the beginning they understood that we had set aside our business, our careers, to work pro bono in support of efforts to bring a new system of thinking to their people. Within a few days of discovering who we were, the people of the West Bank embraced us as they would members of their own tribe who were coming home. They called me al-Ustatha (attorney) Elza and they called Dr. Beck "the freedom fighter." From that day on, we pressed forward in helping the people of Palestine reveal their own capacities to lead, to visualize, and to plan to build a nation designed by its people for its people.

THE VOICES THAT SHAPED MY JOURNEY

I am no stranger to the Middle East. My ancestors roamed the hills and valley of this land for centuries. I was born in the Bekaa valley of Lebanon, less than a three-hour drive to the north of Bethlehem. The town of my birth, Zahle, is the largest Catholic city in the Middle East. When I was ten years old, the fledgling democracy I called home was divided by civil war into sectarian turfs, resulting in the deaths of tens of thousands of people.

I never fully understood why Christians would take up arms against Muslims and vice versa. My father was a businessman who dealt with Jewish partners in Beirut, Sunni suppliers in Syria, and Shia farmers in the Bekaa. I always questioned why and how our values changed from a vision of prosperity and higher consciousness to one that allowed destruction and bloodshed. In Catholic school, half of my classmates were Muslim and the idea that any outside forces could destroy our harmonic existence was beyond the imagination of someone like me, and most of my classmates and our families.

April 20th, 1982, is another day I will never forget. I was sixteen years old and the Lebanese sectarian war reared its ugly head in my own peaceful town. On that day, in the eerie silences between falling bombs, the phone rang at my parent's house. "Elza, please come to the hospital; Carlos has asked to see you." With trepidation and tears welling up in my eyes I quickly ran to the makeshift triage run by volunteer doctors and nurses. Carlos was my high school sweetheart. We had been together in every class since kindergarten. He was an intelligent, responsible, handsome, big-hearted sixteen-year-old.

As I walked down the concrete steps, descending into the basement of this half-completed building, I felt as though I was entering Dante's Inferno. Dozens of wounded people were screaming in pain, laying on stretchers along the concrete floor. Old blankets hung from thin metal wires partitioning the area for some privacy. I looked for Carlos on one of the stretchers. I heard a voice say, "Your friend is in the emergency room."

The emergency unit was a cold, dark concrete room with a door barely hanging on its hinges. I opened it carefully, my heart gripped by fear and anguish. As I entered the room, Carlos' mother's eyes met mine with a deep, poignant sadness—the kind of gaze reserved for those who experience deep loss. In disbelief, I walked slowly toward the boy who had kindled love in my heart. One of his legs was missing, his abdomen was split open and his internal organs were visible. Plastic tubes were protruding from his lungs. He was moaning in pain. I held his hand and kissed his wounded face. "Carlos, it's me Elza." His lips formed a tiny smile. He tried to open his eyes to see me, but couldn't. Before too long, the doctors came in and pushed me away. He needed to be moved immediately to a hospital in Beirut, they said. That was the last time I ever laid eyes on my sweetheart. With Carlos' death, my life took a serious turn. Teenage innocence disappeared.

My confusion and desolation pushed me to question tradition, ethnicity, and religion. At age sixteen, I became disillusioned by the God I prayed to. There was no longer a clear sense of right or wrong. Familiar moorings were blown apart, cast in a million directions. I slowly began to realize that no one was superior, no one upheld a more righteous cause, no one had the one true answer. It became undeniable to me: for better or worse, all human beings were equal. And yet, this shift in perspective was like a dark night of the soul. It was a crisis of faith and a crisis of identity. Nothing in the violent circumstances around me provided direction or affirmation.

Looking back on those first months of Lebanon's civil war, I recognize now that I lost all sense of meaning, whether derived from metaphysical beliefs, family, politics, or tradition. Religion no longer provided an anchor. I could not pray to the saints as I had done in my early years. The magic and sense of mystical reassurance were gone. These were replaced by an inner world of introspection and questioning, seeking elusive truths. I struggled to make sense of what was happening around me. The suffering I witnessed pushed me to look at humanity beyond all divisions and categories. I became consumed by a myriad of unanswered questions:

+ Who is this Christian God that allowed Carlos to feel such pain?

+ Who is this Muslim God in whose name Carlos was killed?

+ What is this war really about—Christians and Muslims fighting against each other?

+ Who are these leaders, who have no sense of history and no sense of the future, who are compelled to open yet another chapter of war and bloodshed?

+ And who are their followers, driving themselves to slaughter like sheep?

+ Who, or what, is the God that is witnessing all of this?

Many Christians in Lebanon blamed the Muslims for allying themselves with the Palestinians and starting the civil war. My upbringing, and later my sense of loss, made me think differently. This was the most significant factor bringing me full circle to where I am today: working on a possible resolution for the Arab–Israeli conflict, and on the elements of a design for an Arab-style democracy.

From the beginning of our mission in the West Bank in 2005, the Palestinians knew that I wasn't ignorant about the role their compatriots played in the destruction of my beloved country. On the Israeli side, my colleagues were equally aware of their destructive role in Lebanon. My desire to overcome my ethnocentric values and align myself with the Palestinian cause was a quality that garnered immediate respect among all Palestinians we came in touch with. My ability to transcend these divisive issues, however, didn't develop overnight. Although I had left Lebanon many years ago, I remained a student of the political culture in the region. Over the years, the evolution of my political views would parallel my personal evolution of consciousness.

Where I grew up, as in much of the Arab World, not a lot was expected of a girl. This fact gave me the freedom to dream, so I dreamt of one day becoming a lawyer who would change laws and empower the equality of women. With the support of a rebellious mother and a loving father I entered the Lebanese University Law School. I thought to myself that the sky was the limit! During this era of Lebanese history, values from the postcolonial French period dominated the university educational system.

Professors with Marxist leaning ideologies, who spent years at the Sorbonne and other French institutions, played a critical role in shaping our young impressionable minds. In my social circle, the works of contemporary socialist and communist Arab philosophers, like Michel Aflaq and Akram Al-Hourani, were required readings. They were the pillars upon which a new Arab identity was being formed. These were the founders of the pan-Arab Baath movement that tantalized the intellectual streets of Cairo, Damascus, and Beirut. They transplanted philosophies born out of the complexity and experience of advanced industrial countries and hoped to apply them in a world that had seen nothing but tribal values and a simple trade and agrarian existence.

On this premature premise, the first wave of Arab Nationalism was born. We all followed the cause believing that this was the system that would bring essential change to our society. Because it values equality and "power to the people," socialism spoke more eloquently to the Arab children (born into middle class values of the 1960s) than any other system of governance. This new ideology (meme) engulfed regional as well as local youth.

In my first year of law school, my circle of friends became part of the very first secular resistance against Israel. We were indoctrinated into the faulty post-colonial thinking that if one Arab brother was being oppressed, then we were all being oppressed. This movement was led by secular Christian and Sunni thought leaders who falsely adopted the view that ancient tribal differences could be overcome if we all fell in line with egalitarian values, a philosophy that was influenced by the existentialist movement in France.

What these thought-pioneers ignored was a factor that would come to dominate my thinking in years to come. It is this: In order for societal values to evolve, all systems must be designed to meet the people where they are, locally. By "systems," I mean the institutions that form a societal structure. The rule of feudal lords over tribal masses has to be replaced by an organizational value-system that the Middle East has had very little experience with.

The transference of foreign ideology brought tyrannical dictators to power under the guise of the Baath Party. As explained by the emerging science of memetics, ideologies born out of Anglo-Saxon values become dangerous tools when applied by feudal lords because they are out of sync with the life conditions and needs of the local people.

Shortly after the death of Egyptian President Gamal Abdel Nasser, the first wave of Arab Nationalism began to crumble. Instead of seeking regional alliances, my generation started to focus on societal reforms within national boundaries. That too, was short-lived, again because existing social and organizational structures favored nepotism and valued clan loyalties over meritocracy.

During my second year of law school something strange appeared on our campus. Over the summer, our Shia classmates completely transformed their appearances. These were young men who were full of enterprising ambition the year before. They had been indistinguishable from other students. They wore Levi jeans and Nike sneakers and freely conversed with women. They participated in heated debates about the nature of governing

and how Lebanon's so-called democracy left out the fair and equal participation of the Shia sect. All that was gone. Dialogue had disappeared. Eye
contact and hand shaking with women became a thing of the past, and so
were many common goals these young men shared with their classmates
just a few short months before.

What happened? These young men could no longer identify with a secular society that denied them equal rights. Now they had a new identity that
gave them a holy sense of purpose. Prominent were their bearded faces,
their black suits, and buttoned up white collars. This was the unmistakable
attire of Iranian revolutionaries. The Islamic Revolution that had swept
through Iran a few years earlier became a new Meme (ideology) for the
oppressed Shia in the region. All the ideology had needed was a new Arab
voice to spread its values and justify its legitimacy as the first modern day
Islamic Revolution. That Arab face was the Shia of Southern Lebanon and
the Bekaa Valley.

Most national boundaries in the Arab world today were drawn by colonial powers. The design of these nations did not emerge naturally through
the creation of common goals and values that bound the people under a
common flag. Colonial clerks who, first and foremost sought the interest
of their own empire, imposed arbitrary geographic boundaries that forced
feuding tribes to compete and claim the new land and its natural resources
for their own tribes. Instead of helping these new nations move forward,
Western interference only constrained their progress.

The values of the Islamic Revolution spoke much louder to these young
men and women than a model for governance designed by French colonialists. The Revolution inspired them. It gave them common purpose and a
personal sense of identity. Suddenly the secular form of resistance to Israel
disappeared. It was replaced by an ideology with the Shia brand of Islam
at its core. This was the birth of an organization that became known the
world over as the Party of God, or Hezbollah.

This was also my first lesson in understanding that places like the Middle East cannot be governed by the same values that govern the West. This
was my first insight into how different values needed different governing
systems, and that if a healthy system doesn't form, a tyrannical system may
emerge. This lead to one of the most important principles on which the
(spiral, memetic) framework discussed in *Emerge!* is based: the design of
local governance that fits.

What I witnessed that year became a lifelong commitment to understanding how cultures develop, and how and why values spread.

- How do certain governing systems vary from each other and why?

- What causes certain cultures to emerge and prosper while others stagnate and fall apart?

- What is it that makes bright young men derive more inspiration out of a speech by a radical cleric than they do out of the teachings of a Sorbonne-trained professor?

The Shia of Lebanon had some government representation, but their struggle was as much with members of their own sect as it was with a French-designed constitution. Shia land barons sought to control any potential competition coming from their own sect by denying basic education to their own people. If this was a microcosm of the region's struggle it represented the internal conflicts within each sect and political party as much as the struggle with external forces. In later years, I learned that regardless of how sophisticated a society is, internal conflicts play as much of a role as external conflicts in any debate, challenge, or struggle. A deep understanding of the nature of conflict is another important principle upon which the (spiral, memetic) framework discussed in *Emerge!* is built.

Regardless of how bright my Shia classmates were, their rise would have been limited by the feudal values that controlled Lebanon's political and economic systems. In spite of outer appearances, this part of the world is still ruled by tribes and dictators who control resources and political destinies. Meritocracy cannot rise past the influence of the Za'eem (Clan Leader), or the Sheikh in today's Middle East. Advancement based on merit in this part of world is a value that requires far more societal sophistication than the reality on the ground. In spite of all the modernity, the most effective mechanisms that deliver services to people are still the religious organizations, Sheikhs, and clan leaders.

- When it comes to feeding the poor, the local church and Mosque are the trusted caretakers.

- When it comes to protection from a warlord seeking bloody retribution, the clan leader and his henchmen are the trusted defenders.

- When it comes to the funding of a development plan, the Za'eem has the final say.

In spite of all the modernity of the Arab world, a formal government is still viewed as an incompetent institution and its employees as corrupt and untrustworthy in this part of the world and at this stage of societal development. These are some of the realities that gave birth to the rebellion against so-called Arab nations, when all they really were was a collection of tribes waging wars against each other.

Today, there are no functioning democracies to speak of in the Arab World. Short of benevolent monarchies, there is not wide acceptance of other forms of political leadership. The Arab Spring is taking the region by storm as the people look to undo the injustice of the past. Would all the bloodshed and destruction that accompanies the Arab Spring be just another false start? Would it be just another contrived ideology that would fail, or would it result in the true emergence of nation-states in the region? As bloody as the Arab Spring has been, it is the first sign of the rise of the indigenous intelligence, the primary catalyst that drives the human spirit to collectively carry on its quest towards self-determination.

Many years after graduating from law school, I continued my search for ways to help the region emerge by exploring different theories and methodologies. I knew I needed to mature intellectually, spiritually, and empathetically before I would be able to help develop societies or organizations. I delved into various consciousness studies and psychological theories, and mastered their primary principles enough to teach them. For a few years this was how I learned more about myself and the evolution of societies. I learned enough to develop the deep internal strength needed to serve a larger cause.

AN EVOLUTIONARY MODEL FOR POLITICS

In parallel to my spiritual development, I sought scientific knowledge that might enable me to decipher the complexities of culture. I wanted to study the mechanisms that made certain cultures prone to development while others remained resistant. My inquiry into the Western mind led me to Ken Wilber, an integral philosopher who synthesized various theories into a new developmental model called All Quadrants All Levels. (AQAL).

I met Wilber in person at the Integral Institute in Boulder, Colorado, when I trained in the first Integral Leadership Program. At the seminar there were many references to Dr. Don Beck and his pioneering theory of Spiral Dynamics Integral. I had been reading about Spiral Dynamics and memetics on and off, but hadn't seen wide applications based on its teachings. Theoreticians like Beck usually receive attention posthumously, but to my surprise, Wilber spoke of Beck as a contemporary who was currently offering training seminars and helping governments around the globe. I wanted to meet the man who seemed to be a global agent of change. I suspected he could have different views and philosophies on which governing systems work for different cultures.

On the first day of the Spiral Dynamics seminar, Dr. Beck detailed his involvement in South Africa with Nelson Mandela and F. W. de Klerk. The experience was still fresh in his mind as he explained the different strategies he employed over the years to help South Africa transition from apartheid. At the end of the first day, Dr. Beck handed me a white paper he had written in 2002 about a "stratified approach" to solving the Israeli-Palestinian conflict. For the rest of seminar I listened intently, conscious of the possibilities in the Middle East and the possibility of what a potential partnership with Dr. Beck might bring.

By then I knew the cultural "Memes" and the history of the Middle East and the nature of the conflict. Dr. Beck knew the large-scale framework and the design process—a scaffolding upon which we might leverage all of my knowledge. This was a man who thoroughly understood the nature of tribal and feudal cultures. He could decipher the anatomy of any conflict, be it in hot spots in immediate crisis or more complex pathologies in first world countries. Far beyond any ideology or "ism," his vision challenged the fundamental construct of how to approach solutions for the developing world. Eventually, Dr. Beck and I formed the Center for Human Emergence Middle East (CHE-Mideast) and designed the elements of the Build Palestine Initiative, which will be discussed in detail later in this book.

Throughout *Emerge!* I use the terms "memes," "memetics," and "value systems" in referring to many of the constructs underpinning the framework we apply to regional and organizational systems. These ideas are at the heart of the specialized field of social psychology called Spiral Dynamics. By explaining the genesis of these concepts, I hope to give you, the reader, a better understanding of the theoretical origins and the academic research behind the use of these strategies, templates, and concepts.

The word "meme" is a term originally coined by evolutionary biologist Richard Dawkins. (It rhymes with gene.) Just like a gene that carries the codes that define human characteristics, a meme carries the codes that define societal characteristics, such as values and ideologies. A meme is a unit of cultural DNA, a behavior or an idea that is capable of replicating itself. Memes are expressed in music, fads, fashion, and so on, and define our lives in terms of religion, philosophy, politics, and economics. In Spiral

Dynamics theory, Dr. Don Beck and his former colleague Christopher Cowan coined the word "'MEME," meaning value-systems memes, to rebrand what founding developmental psychologist Dr. Clare W. Graves called "value systems." Dr. Graves conducted research over five decades and described the value systems concept as follows:

> Value systems are: a hierarchically ordered, always open to change set of ethics, values, preference, priorities and purposes by which individuals, groups and cultures can come to live.[1] These value-systems have a spectrum of meaning for words and expressions at every level of personal and cultural development.

Dr. Beck and my work focus on determining the existing and emergent values systems for a culture, specifically identifying its unique local expressions. This focus on the indigenous content of a value system provides a memetic interpretation of what is critical to the design of governance, and explains why governing systems adopted from the West—which are unaware of the indigenous memes—are destined to end in failure.

Emerge! is not about faulting the West for its past mistakes or blaming Arabs for their lack of collective visionary leadership. It is about political designs with an appropriate cultural fit. It is about employing a scientific approach to assess where a culture is in its social emergence, and to design the institutions that are appropriate for supporting particular levels of development.

Emerge! is about teaching young men and women how to build institutions that are indigenous to their culture in order to be sustainable long after the designers are gone. The Anglo-Saxon model for social advancement has been centuries in the making and has evolved and adapted to the unique challenges arising from the uniquely Western experience. From the dark ages of the Spanish Inquisition, through the European Renaissance to the Industrial Revolution and the Enlightenment Era, these historic milestones shaped Western culture into what it is today.

In contrast, the Arab world had very little experience with Industrial Age values that ushered in the nation-states of Europe. Yet the appearance of oil in the region a few decades ago changed the trajectory of regional development. Suddenly, modernity could be purchased by oil wealth. The "hard work ethic" of the industrialized West became unnecessary for building cultural capacities in the Arab world.

Great thinkers throughout the Arab world, preaching the ideals of nation-states, did not have the chance to see their dreams come true. The natural process of developing a successful economy from the skills and labor of a working class that progresses into a formidable middle class did not occur. This stage was replaced by top-down planning by governments that controlled the sudden acquisition of wealth from oil resources. Western powers encouraged dictators and weak leaders in the region to squander the national wealth without long-term planning aimed at institutional and human development.

This became an unprecedented experiment in what happens when cultures that remain centered in tribal and feudal values are suddenly thrust into great wealth that causes the evolution of their values to a higher level to be arrested. Unfortunately, as a result, having all that money could not in itself develop a resilient society to compete with Western ingenuity and innovation.

THE NEED FOR A WHOLE-SYSTEMS APPROACH

Many books have been written about the miraculous transformation that the resources of oil brought to the Middle East, and much criticism has been leveled at the extravagance that resulted from this wealth. Western think tanks offered to develop the region's infrastructure, but fell short on developing sustainable capacities within the Arabs. The reason this continues to be a reality today is because non-indigenous plans tend to miss one pivotal element of cultural development: the value system of the people they are designing for. Development in the Middle East has been focused on what to do with oil wealth. Should oil disappear in the next fifty years, as much of the research suggests, where would the region be? These are some of the concerns that are addressed in this book and the reasons why I call on the leaders of the region to start focusing now on developing our full human capacities, especially in women and the Millennial Generation.

Will the Arab Spring be another passing phase of disappointment, or will it be the spark that marks the beginning of real and lasting change? My bet is on the latter—if certain internal and external conditions coalesce to accomplish what needs to be done.

Emerge! delineates *life conditions* from a whole-systems perspective. Like the Center for Human Emergences' work in Palestine, this book presents design solutions that fit the indigenous culture and that will place the region on an open path towards self-reliance and global inclusion. Women and Arab youth play a crucial role in that vision.

I have spent time with young men and women from every walk of life in the Middle East, from the remote village at the epicenter of the Syrian uprising to the cosmopolitan streets of Abu Dhabi and Kuwait, to the Millennials in Egypt and Palestine. This is the generation that's helping

Arab societies transition from a historical patriarchy to a newly dawning meritocracy. My aim is to provide some guidelines for policy makers on how to design institutional reforms based on this emerging science of value systems. Included are the details based on our approach, and an analysis of why this approach is different than any other. I articulate the whole-systems design that holds the potential to transform the future of the Middle East, chapter by chapter as follows:

In Chapter One

Chapter one, "From the Clash to the Confluence of Civilizations," makes the initial case for why we should begin to view the history of the region through value systems lenses. This is where a shift in thinking begins.

After a society reaches a certain level of complexity, a leap in social perspective must occur. The value system of the natural indigenous intelligence turns from a culturally specific frame of reference to a frame of reference that recognizes all of the cultures' existing societal strata. This chapter makes the case for why the Arab Spring represents the region's long-awaited quantum leap to a new perspective. This chapter reframes the evolution of Arab society through a unique prism rarely explored by most historians, scholars, or policy makers: a history reframed through memetic lenses provides a realistic developmental view of the region.

At the CHE-Mideast the study of value systems and memes defines a culture or an entire society. Chapter one examines the tribalistic nature of the Middle East through the prism of value systems. We examine the culture historically from the days of the Prophet Mohammed through the end of the Ottoman Empire. Then we take a closer look at the misalignment of the governing structures left behind by colonial powers. Many of the fallacies of Arab Nationalism are examined, and a deep memetic analysis explains why all of these governing styles were misaligned with the *life conditions* within the culture.

Chapter one sets the stage for the reader to understand that the era of dictatorships was just a passing developmental stage along the journey towards the formation of nation-states. It also examines how oil wealth has arrested cultural development and has given the region a false sense of economic security. Memetics explains why this current transition, the toughest for tribal and feudal cultures, is a pivotal stage and necessary prerequisite for the formation of nation-states. It is reminiscent of the feudal and tribal Middle Ages of Europe.

This chapter distinguishes why the Arab Spring, empowered by the information age, women, and the Millennial Generation, is representative of a culture that can no longer accept oppression. It looks at how the confluence of these forces became the catalyst that sparked the search for a new paradigm and future vision.

Just as democracies in the new world were different than the social democracies of Western Europe, democracies of the Middle East will be vastly different from any we've seen. They will be shaped by the unique memetics of Arab culture that reflect democracies created by these specific people for these specific people and their *life conditions*. This chapter opens the doorway to thinking in terms of evolving systems. Social and governing systems must change in response to changing *life conditions*, or become toxic and pathological to their societies.

In Chapter Two

Chapter two introduces the main theoretical framework on which the book is based, and is titled "Governance and the Stages of Human Development."

The work of developmental psychologists Dr. Clare W. Graves and Dr. Don E. Beck represent the most ambitious effort ever undertaken in the mapping of human existence. This chapter details the academic history and theoretical background of Spiral Dynamics theory, described by the Canadian publication *Maclean's Magazine* as "the theory that explains everything."[2] In this chapter I provide the reasons why I developed specific ideas that support this approach and relevant data and experiences that are specific to the Middle East in an effort to tailor academic Western concepts to the regions' experiential reality. Many of the models Dr. Beck and I developed in the field are being published here for the first time.

Spiral Dynamics is based on a bio-psycho-social approach to measuring human values. It describes how cultures emerge and why. This chapter conveys not only the history of the Spiral Dynamics conceptual framework, but also our application at the Center for Emergence-Mideast of the Spiral Dynamics principles to the unique values of the Middle East.

This chapter describes how cultural values are measurable through the eight-known levels of human existence. Each system has distinct value preferences and unique characteristics, including social, political, and economic inclinations; life priorities; ways of thinking; and an array of other metrics. The reader can gain an understanding of what research now confirms: value systems exist as structures in the brain, as well as within groups and within cultures.[3] This chapter presents different ways of governing based on value systems preferences from around the world. It analyses how Western and Middle Eastern leaders have been approaching the issue of governance from what Graves called "the values of subsistence."

In Chapter Three

Chapter three is titled "MEMEtocracy—What Makes Democracy Functional." This is a concept that I have developed as a result of my experience with and exposure to the value-systems framework over the last decade. This is a conceptual framework for nonlinear democracy. This chapter details the Operating System of the framework. Democracy is injected with certain evolutionary concepts that keep it from becoming toxic. I describe the genesis of the framework and how I came to believe that this is the best model for the future of governance.

This chapter also illustrates the science behind political cycles, the natural phases of political systems, the value-systems approach to politics, and the concept of Seventh-Level Yellow political leadership. We pay close attention to the essential value-system transition phases, which are often missed in political structures. This all-important model also defines the character and the qualifications of individuals who will inform the future of political design. Through the illustration of this conceptual framework, the reader will gain an understanding of how politics naturally shift away from the divisive language of bi-partisanship to higher values of trans-partisanship or the "Third Way." The nature of Seventh-Level Yellow political leadership shifts the polarity from rightist and leftists to centrists and functionalists, and from win or lose to a win-win . . . with a third win for the entire electorate and for the future of governance.

In Chapter Four

In addition to Dr. Beck's groundbreaking work with Graves' value-systems framework, Beck developed many of his own concepts in Large-Scale Psychology. Chapter four is the first place where much of this work is published, along with what Dr. Beck and I developed together at the CHE-Mideast for our joint work in Israel and Palestine.

Chapter four is titled "Mapping the Anatomy of Conflict and Identifying the Spectrum of Values." Many of the concepts in this chapter illustrate the bigger framework through which the concepts of MEMEtocracy can be applied. MEMEtocracy thoroughly examines many prominent social psychology theorists and adds the dimension of the value systems to the existing body of knowledge. Large-Scale Psychology was a new branch of study that Dr. Beck and I introduced to the American Psychological Association in 2008.[4] In this chapter we examine conflict resolution at its core, including the value-systems approach to the Assimilation Contrast Effect model. I developed two unique constructs, which are presented next:

the critical *Indigenous Intelligence* component for social design and the Anatomy of a Conflict Model.

Many other Large-Scale design concepts, such as Natural Design and Functional Flow, and the Hearts and Minds Strategy that were designed by Beck for South Africa, are discussed in detail. The chapter ends with the placement of all these concepts into a grand model called MeshWORKS Solutions. This is the final piece of the framework that makes this applicable theoretical approach to conflict resolution and cultural change operational.

In Chapter Five

Chapter five, "Uncovering the *Indigenous Intelligence*: A Case Study of Israel and Palestine, introduces the reader to the application of these methodologies via a real-world case study: The Build Palestine Initiative at the CHE-Mideast. Here we detail our experience in building the very first integral emergence model in the entire Arab world. I describe the value-systems obstacles we encountered and how we dealt with embedded beliefs and mores that played a big role in preventing Palestinian and Israeli societies from moving forward.

We show how we used references to colors in the Spiral Dynamics theory that represent the different developmental stages to diffuse the polarization among various groups of Palestinians and among disparate groups of Israelis that continue to fuel and exacerbate the conflicts between Palestine and Israel. This case study familiarizes the reader with the unique approach that ultimately led to the empowerment of thousands of Palestinian change agents. It details the steps on how to assist in the creation of *Superordinate Goals* that are unique to every culture. This chapter specifies the full meaning of the concept of *Indigenous Intelligence* and what its implications are within the parameters of this methodology.

I also explain the unique mapping that we undertook in order to understand the total forces shaping the Palestinian experience, including the issue on how to deal with the asymmetry that exists between the Palestinians and the Israelis. Memetic mapping is important prior to designing any developmental programs because of the asymmetries it can reveal. I list the painstaking steps that were involved in shifting the focus of people in both cultures away from the historic patterns of conflict, resolution initiatives, and negotiations. Memetic mapping helps focus the respective cultures on building their own capacities in order to level existing asymmetries so that negotiations are functional.

This chapter introduces the concept of *Seventh-Level Yellow listening* and the *5-Deep strata* where I show the difference between how the world has approached negotiations from a surface level, and how our method-ologies dig into four deeper layers of cultural complexity to identify and address the issues at their roots.

There has been no other large-scale application of value system-based conflict resolution than the Build Palestine Initiative. The chapter concludes with the grand design that culminated in the events of February 2, 2008. This was the day the Palestinians acknowledged ownership for designing their own future state. The experience described in this chapter contributes to the design of an "emergence template" that has the potential for region-wide applications, needing only minor adjustments for each culture.

In Chapters Six and Seven

The last two chapters of the book represent the design section for the future of the Middle East. Chapter six is titled "Functional Governance Empowered by *Functional Capitalism*." It starts with the empowerment of *prosper and let prosper* values. This is a historic catalyst for cultural emergence.

Chapter six also takes a look at my first-hand experience with the corporate world of the Middle East, visualizing how to make the memes of prosperity at the organizational level more sustainable. I introduce my whole-systems approach to corporate consulting and how the adoption of the values paradigm at the organizational level can lead to culture-wide sustainability. The goal in this chapter is to empower business pioneers to take the lead in designing sustainability practices that go beyond the age of oil. In the process, these new business values inform the culture and the political process.

With functional governance comes *Functional Capitalism*. In this chap-ter I analyze the value-systems challenges facing many Middle Eastern corporations as their leadership transitions from heroic and ad-hoc values to more tempered and strategic values. This is where we present the tools needed to shift organizational practices from an approach that copies Western strategies. Instead, we build layers of functionality that facilitate the creation of resilient ecosystems based on indigenous intelligence in the Middle East. These are the half steps in Mideast business that will transform the culture at large.

The elegant design of resilient organizations relies upon knowing when to use best practices and where. From government institutions to large businesses, the reader will understand how designs that are informed by memetic profiles of individuals, their capacities and potential make for very effective forms of management. We will see how corporations and government agencies can be run more efficiently and learn how businesses can be made more profitable. Readers will also understand the steps Western businesses need to take to alter their views of the region and how to become trusted partners that contribute to common future goals. This chapter concludes with strategies on how to empower a new corporate ethic that can attract a more scientific mindset, which has defined the first world and its evolving corporate culture for many decades.

The book concludes with discussion of how to safeguard political stability in the Middle East. This seventh chapter, titled "The Arab Memome Project: Designing for the 21st Century Arabic Renaissance," is based on a project that has been more than ten years in the making at the CHE-Mideast: *The Arab Memome Project.* This project details a preliminary road map for the future development of the Middle East that must begin in earnest now. While many countries and global corporations have participated in the physical infrastructure development of the region, very little attention has been given to building memetically-fit institutions. This chapter outlines our ambitions to memetically map the entire region in order to facilitate its emergence.

The Middle East today suffers from the worst form of income inequalities. Should oil disappear without a sustainable economy in place, the Middle East could become the poorest region in the world. Crucial to the development of the future of the Middle East is the empowerment of a middle class. We will examine the necessary steps needed to make this goal a reality. We will take a closer look at the miracle of Dubai and Abu Dhabi and evaluate their modernization experience, choosing best practices to inform a region-wide design for a sustainable economy.

This last chapter outlines the need to create a regional superordinate goal that has the capacity to transcend the current dysfunction and bloodshed in the Arab world. It describes how to strategically align the future of governance and corporate practices to that new superordinate goal, and how to uphold the new vision of a prosperous future for the Middle East.

At the core of the reforms that the Arab Memome Project seeks, is the reform of the educational system and a focus on the future of the Arab child. This is a far-reaching program that addresses the structural faults at the heart of the region's inability to create middle class values. It provides an "ecosystem" approach. The chapter concludes with the mythological *hero's journey* and how that journey compares to what the Mideast is experiencing today. I explain why, in spite of all the pain and bloodshed, this hero's journey must begin in earnest or the entire region will be relegated to a footnote in humanity's cosmic reality.

The ideas presented in *Emerge!* are based on the belief that whole-systems thinking is the way of the future. By applying the unique principles of the emerging science of values systems, the tools of Large-Scale Psychology, and the concepts of MEMEtocracy as described in the book, a far more resilient development model can emerge.

An essential part of designing the whole-systems model is a keen awareness of the values of the specific society that we are designing for. We will no longer utilize models that impose unnatural and contrived systems on indigenous people. The concepts detailed in this book provide the optimal example of leadership that works.

The linearity of past models for democracy is "out." The complexity of the models of MEMEtocracy is "in." Imposing non-indigenous models is outmoded and inoperable. Meeting the *Indigenous Intelligences* where they are is the effective method to achieve a functional, flourishing democracy. These models are empowered by the virtues of full transparency and resilient design. This is the future of political leadership emboldened by a global village that can no longer tolerate its leaders' complacencies and corrupt practices. Old and corrupt political systems are obsolete. Models for evolutionary politics are the basis for renewal.

Emerge! is about 21st century leadership, changing the game of politics not just for Arab leaders, but for anyone who is inspired to serve in an open system society, empowered by cutting edge practices that exude humanity's highest virtues.

ONE

From the Clash to the Confluence of Civilizations

There are very few moments in our lives where we have the privilege to witness history taking place. This is one of those moments. This is one of those times. The people of Egypt have spoken, their voices have been heard, and Egypt will never be the same . . .

President Barack Obama
February 11, 2011

The world joined the Egyptian people in celebrating the joy that comes from the breaking of shackles and the downfall of tyrants. Now, more than three years have passed since the U.S. president made this statement. What started as an anomaly in Tunisia in January, 2011, crystallized into a powerful meme taking the Middle East by storm. The West called it the Arab Spring. Arabs were too divided to give a meaningful definition to what was happening. On this day of February 11, 2011, after thirty years of rule, Hosni Mubarak was ousted from power. Egypt stood on the threshold of a return to past glory. In Tahrir Square the tweeters tweeted and the facebookers posted exuberantly. Voices rose from young crowds in unison, inflaming the passions of revolution, "Lift your heads up high. You are Egyptians!" was the cry in endearing Egyptian Arabic. The response from other parts of the square came in repeated bursts of "Allah-hoo-Akbar!," the exclamation that means "God is Great."

Weeks before this day, Tahrir Square lived up to its name, the square of liberation. Egyptians from every walk of life had come together as a microcosm of Egyptian culture united in the pursuit of a better life. Sunnis, Shia, Copts, and Salafis relinquished their historic differences in favor of a vision of what a future without Mubarak could be. Christians encircled Muslims at evening prayer, protecting them from attacks that might have come from Mubarak's *Baltagia,* hired mercenary gangs and plain-clothed police who would have used brutal intimidation tactics. Anyone standing in Tahrir Square on that day was engulfed with the euphoria of a vibrant promise for the future of Egypt and the rest of the Middle East.

For centuries the people of this region have called Egypt *Um el Dunia*, the mother of the universe. On this day, after a brief absence that clouded her leadership, she was reclaiming her rightful place in history. On this day, the future of her people never looked brighter. In scenes reminiscent of the social revolution that engulfed the West in the 1960s, Egyptian youths with iPhones and BlackBerrys in hand were ushering in their own brand of change. The power of people unfazed by fear was contagious. Egyptians converged from every part of the country to bear witness to history being made in their lifetimes.

Exiled politicians returned in droves and gave lively interviews to every reporter with a microphone and a camera. Their command of the English language was flawless, as was their deep awareness of the direction Egypt needed to take in the future. These exiles were the pride of Egyptian culture. They taught at Western universities and came from a national lineage of Nobel laureates in peace, poetry, and literature. Their analysis of the future of Egypt paralleled the sophisticated intellectuals of Western think tanks who had shaped Middle Eastern policy for decades.

With Mohamed el Baradei at their helm, an agreement was negotiated with the army that could transition Egypt into a civil society with democratic institutions and elections. From here on the Egyptian people would utilize a democratic process. After the overthrow of Mubarak, the world was assured that Egypt would rejoin the world community as a newly-minted democracy with vibrant institutions represented by the faces that defined the rebellion. Western media assured the world that democracy in the Middle East was born.

Just a few days after Egypt's moment in the limelight, things began to change. Members of the Muslim Brotherhood, who sat out the revolution and allowed it to have the face of spontaneous rebellion, became more visible. Suddenly, Wael Ghoneim, the Egyptian Google executive whose social media efforts helped start the revolt, was booed off stage at a rally in Tahrir Square intended to honor his contribution.

The crowds were far more interested in hearing from the older and wiser Sheikh Qaradawi and what he had to say about the future of Egypt. Qaradawi, an elder but also a charismatic Muslim Brotherhood cleric, had been exiled from Egypt for over three decades. His sermons, however, inspired millions of Muslims on the Arab Satellite network Al Jazeera. While Ghoniem represented the elite and the educated in Tahrir Square, Sheikh Qaradawi represented a majority of Egyptians who had been disenfranchised and marginalized in the Arab World, those who lived in poverty. Qaradawi's journey was a hero's return.

The loud speakers repeatedly urged the jubilant throngs to make room for Doctor Yousef Qaradawi. Just as the Shia revolution had Khomeini's face emblazoned to it after the fall of the Shah, the Sunni revolution looked to Sheikh Qaradawi after the fall of Mubarak. Qaradawi spoke to the values of people from every sect and religion. He stirred the passions of the people who shared the common plight of being left behind. Within a few minutes the crowd swelled to over a million people. The chants grew louder repeating a new catchphrase: "Al Sha'ab yurid tahqeeq al'umneeat": "The people want to make the promise a reality."

The Sheikh did not disappoint his followers. Interrupted by constant applause, Qaradawi urged Egyptians of every sect to denounce the tyrants of the past and unite in building the future of Egypt. He warned Arab leaders not to stubbornly resist the wave of change or stand in the way of history. In rhetoric guaranteed to stir the passions of the Arab street, he ended by calling on Allah Almighty to help the Palestinians reclaim the Aqsa Mosque in Jerusalem and pave the way for him to preach there in safety.

Inspired by its resurging popularity, the Muslim Brotherhood's leadership decided to form a new political arm, the Freedom and Justice Party. This was just in time for the National Conference elections of the new parliament. In early 2012 the Freedom and Justice Party's newly-formed political arm won a majority of the parliamentary seats and became an unstoppable force. By June it became allies with both liberals and extreme Salafis, uniting opposing forces as it created the Democratic Alliance, a secular coalition of which the Freedom and Justice Party was the largest organization. This victory ushered in Mohamed Morsi, the first democratically elected Egyptian president.

The *"one-person, one-vote"* model for governance worked. Now every nation operating in the region, from Saudi Arabia to Israel and the United States, had reason to worry. The older ideology swayed the masses, rather than the new. Why did the people make this choice? How could the analysts have been so far off in their assessment of the values and belief systems of the majority? Caught by surprise, the West and other national leaders rushed to offer opinions on whether the Brotherhood's victory in Egypt would inspire the underground Muslim Brotherhood factions to rise and topple the oil monarchies.

Panic set in everywhere. Would Egypt become a supporter of state-sponsored terrorism? Would Egypt's long-standing peace with Israel become a thing of the past? And in one of the most debated questions (that is yet to be answered), in the absence of the active engagement of U.S. foreign policy would this important U.S. ally turn its back on thirty years of regional cooperation and become a destabilizing force in the Middle East and North Africa?

In the new Middle East, rising from the ashes of dictatorships, the world expected and rejoiced at the Egyptian democracy. But a closer look at the intricate dynamics in the region suggests a narrative that is far more complex than just ousting the dictator in charge. Western leaders were not aware of the memetic structures and historic patterns in the Middle East. This led them to expect that the outcome of Arab revolutions would resemble that of past revolutions around the world. However, with democracy comes transparency.

In this case, democratic transparency demonstrated that the majority of Egyptians resonate more to the aspirations of the Muslim Brotherhood than to liberal democratic ideals. Although Mohammed el Baradei and Amro Mousa are well known on the world stage, their platform spoke to very few Egyptians. This event also uncovered a reality that very few non-Arabs understood, the indigenous assessment of where the Middle East stood in establishing its social institutions.

More importantly, what was missing was an indigenously-informed approach to how to design for the emergence of such institutions. The memetic insights that can be learned from indigenous intelligences in the local environment are a critical assessment. In order for the Middle East to move forward with prosperity and self-reliance for its citizens, not just past the dictatorship era, but well past the Age of Oil, this crucial step in the evaluation of the local *life conditions* and values cannot be over emphasized.

In the history of modern humanity, many theories have been applied in helping different regions of the world fill in developmental gaps, from the Modernization theory on which much of Western emergence was based, and that continues to prove its success in China and India today, to Ataturk's systemic reforms (called Kemalists) that brought Turkey into modern-day existence. Ataturk's reforms still more closely parallel the values of the region today. It is Islamic by nature but is secular in its inclusion. The key questions for the region's development are these:

+ In a region where the center of gravity of the culture is embedded in tribal and feudal mindsets, how can a model like that of modern-day Turkey serve to accommodate the region's transition to true nation-states?

+ Could the Ottoman Turks, who created the first model for governance and the rule of law in the Muslim world, be a guide to other Muslim and secular countries in the region?

To answer these questions, we have to reexamine the region's history through lenses rarely used or understood by historians or political scientists: the lenses that examine the evolution of value systems in the region.

MEMETIC HISTORY OF THE MIDDLE EAST

Before the dawn of Islam, the Middle East was a vast nomadic desert mostly identified with feudal lords who led their tribes in the conquest and domination of other tribes and clans. For centuries, warrior kings dominated the landscape and ruled the region. The Byzantines and the Sasanians sponsored these powerful nomadic mercenaries to help them exercise control over vast lands and to quell any aggression. The alliances created by competing dynasties, the Byzantines and the Sasanians, kept local Arab tribes divided. There was no reason to seek unity among themselves.

The old adage of divide and conquer worked well in the age of antiquity, until something far more meaningful united the Arab tribes against the will of their emperors. As disease and war weakened the Byzantines and the Sasanians, the region witnessed the birth of Islam. The dawn of this new religion brought order and structure to the time known in Islamic literature as the pre-Islamic Age of Ignorance (Al Jahaliyyah) that symbolized Arabian tribal living.

The rise of Prophet Mohammad presented these tribes with a new sense of purpose that ushered in an era of order and the rule of Sharia Law. This was a powerful upward movement in human social evolution from the nomadic structure of tribal living to an orderly purpose-driven societal structure. The same tribes that had feuded for centuries suddenly found common purpose through Godly guidance, a law that required self-restraint and adaption to values beyond those which defined nomadic life.

Rituals provided a means for adherence to the rules of everyday living. These daily rituals supplanted the celebrations of tribal conquest. The drive for instant gratification gave way to the Abrahamic notion of sacrificing now to make gains later, in a meaningful world of inward reflection and self-discipline. This was the first social and spiritual structure that made sense to tribal reality as the next stage in its cultural evolution.

The promise of Islam spread by leaps and bounds through every village and town. In its early days, the rule of Islam (Al-Khilafah) was representative of a direct democracy or an elective monarchy. Orderly, yet simple and effective in its prescription, Islam provided unity to indigenous cultures at similar levels of development. It provided a common lens through which its people could visualize a safe and certain future. The values of Islam spoke to the masses and united them under the strength of godly fear. Cultural harmonies evolved into political unity under the rule of Khalifah, spreading Islam as a complete and orderly social system.

Socially, politically, and religiously, Islam overtook tribal law as a superior model for governance. It spread faster than any one might have predicted. It is said that within the lifetime of the children who met the Prophet Mohammed, Arab armies controlled vast lands extending from the Pyrenees Mountains in Europe to the Indus River in South Asia, an area that spanned more than five thousand miles.[5]

According to Ottoman understanding, the state's primary responsibility was to defend and extend the land of the Muslims and to ensure security and harmony within its borders. While Europe was going through the Dark Ages, the values of Islam continued to spread. The Turkish Ottomans took on the mantle of the Khalifah rule led by a sultan and spread its virtues.

During the first three hundred years of Ottoman rule, scientific and medical discoveries thrived. Philosophy and astronomical exploration reached new heights. Cairo, Baghdad, Istanbul, and Andalusia were places where Islamic scholarship became the source of cultural advancement. Arab intellectuals translated the works of Chinese and Greek philosophers. It was their translations, from Socrates to Aristotle, which preserved the philosophy in the Arabic language. The later translation to Latin of these voluminous works by Arabs became the catalysts that reignited the European Renaissance. However, with unchallenged powers, the empire became complacent towards the end of the fourteenth century.

By the late fifteenth century, with its governance overtaken by religious conservatives, the Ottoman Empire began to see its renaissance wane. The Islamic system that provided for the welfare and spiritual needs of its believers became increasingly focused on Islamic puritanism rather than on the full system of teachings that were essential for the governance and maintenance of an empire. The conservative shift came at the cost of science, medicine, and technological advancement, as well as philosophy and art.

At the same time, new trade routes between Europe and the Americas weakened the monopolistic Ottoman grip on historical trade routes, contributing further to the decline of the Ottoman Empire. By the seventeenth century, the Industrial Revolution took Western Europe by storm. The dawn of a new era of values in Europe and the West brought science and technological advancement to the fore in that part of the world, and brought military superiority to Europe. The Ottomans simply had neither the infrastructure nor the know-how to compete.

By the mid 1800s the Ottomans, unaware of the shortcomings of a patchy and decentralized system for governance that placed religion over all else, could not maintain control over some of their territories. Parts of Europe, previously complacent under Ottoman control, now sought to free themselves. The Ottomans couldn't stop them. The social order and spiritual energy that helped spread and maintain the influence of Islam for five hundred years came face to face with a fierce enemy—the likes of which no sultan has seen—a value system infused with the energy of technological innovation. This very different driving force had produced superiority through military technology. The empire did not value and prioritize innovative advancements at this time, and the Ottomans struggled to catch up and gain a competitive technological edge to no avail.

It took less than fifty years for the Ottoman Empire to lose control over most of its vast territory. In an effort to salvage Ottoman dominance, Islam was pushed aside by the revolution of the Young Turks in 1908. The Ottoman Empire became a state with a constitutional monarchy and the sultan no longer had executive powers. A parliament was formed with representatives chosen from the provinces, but it was all too late. After decades of gradually losing its economic and military superiority, the remaining hollow and obsolete structure of power came crashing down. By the end of WWI, the Ottoman Empire was reduced to the size of modern-day Turkey. Regional Islamic leadership had disappeared. Without a sustainable infrastructure in place, the entire region of tribes led by feudal lords, with few skills for modern self-reliance, was left in the hands of Western colonialists.

During the period of English and French colonial mandates a general from the West, with no understanding of the local culture, replaced the Turkish governor (the Wali). The citizens of the governorates hoped that the rule of English and French would be temporary. They expected that within a reasonable period of time foreign powers would be replaced by local leaders. Then, once the local leadership had an understanding of how Western democracies operate, the region could begin to thrive and resume its journey along the path to modernization. But the colonizing governments soon developed strategic interests that did not necessarily include helping the region emerge into modern-day democratic states. They were anxious to secure natural resources to fuel technological progress, and this altered their objectives. Instead of securing trade channels, the colonial governments now sought to actively explore and occupy the region before carving it up into partitions that facilitated natural resource management.

In a few short years, the Middle East was divided into arbitrary partitions, countries with boundaries that had no alignment with the existing tribal or clan allegiances but favored the colonialists' exploitive interests. These newly formed countries were recognized by The League of Nations and later the UN, but were left to their own devices after a relatively short period of administrative guardianship. The entire colonization process ignored thousands of years of tribal and ancestral history.

However, as long as the local population paid taxes and obeyed the law, there was little intrusion into their way of life from the colonial government. The Ottomans never gave the citizens of their governorates a reason to rise up in protest. They never inspired a national sense of patriotism. A defined national identity would have been the next social development stage, but that needed decades to emerge. The region wasn't ready for it.

This was a critical time in the modern history of the Middle East, a time when hundreds of years of tribal safety and trust in the old ways were threatened by two major factors that still shape the region till this day.

The first was the disappearance of the fatherly values of Islamic law and order.

The second was the sudden appearance of nation-states designed by Western colonialists who knew very little about the historic value systems (memetics) of the region.

Colonialism provided an illusion of sovereignty. Historic, religious, and territorial disputes were expected to disappear once a common flag was flown over the newly drawn borders. However, Western abstract values and ideals had no real-world connection to the history and *life conditions* of the people in the Mideast, and thus created sadly dysfunctional forms of governance.

To secure their economic interest in the region, Western powers initially appointed kings thought to have historic ties to the land. Confident in the implementation of their strategic grand design for the region, the mandates came to an end in a few short decades as kingdoms cropped up all over the Middle East. Tunisia had King Mohammad VIII, Libya had King Muhammad Idris AL-Senussi, Egypt had King Farouk, and this pattern spread through the rest of the region, including monarchies in Syria, Iraq, and Alhijaz, (now Saudi Arabia). To the inhabitants of the region, the imposition of monarchies by the West was tantamount to a return to Ottoman rule. Although these monarchs were in touch with the historic values of the subjects, they simply were not in step with their changing needs and minds that were now open to many different political ideologies of the West. Within a few short decades, these monarchies were toppled as the arduous search for identity continued.

THE MEMETIC INTERPRETATION OF ARAB NATIONALISM

In its initial phases, Arab nationalism was culturally defined by one's ability to hurl insults at the imperialists—including the United States. As a child I remember my uncle taking me to the meetings of the Syrian National Party, one of many Arab nationalists parties in Lebanon. The Syrian National Party sought to reunite Syria and Lebanon under one flag. During those meetings, attendees escalated the rhetoric to levels where I thought military action was imminent. Shouts came from every corner of the room: "Those Imperialist dogs have not felt the wrath of the Arabs," and "We will slaughter them all." Then coffee was served with freshly made Baklawa and we all went home. This scene repeated many times over and nothing was ever accomplished.

In retrospect this was my earliest introduction into the Arab political mindset. I had a front row seat near the stage upon which the future of the entire region was being defined. The new Middle East was expressing itself through individual feudal aspirations that had innumerable generals but very few, if any foot soldiers. These values confused rhetoric with action and were more of a way to blow off steam than a real plan to recruit people, develop their capacities, and get things done. This reflected the frustration of the culture during that developmental stage. Up until the start of the Arab Spring, these were the values that still defined the majority of the region and the mindset of the Arab street. In addition to the imperialists, the Zionists and dictators were on the receiving end of those insults.

The nationalistic ideal has been a part of the political landscape as far back as the 19th century. Under Ottoman rule ideas on nationalism were discussed in secret. In a postcolonial era that sought individual freedoms, those ideas could no longer be kept as a part of the underground. Christian and Sunni intellectuals, borrowing from several Western romantic notions on nationalism, started to preach the virtues of unity for the Arab nation. Shia, being a sidelined sect, always suspected that the whole notion was a Sunni ploy for regional dominance and never joined in its calling.[6] Prominent thought leaders like Sati' Al-Husri, and Michel Aflaq competed to define the nature of the movement in the minds of the Arab street. This self-seeking could be viewed as the most difficult stage of cultural evolution. The Arab world not only needed to be defined by a uniquely Arab nationalist philosophy, but also required institutional planning aligned with the defining characteristics of this emergent stage of social development.

The intellectuals of the day didn't care much for the existing form of governance, nor did they care to advocate for functional social institutions. They focused on finding a charismatic Arab leader to unite all Arabs. Since it was commonly believed that what determined a nation was people who were bound together by a common language, culture, religion, and historical heritage, the conditions for nation building have historically been present. This was the presumption of these influential thinkers.

Husri's thinking on nationalism was influenced by the German school of nation building that advocated for the unity of all Germans. He advocated German-style nationalism, but his assessment of the capacities of Arab people and their leaders lacked foresight. Outside of simple tribal leadership, the region had no formidable forms of governance that could transcend and include their tribal identities. Aflaq, a Syrian Christian and French-educated philosopher, was the ideological father of the Ba'ath movement. He had advocated for many restrictions and harsh treatments of citizens as a way to discipline them into developing national values. Cruelty was identified by Aflaq as the most reliable means to bring about the desired transformation of the people.[7] This was fascism 101. Cruelty was necessary, he thought, in order to shock people out of their ignorance. This became an expedient meme (ideology and value) that spoke volumes to rising leaders.

A German-style of nationalism and disciplined cruelty were popularized by Stalin and became the two dominant ideologies adopted from the West. The proponents of these ideologies competed for the hearts and minds of the Arab street and its leadership. These memes actually still define much of the values of leaders today.

In later years Aflaq took on the tyrannical Saddam Hussein as his most prized pupil. Hussein elevated violence and cruelty to a new level in order to make up for his intellectual limitations. Aflaq needed an apprentice who could eliminate opposition to the Ba'ath philosophy, and Hussein was the perfect fit. Hussein thought of Aflaq as a father figure and emerged as the enforcer of the Ba'ath cruelty measures.

The classical nature of Husri's philosophy attracted far more willing believers than the punitive nature of Aflaq's philosophy and the Ba'ath movement. In the search for what Arab nationalism represented, the misguided call under which Arab nationalism thrived in the 1950s and 60s was the simple belief in the strength of the commonality of language.

Soon Egypt, *Um el-Dunia,* delivered a charismatic trailblazer, Gamal Abdul Nasser, who promised to lead the region into a new frontier where the glorious past would be transformed into a splendid future. Nasser represented the region's hero archetype upon whom the people projected all their aspirations. He was tall and handsome, with great oratory skills and the Arab knack for the rhetoric. Always dressed in the latest Western suit, his pictures adorned the walls of every living room where people believed in Husri's brand of Arab Nationalism.

Within two years after becoming the president of Egypt, in an act that was designed to galvanize Arab pride, Nasser nationalized the Suez Canal. This dealt a significant blow to British and French influence in the region. His program of nationalizing all that was owned by Western interests, along with land reforms that gave power to the people, made him the face of new and powerful Arab memes. The imperialists were finally gone and the hard work of reformation and building the next phase of Arab identity had begun.

Nasser then set his sights on regional alliances by creating the United Arab Republic. The UAR brought Syria and Egypt under one flag. The future looked bright as Nasser was carried on the shoulders of crowds anywhere he spoke in the Middle East. The land barons who controlled the Arab wealth were no longer protected by the Ottomans and the colonialists. This era was coming to an end. The average Arab on the street hailed this radical redistribution of wealth as the dawn of an era of equality and economic prosperity. Land barons, the traditional power brokers throughout Egypt and the Levant, had every reason to worry. Nasser modeled his leadership style after the Soviet Union.

The Soviets had a culture rich in classical music, Western literature, innovations in science, industrial production, and advancements in agriculture, but Egypt was relatively behind on developing most of these cultural capacities. To the Egyptians, these were their first steps toward a new, untested system, and there was very little infrastructure in place to support it all. Historically, for example, agriculture was in the hands of Egypt's big landowners, who knew how to use the land, maintain it, irrigate it, rotate its crops, and market their products. Land reforms gave plots to small and often uneducated farmers who had few skills to insure the success of Nasser's policies. Without long-term development plans guided by a competent government that provided support and education to these farmers, the reforms had a low chance of success. Land reforms and nationalization of economic activity required leadership far more sophisticated than the existing system could deliver. The modern development of every nation requires long-term planning and support structures at each node of a productive process.

Today, five, ten, and twenty-year development plans are required by organizations like the IMF or the World Bank, even from the poorest countries in the world. Arab Nationalism under Nasser's leadership had little long-term planning in place as these ideals were founded more on arousing the passions of crowds for a day to gain populist fervor. Political unity also brought together the masses under the rhetoric of a common enemy. This garnered far more emotion and inspired more action than the discussions about long-term prosperity. This was Nasser's style for gaining regional dominance. He preached the propaganda that people wanted to hear without having a full understanding of the hard long-term commitment needed to make the dream a reality. If it was language that united a people, Nasser's rhetoric definitely delivered.

Around the same time that Egypt united with Syria, Iraq and Jordan declared their own union as a slightly different Arab Federation. King Faisal II of Iraq and his cousin King Hussein of Jordan reunified the Hashemite Kingdom as an answer to the growing popularity of Nasser. Not to be upstaged in his regional leadership, Nasser immediately welcomed the Arab Federation and declared that any enemy of the new federation was an enemy of the Arab nation. However, having to answer to far more pressing political and economic issues coming from within Iraq and Jordan, the Arab Federation fell apart within six months of being created.

Nasser spent a few years jockeying for power among Syrians who remained divided regarding which ideology to follow. Many Syrians were loyalists to Aflaq, their native son, while others were divided between Nasser's brand of socialism and pure communism. These were ideological perspectives born in Western value systems and adopted by Western-educated Arabs without proof that any of these ideas might ultimately be functional in the Middle East.

Nasser had no tolerance for communism and radical leftist ideologues. In a few short years, Nasser's platform emerged as a socialist style of leadership and fell into the polarizing reality of the Cold War. To the West, Nasserism by default became the acceptable alternative to communism. As he pushed for more centralized control, the economic reality in Egypt and Syria began to expose the misalignment of this political ideology with the needs of the Arab people. By September 1961, a group of Syrian army officers declared Syria's independence and the first experiment in Arab nationalism came to an abrupt end.[8] Nasser declared that he would never give up on his dream of uniting the great and dignified Arab people, but there were fewer people cheering him on this time.

Arab nationalism was still only an idea. However, those decades of soul searching dislodged historic power from tribes and monarchs and placed it in the hands of the emerging middle class and the military elite. Bloody, rhetorical, and chaotic, Arab socialism as a system for governing proved to be a misfit with the *life conditions* and the reality on the ground. As the notion of pan-Arab nationalism was dying a slow death, it dealt the Arabs a final moral blow in the 1967 Arab–Israeli War.

While Israel was advancing into Arab territory on many fronts, Nasser, desperate to reclaim his past glory, erroneously announced to the entire region that Israel was being destroyed at the hands of Arab armies. In reality, the 1967 Six-Day war with Israel had dealt a military blow that went down in history as the most humiliating defeat the modern Arab world had ever seen. Nasser went down in flames. Two decades of rhetoric about the unification of Arab people, to be united by a struggle against a common enemy, came to an end. Many who followed Nasser still believe he died of a broken heart because he lacked the skills to advance the cause he so passionately believed in. This will remain Nasser's legacy, and Arab nationalism will remain an essential building block defining the emergence of the region for many decades to come.

Revolutions that seek socialist equality, which result in true nation building, are sometimes based on abstract notions like "liberté égalité fraternité." These are the pillars upon which modern day nation-states like France and the United States were built. These values are codes from a cultural development stage that is just beginning to emerge in the Arab world today, and will take many decades to define. By falsely trying to adapt Western values within a culture that had very little capacity to sustain them, these developmental codes placed the region on quicksand in the form of a hollow framework of power that was incongruent with the realities and needs of the local people. The Arab world is divided by sects, religion, and clans. A proper governing system must deal with polarizing dynamics in order to neutralize their historic divisiveness first, before a platform for nationalistic values becomes feasible. Reality in the Middle East of the 1960s was one of rampant illiteracy. The experiment with socialism illustrated the need for bringing the goal of education to the forefront of the entire region as a catalyst for development.

THE CONSEQUENCES OF ABSOLUTE POWER

With the failure of Nasser's Pan-Arabism, Aflaq's Baathist ideology began to appeal more to the remaining leaders who had historical ties to various geographic regions. These leaders were mostly military men who had abandoned ideas of regional power and instead focused on the Baathist doctrine, shocking people out of ignorance and into developing the discipline needed to build a nation-state. Although a Christian founded the Baathist ideology, this construct drew heavily from Islam. Aflaq described Ba'athism in a five-volume work that connected pan-Arabism to Islam. This work represented an idealistic community and called upon all Arabs who had fallen under the rule of the Ottomans and Europeans to reclaim their glory through modernization and a socialist system with uniquely Arabic characteristics.[9]

Ba'athist Party chapters began appearing in every country, from Saudi Arabia to the East and as far West as Libya, taking on local flavors. Developing national values among more homogenous people within smaller geographic confines was a far better solution than Nasser's grand design. If successful, this phase had the potential to build the social institutional systems and the robust infrastructure needed within each individual nation, setting the stage for regional unity in decades to come.

But alas, Aflaq's cruelty took on a completely different meaning when implemented by feudal military men. In the 1970s the region witnessed the rise of military rulers who, after being in power for brief periods of time, turned their countries into dictatorships. The interpretation of cruelty and the goals of a uniquely Arab brand of socialism took on a far bloodier dimension than Aflaq or any ideologue would have ever imagined.

In absence of strong social institutions, absolute power began to define Arab politics. It was an era of feudal lords with modern weaponry and the resources to finance egocentric ambitions whether the people willed it or not. It was the era of absolute dictatorships: Saddam Hussein in Iraq, Hafez Assad in Syria, Zein al Abidine in Tunisia, and Muammar Al Gaddafi in Libya. The entire region of so-called nations became closed societies, their leaders administering punitive punishment to whichever sect, group, or religion opposed their platform. Under the guise of socialism, leaders squandered their nations resources and used them to enrich themselves and their inner circles. Under the guise of Ba'ath, Hafez Assad slaughtered tens of thousands of his people in the town of Hama, and Saddam Hussein gassed thousands of Kurds in Halabja. Everywhere in the region contrived ideologies of all types ran head-on into each other, leaving hundreds of thousands dead in their path. Leading ideologies developed many characteristics in common. These characteristics defined modes of oppression for many decades within the Arab nations, until the onset of the Arab Spring.

Also, by invoking Arab pride and branding Israel as a common enemy, and the United States as Israel's imperial ally, Assad, Hussein, Gaddafi, and other leaders justified their actions. Israel's peace agreements between Egypt and Jordan limited the rhetoric about this conflict, but the peace agreements did very little to gain the hearts and minds of the Arab street.

Anwar Sadat, the third president of Egypt, was a visionary who wanted to create the Egyptian Industrial Revolution for the forty million *Falahine* (farmers). He wanted to empower a democracy that guaranteed a larger, educated middle class, but he was ineffective in eliminating corruption within the political and military machinery. As he ambitiously sought reforms and peace with Israel, the radical elements in his country rallied to assure that his plans were short-lived.

But Mubarak was satisfied with running Egypt as a police state. He exercised selective repression that was equivalent to dictatorial practices. By appearing to curb radical Islam and maintain the peace with Israel, he assured the massive flow of Western aid that enriched the embedded political and military establishment. In order to understand how effective the current revolutions were in the region, it is imperative to assess the damage and the impressions these decades of dictatorships left on the collective psyche of the larger Arab population.

Dictators were able to oppress their people and enrich themselves openly because these societies lacked the capacities and vision to build complex social institutions that oversee and care for a variety of essential needs in modern society. This level of societal sophistication only comes after the majority of a culture has moved from a tribal or feudal stage, through an order-driven stage of social development, and comes to believe in the power of institutions and systems over the power of a few charismatic leaders.

In the research I've done for this book, I have uncovered many commonalities among Arab leaders during this critical phase of development. Here are some unmistakable patterns of behavior that I have observed:

The Manifesto of an Arab Dictator:

First: Convince the people that the primary reason for their misery is the presence of the State of Israel and build a regional political alliance that confirms the myth.

This belief has been pounded into the psyche of every man woman and child on the Arab street for more than five decades. Projecting blame for the collective misery on the "evil enemy" worked well as a relief valve through which pent up anger was channeled. This ideology was spread further by firebrand Imams who championed the idea of the United States as the greatest evil because of its blind support for Israel.

As this ideology festered into pathology, every extremist wanting to start an Al-Qaeda-like chapter—from Detroit to the Philippines—invoked the Palestinian cause. It is worth noting that the Arabs collectively abused the Palestinian cause and used it for political and monetary gain more than anyone else. To this day, Palestinian and neighboring Arab politicians squander the aid intended to ease the plight of the refugees who are still kept in camps.

The United Nations defines Palestinian refugees as those who lost their homes and livelihood due to the 1948 conflict, which was a period of time that stretched between June 1st, 1946 and May 15th, 1948, and includes all their descendants. Today, they estimate the number of people living in camps has increased from 750,000 in 1948 to almost five million people. There are eight camps in Gaza with 1,200,000 refugees, ten in Jordan with over 2 million refugees, nineteen in the West Bank totaling approximately 740,000, at least ten in Syria with approximately 500,000, and ten in Lebanon with approximately 450,000.[10]

Second: Suspend most (if not all) civil liberties and impose emergency laws. This occurs under the guise of a government need to assure peace, which requires an absence of the right to due process.

The absence of civil liberties and due process horrified free thinkers everywhere. Those who dare to speak out against totalitarian regimes were hauled off to prison never to be heard from again. The fate of these so-called infidels was intentionally well publicized, and the fear of speaking out spread at a systemic level.

Third: Produce carefully constructed propaganda disguised as the truth, and disseminate this within the educational system. The antiquated educational system thus serves to praise leadership for preserving Arab dignity and safety and cautions against the adoption of Western values.

Of all the dictatorial policies, the manipulation of the educational system was the most damaging to the development of long-term capacities within Arab culture. Education and the expansion of the mind, a thinking public, was a dangerous thing in the eyes of a dictator. In 2006 The United Nations Development Program reported that the region suffered from illiteracy rates as high as 80 percent.[11] On average the entire Arab world produces less than one tenth of the scientific papers per capita compared to developed countries. The basic institutions that build human capacities simply do not exist.

Fourth: Build a military and a ruling class whose primary purpose is to keep the dictator in power.

This was a common and very pervasive policy that assured the anchoring of the regime, particularly where rich natural resources or sources of foreign aid exist. In most cases, without a national development plan, working for the regime was a good opportunity to earn a living. Generations of people became overtly loyal to the regime because they knew that this privilege could be taken away at the first sign of dissent. This also created an internal division—people seeking to preserve the status quo prolonged the demise of a dictator when his time had come. Examples abound, including Tahrir Square and demonstrations on the streets of Damascus, Tripoli, Sanaa, and Tunis.[12]

HOW OIL ARRESTED SOCIAL DEVELOPMENT IN ARAB CULTURES

In oil-rich nations that didn't adopt Arab style socialism into their governing philosophy, social evolution was constrained or limited in other ways. Before the region could emerge into an evolutionary stage that valued institutions common to nation-states, such as the rule of law, equal rights, respect for labor unions, and social justice, the discovery of oil was an arresting factor in social evolution. This discovery lulled societies into a false sense of prosperity. In comparing the differences between a less developed society of an oil-rich country in the Middle East to another oil-rich country with developed institutions like Norway, one can see the vast difference in how money and wealth are perceived through the prism of value systems.

In the Middle East, aside from developing some of the physical infrastructure necessary to manage related resources, oil revenue was pocketed by the extended royal circle, the merchant class, and tribal leaders. In Norway, no more than 4 percent of oil revenue is used to help pay for public services and the rest is invested in a National wealth fund to support future generations of Norwegians.[13]

In addition to developing social institutions, there is a need for the creation of economic policies to invest in advancements aimed at placing these countries on track to compete with other emerging economies. Without developed social institutions and future-looking economic policies, a high percentage of oil revenues will continue to be squandered. It is estimated that within fifty years oil wells will begin to dry up in the Middle East. By then, it might be too late for the region to start building their most sustainable resource—the human resource. It was only recently that King Abdullah of Saudi Arabia took on the visionary mantle by creating a long-term plan, a national development program that goes beyond the age of oil.

Between 2005 and today, King Abdullah institutionalized scholarships for study abroad in the West, allocated 25 percent of the national budget to education, established a co-ed University for Science and Technology, created developmental energy projects, sponsored public health engagement (including breast cancer awareness) and Center for Disease Control cooperation, established a crackdown on terrorist ideologies within the country, gave women the right to vote in some municipal elections in 2015 and to participate in the Olympics, criminalized domestic violence (psychological, sexual, and physical) and workplace violence, instituted numerous other reforms, and called for interfaith dialogue.

THE ARAB SPRING REDEFINED

No one questions the role that social media played as a catalyst that mobilized young Arabs to rebel against their leaders. Tweets (*taghreed* in Arabic) and text messages enabled crowds to gather at the speed of light, and citizens' videos of police brutality were broadcast all over the world. Technology has enabled the oppressed to rise over the oppressor.

In the 1800s, Europe's Industrial Age and military might broke the grip of the Ottomans. Today, the information age is breaking the grip of dictators on the people of the Middle East.

One of the biggest flaws inherent in a closed-system dictatorship, especially in Syria, is the arcane intelligence apparatus, a relic of the Cold War. When my work with The Harvard Group's Abraham Path Initiative took us through Syria, the phones in our hotel rooms were always tapped. We could hear the clicks, breathing and whispering of agents listening to our conversations. The tapping of phone lines and eavesdropping on conversations were easily circumvented by the young generation, children of Google, Facebook, Skype and Yahoo. Young Syrians communicated with people all over the world, freely accessing unfiltered information. They saw how the rest of the world was passing them by. They exchanged dreams, ambitions and love songs with their peers from every part of the world. The dictatorial barrier of fear that their parents experienced did not exist for them, as they were able to witness and experience what freedom felt like over cyberspace.

As the Arab Spring rolled through different parts of the region, it took on different forms:

In Libya

After Gaddafi was killed, the Libyans started on the long road to organize and structure their society, which was still centered in exploitative tribal value systems. While Libya stayed out of the news after the attacks on the American embassy, it became clear that Al Qaeda factions had a strong presence there. The future of Libya is not as promising as NATO made it out to be.

In Syria

Syria's pattern of emergence looks a lot different than the patterns in Egypt, Libya, or Tunisia. NATO and the West were careful not to meddle with Iran, Syria's protector and benefactor. Meanwhile, Syria, Iran, Iraq, and Lebanon's Hezbollah formed a regional alliance called the Shia Crescent. Any military interference there could lead to a regional conflict between Shias and Sunnis. Assad so far has followed in the footsteps of his father and shows no signs of relinquishing power. Although Syria denied the use of chemical weapons against its own people, it allowed Russian President Putin to negotiate the removal of such weapons from the country.

Ironically, while Assad allowed the most radicalized Al-Qaeda affiliates from all over the Middle East and North Africa to train in Syria in order to infiltrate Iraq and Lebanon, those same radical groups began to fight Assad himself. In Syria the revolution against the Assad regime became the most violent in the region. Assad regained the upper hand, but innocent citizens continued to die by the thousands and refugees continued to flee to neighboring countries.

At the same time, the smaller, opposing groups that make up the Syrian opposition went through their own bloody battle for dominance. Several offshoots of Al Qaeda assassinated Syrian opposition leaders one by one. The entire opposition seems to be a disorganized rag-tag band of warriors without a coherent agenda, divided and unpredictable.

If the Syrian regime collapses, it will have dire ramifications for Lebanon, Jordan and Israel. The only organized movement to fill the power vacuum would be the Muslim Brotherhood. In Syria, the Muslim Brotherhood is far more radicalized than in Egypt.

In Egypt

Cultural emergence will usually be tumultuous. For example, after only a year in power, Mohammed Morsi was ousted as Egypt's President. The crowds in Tahrir Square that ousted him were even larger than the ones that ousted Mubarak. Morsi's inability to revive a worsening economy, his autocratic style in claiming power, and placing himself above the courts, were all viewed by the military and the opposition as the Brotherhood's plans to monopolize power over the future of Egypt.[14]

The most disturbing sign of Morsi's weak leadership came when he turned a blind eye to the terrorist activities in Sinai by Islamist factions. Some even believe that by not supporting the military in its fight against these factions he was a de facto supporter of their activities. In Egypt, the one-person-one-vote system of democracy elected the Muslim Brotherhood to lead, but they proved to be too weak to control the radicals within their own party, and this caused their own demise. In December 2013 the interim Egyptian government backed by the military declared the Muslim Brotherhood to be a terrorist organization. The government outlawed the country's most successful recent political movement and vowed to treat anyone who belonged to it as a terrorist.[15]

It took the Muslim Brotherhood more than seven decades to achieve a gradually- increased acceptance into Egypt's political system. They missed a prime opportunity to become a significant part of the political process as their long effort crashed in less than a year. Their leadership may realize now that the doctrine upon which they built their political platform no longer serves the majority of Egyptians' values today. If the new leadership fails to involve the more moderate members of the Muslim Brotherhood in the political process, the movement will go underground. It may resurface at a later stage with an even more radical agenda.

In Iraq

In Iraq, a natural disintegration took place a few years after the Multi-National Force led by the United States invaded and failed in its attempts to impose a Western-style democracy. The Kurds in the north formed a semi-autonomous state with oil revenues bolstering the coffers of the tribal government led by the Barazanis and Talibanis. Baghdad and its surrounding areas are becoming the stronghold for Sunnis, while the south is very much influenced by Iran as they become a Shia stronghold, including Basra and the two main Shia holy cities of Najaf and Karbala. These geo-political, canton-like, pre-nation formations fit the values prevalent in the region. They might become the natural solution to ending the violence there.

Throughout the Mideast

The Mideast region is torn between radicalism and globalism in its search for its own new identity. Whether guided by the West, whether it develops its own superordinate value system, or if driven by a unique combination of the two, this critical stage of societal emergence will continue to take years, if not decades to form.

The desire for larger nation-states can only come to fruition after a culture with a tribal or feudal type of social structure naturally outgrows the values that define it. Even as a population grows, and a more sophisticated, complex societal structure becomes necessary, prevailing values are likely to constrict natural development of appropriate governance and infrastructure. This is what we are witnessing in the recent decades of upheavals in the Middle East. If natural emergence does not occur through reform, social crises will continue to inspire revolutions.

This process is a glimpse of what we call *Natural Design*. The Mideast must forge a common bond based on coherent nationalistic values first before it can join in the values of an increasingly competitive, sophisticated, and complex world.

Cultures cannot skip a developmental stage during the pangs of nation building. The task ahead for the entire region is a formidable one. Importantly, each nation must develop principles whereby everyone is equal under the law before they can truly compete on the global stage.

The history of cultural emergence in the Middle East is filled with so many false starts. Today, the human experience, like the paths taken by France and the rest of the West, is proving to be a blood-soaked journey. The saving grace is that the journey seems to be giving birth to liberty, equality, and fraternity. Without the high personal cost, nation building in the Arab world would remain a foreign imposition. Today, the long awaited battle for self-determination has begun. Today's revolution is led by women and globalized Arab youth. They have answered the call for change and are beginning to realize and accept the high cost of self-determination. The collective mind, much like the individual search for identity, must go through the dark night of the soul in the quest for freedom and democracy.

ALIGNING THE MIDDLE EAST
WITH EMERGING GLOBAL VALUES

Political experts and analysts have offered many opinions and considered many potential trajectories with regard to how the Arab Spring might evolve. Without having the deep understanding of the underlying cultural tectonic plates moving across the Mideast landscape, very few of these predictions are realistic.

In planning and decision-making, Western governments and political advisers lack a deep understanding of culture that comes from studying and analyzing the memetic profiles of the people in the region. This emerging science cannot be ignored if we are to move from the clash to the confluence of civilizations. The use of memetic technology, based upon decades of scientific research and applications, confirms that an effective governing structure has to meet people where they are and design for their future from that point in a systematic process of social evolution. A design scheme specific to the Middle East is the primary focus of *Emerge!*

Experts in the field of memetics are called *Integral Design Architects* (IDAs). We architects, who work closely with *Indigenous Intelligence Experts* (IIEs), are pioneering the application of these principles in the Middle East. (A full description of the qualifications of these two types of individuals and the crucial roles they play in the future of the Middle East will be discussed in more detail in Chapter 3.) In general, IDAs can design for different cultures, while IIEs are experts in their own field within the context of that specific culture. Both types of expertise are essential to the natural design process, which identifies the challenges in any given political system and offers sustainable solutions that fit the culture.

More credible than traditional political science, the reframing of the region's history through Natural Design and memetics is a process informed by the deeper metrics of the culture. Middle Eastern cultures were shaped by chaos, repression, and passive engagement. Attempts at reform have been overwhelmed by ancient value systems, inhibiting transformation.

For example, a few hundred years ago, the Middle East failed to success-fully integrate the values of the Industrial Revolution into its culture. As a result it lost its chance to make middle class prosperity a dominant part of its current economic expression. Today the total productive output of the fourteen nations that make up the MENA economy barely surpasses the GDP of the two largest states in the United States.[16] Would Industrial Age values that were born out the Western Era of Enlightenment have changed the political and economic trajectory of the Middle East? The conditions that would have moved the culture from simple trade to the mass produc-tion of the Industrial Age were not present, nor did the leadership help make such conditions a reality. Any attempts at social or economic reform were supplanted by the feudal mindsets present in the region.

My partner Dr. Don Beck points out that the next natural step after revolution is the dismantling of toxic systems—those that were the glue that held these societies together. Without visionary, memetically informed leadership to replace dictators, the region could descend into chaos for decades or even disintegrate into feuding tribes.

As events continue to unfold in the Middle East, Dr. Beck's views seem to be confirmed. The short-term future of the region might not look as bright and euphoric as Tahrir Square did on the day Mubarak was ousted, but a few decades after the chaos is sorted out, elements of uniquely Arab democratic institutions may emerge. They may not look like Western democracies, but if they are designed from a value-systems perspective, they will be appropriate to serve a functional purpose in helping the region emerge into the global community of nations.

It's not too late for the region to adopt economic philosophies that can help political strategies evolve. Educational reforms that align skills with employment opportunities will afford much of the disenfranchised a sense of purpose. Redistribution of wealth by creating employment opportunities for the working and middle class will be a far better approach than the failed socialist agenda of the past century. With its wealth in natural resources, leadership in the region can undertake a number of strategies to make this goal a reality.

King Abdullah of Saudi Arabia has provided some leadership examples. China became the second largest economic power in the world in just three short decades, another awe-inspiring lesson in modernization. The Marshall Plan after World War II forever changed the face of the global map, but is this type of plan appropriate for the Middle East? Could China's central planning model provide lessons for Middle Eastern political and economic leadership?

In Turkey

There is one additional success story in the Mideast's modern history: Kemal Ataturk, Turkey's first President, undertook political, economic, and cultural reforms to modernize the former Ottoman Empire into a modern secular state. This ideal may represent a next phase in the region's cultural evolution. Kemalism, as the reforms were known in the early twentieth century, brought modern institutions to Turkey. One hundred years later, its basic tenets still represent the next phase for the rest of the Arab world.

Today Turkish soap operas portray the equality of women, individualism, meritocracy, and success through hard work. These are the most popular TV shows on Arab satellite networks.

At the same time, Turkey is a NATO ally and a friend of Israel, but has vehemently defended Palestinian rights and is playing an increasingly crucial role in regional politics. The underlying tenet that created modern day Turkey was explained by Ataturk himself: all laws of the Republic of Turkey should be inspired by actual needs here on Earth as a basic fact of national life.[17]

- ✦ How can one create a political platform that balances and honors the past, that deals with the challenges of the present, and has resilience for the future?

- ✦ Can progress be measured without reforms like those which modernized Turkey?

- ✦ Can a modernizing design in the region include the separation of state and religion and still be successful?

- ✦ How can equal rights for women and protection of minorities and religious sects be guaranteed?

- ✦ What would the educational systems have to look like to lead the region towards self-reliance and scientific inquiry well past the age of oil?

The expression of irony that I often hear in the Middle East is that they live in the richest region in the world but have the poorest people. How can we create a middle class, which in the West has proven to be a key for economic and political stability?

This book is not about providing all the answers to what ails the Middle East. Nor does it adopt a certain political ideology for expediting the evolution of the culture. It is not beholden to certain ideologies that preach the virtues of past glory or perpetuate the blame game.

Emerge! honors the past, yet it is intended to guide future generations to develop capacities for nation building. This book is my attempt to explain from a fresh perspective the role that value systems play in defining the success or failure of the societal evolutionary process. My hope is to create a way for the reader to understand how government in the Middle East can be made wiser and run smarter, how business practices in the region can evolve and become more innovative, and how IDAs can design for an infrastructure of the region from a unique value-systems perspective that goes beyond the age of oil.

The Arab Spring did not usher in democracy. Instead it removed barriers that have stopped the human evolutionary process from continuing on its endless quest along the upward spiral of social existence. It is through understanding the various levels of social development, understanding this journey, that we begrudgingly come to accept that the bloody and gruesome battles that are still taking place on the streets of Middle East are the unfortunate price people have to pay in order for their countries to move up to the next stage of social evolution and a promising future.

Governance and the Stages of Human Development

The question is not whether such democratization is possible, but instead how to meet the yearning of the masses in the Middle East for democracy; in other words, how do we go about achieving democratization in the Middle East.[18]

—Recep Tayyip Erdogan
Prime Minister, Turkey
January 30, 2003
Harvard University Kennedy School of Government

A witness to the historic Egyptian revolution first hand was Nafiz Rifai, our partner at the CHE-Mideast and one of the leading *Integral Design Architects* (IDAs) in the region. Over the course of several meetings we discussed the revolutions that were sweeping the region and what might be next for Egypt and the rest of the Middle East. Nafiz had visited Cairo several times and was surprised at the Western media's general ignorance about the events in the Mideast and their premature talk about democracy. In several Natural Design sessions with Dr. Beck, Nafiz and I discussed what natural form of government might replace the dictatorships. In our very first conversation after the Tahrir Square demonstration that ousted Mubarak, Nafiz had asked: *"What does Western-style democracy have to do with us?"* This very simple question defines the nature of the CHE-Mideast approach and the unique principles we use to view the world through a different lens. The Natural Design of governing systems for "us" is what will determine the success or failure of these revolutions.

In order for governing systems to be effective they must be designed from a framework that diagnoses and captures the prevalent beliefs, values, and levels of social development of the local culture. The Natural Design process places a culture on a trajectory that makes an indigenous form of democracy possible. This is the same approach (based on more than a half century of research and field applications) that helped South Africa transition from apartheid, inspired Palestinians to build the infrastructure for their future nation, and informed the Icelandic government of the imperative for redrafting its national constitution.

What is unique about our approach is that it focuses as much on the psychological systems of an evolving culture as it does on the psychological systems of the individual. It takes into account the ever-changing nature of both the environment and the human beings living there. What was missing in Nasserism, Ba'athism, and the myriad of social concepts deployed during the Middle East's brief march towards nation-states, was a reliable way to measure the stage of development of the region before proscribing a solution to its most pressing needs. If metrics were in place, a more functional form of governance could have been produced. Today, we have at our disposal the technology that can measure the memetics of a society and recommend a design strategy for functional governing institutions. Natural Design structures fulfill the needs of a culture while simultaneously placing it on the path toward its next stage of societal development.

THE SCIENCE BEHIND VALUE SYSTEMS

The late developmental psychologist, Professor Clare W. Graves of Union College, New York, pioneered a new and revolutionary paradigm, which took a lifetime of research. The principles behind the work of the Center for Human Emergence in the Middle East are steeped in Graves academic research and have been field-tested in both global hot spots and first world societies.

Theoretical Development

Professor Graves was a contemporary of Dr. Abraham Maslow, one the first psychologists to identify the hierarchical nature of human development in his famous *Hierarchy of Needs.* As peers, Graves attempted to verify Maslow's work in order to shape a more unifying theory of human psychology. Graves devised deeper testing methods and became convinced that Maslow's model didn't adequately express the dynamics of human nature. Instead of defining variations of existing psychological models and theories, Graves set out in search of the reasons for these multiple, shifting views of human nature.

After working with thousands of Maslow's students over the years, it became apparent to Graves that the *needs* in Maslow's model appeared to relate to what Graves called *levels of human social existence.* Graves identified a series of psycho-socio-cultural systems within an open-ended framework that characterizes our species' development.[19] This framework provides the definitive answer to why the Middle East is going through such a gruesome phase in its social and cultural evolution. The situation looks far less overwhelming once events are viewed through the rich hierarchical lens of Dr. Graves' *Levels of Human Existence*. Below is his summary of the framework and how he perceived human nature:

> Briefly, what I am proposing is that the psychology of the mature human being is an unfolding, emergent, oscillating spiraling process marked by progressive subordination of older, lower-order systems to newer, higher-order systems as an individual's existential problems change. Each successive stage, wave, or level of existence is a state through which people pass on their way to other states of being. When the human is centralized in one state of existence, he or she has a psychology, which is particular to that stage. His or her feelings, motivations, ethics and values, biochemistry, degree of neurological activation, learning system, belief systems, conception of mental health, ideas as to what mental illness is and how it should be treated, conception of and preference for management, education, economics, and political theory and practice are all appropriate to that state.[20]

What Graves created was the very first model for understanding the belief systems and behaviors of cultural groupings. By digging deeply to uncover the source "code" behind the motivations of human groups, he was able to propose that individuals, groups, and cultures function on the basis of several natural constructs: biology (brain capacity), psychology (why people think in a certain way), and sociology (how and where people live). Understanding the interplay of these factors was necessary in order to design institutions and governing systems that could facilitate the emergence of societies to meet the needs of increasingly complex societal structures as humanity evolved.

Through his research, Graves identified eight-existing hierarchical social structures that encompass the bio-psycho-social factors of a human group at any given point in time. He called these social structures *"value systems."* Graves formed the very first comprehensive psychological map of the human experience, which became known as the bio-psycho-social systems framework. In its abbreviated form the theory was known as the Emergent Double Helix Cyclical Levels of Existence Theory.

Dr. Don Beck dedicated his life to bringing Graves' academic work to worldwide audiences. After many years of working closely with Graves, Dr. Beck turned his effort to real-world applications of the theory. He then further augmented the bio-psycho-social systems construct with his own research. Beck, along with his former associate, Christopher Cowan, put much of Graves' comprehensive work into a theory called *Spiral Dynamics.* Together, they co-authored a groundbreaking book of the same name: *Spiral Dynamics: Mastering Leadership, Values and Change.* The updated theory included Richard Dawkins concept of memetics, which explains how human groups express and spread ideas within a value system, and how values morph to manage crises and within the evolutionary spiral process.

On the theoretical end, both Beck and Cowan continued to verify the vast amount of Graves' research through different applications and methodologies. Beck has compared Professor Graves' *psychological mapping* to the Human Genome Project, and has often shared with me his dreams to fund a similar project he calls the Human Memome Project. This influential research into the nature of human values and human socio-cultural evolution continues to unfold through many third generation Gravesians who have been trained throughout the world.

This research is also the foundation upon which much of today's *integral philosophy* is based. Since the Spiral Dynamics theory was published, Don Beck has collaborated with integral philosopher Ken Wilber on creating *Spiral Dynamics Integral,* which added four quadrants to the model. These additional components make up the All Quadrants All Levels (AQAL) model which has defined much of Wilber's work ever since:

"I" (individual, intentional, subjective interior),

"IT (individual, behavioral, objective exterior),

WE (collective cultural, intersubjective, interior),

ITS (collective, social, systems, intraobjective, exterior)

Don Beck is the acknowledged trailblazer in the field, successfully applying the principles of the emerging science of value systems to global hot spots, organizations, and in consultation with world governments. Over a ten-year period he played a major role in designing South Africa's transition from apartheid, and in 1991 he co-authored a book entitled *The Crucible: Forging South Africa's Future.*[21] *The Crucible* defines the importance of understanding the "macro-memetics" of cultures in order to design effective political and economic policies for each respective country.

I have heard Dr. Beck speak countless times about his experience in South Africa and the advice he gave Nelson Mandela and F.W. de Klerk. Nothing crystallized that experience in my mind better than a recent meeting in Oslo where Beck and de Klerk came together to converse like old friends, once again long after significant lifetime events have passed.

On May 3, 1995, both houses of the Texas State Legislature Texas (Beck's home state) adopted a resolution (S.R. No. 901) presented by the President of the Texas Senate which commends Beck *for his invaluable contributions toward the peaceful creation of a democratic South Africa.*"[22] Beck was invited to return to South Africa in November, 2013, as a key presenter for the University of Stellenbosch Business School Executive Development Event "Africa Leads" on sustainability and leadership at the conference Responsible Leadership for Africa and the World.[23] According to the University program announcement: *"Beck's spiral dynamics approach was the basis for the creation of the Peace Committees and subsequent CODESA process in the run up to the first post- apartheid elections in 1994."* This event was sponsored in partnership with the Globally Responsive Leadership Initiative,[24] a United Nations based world-wide partnership of companies, business schools and learning organizations working together to develop a next generation of globally responsible leaders.

Dr. Beck's work in recent years has influenced decision makers in Europe, South America, and the Middle East. I have had the privilege of working with Don Beck since the turn of the century. By applying his framework, I learned much of the intelligence behind the principles of Spiral Dynamics for managing large-scale change initiatives. Together, Dr. Beck and I co-founded the CHE-Mideast, a think tank that applies the Beck/Graves methodologies to large-scale social and organizational systems. Since 2003 I have authored several papers that detail our methodologies and continue to offer fresh perspectives on the application of this resilient framework.

Today, Beck is well into his 70s and is working on yet another evolution of the Spiral Dynamics theory tentatively named *Humanity's Hidden Code.* For the first time in human history, a measurable, predictable large-scale psychology is able to replace arcane linear ways of looking at what motivates groups and cultures. It is that paradigm shift—seeing the world through the stratified lenses of value systems as presented through the Beck/Graves framework—that I wish to bring to the readers of *Emerge!.* My hope is that policymakers dealing with all aspects of global geopolitical challenges, not just the Middle East, bring the science of value systems into their decision-making framework.

I would like to take this opportunity to reframe my life-long involvement in the socio-political and business circles of the Middle East through the lens of *Spiral Dynamics*. Following are on-the-ground examples from my experiences in the Middle East. The macro-design elements represent the evolution of Beck's work into a field called *Large-Scale Psychology,* which was presented as a new branch of psychology to the American Psychological Association in 2008.[25]

SPIRAL DYNAMICS:
THE BIO-PSYCHO-SOCIAL SYSTEMS FRAMEWORK

To recap briefly: Spiral Dynamics models a new way of framing and under-standing the forces of human interactions and behaviors. It integrates Dawkins' theory of memetics and Graves' stages or levels of human socie-tal development to explain individual, organizational, and cultural behav-iors, or value systems.[26]

Memetics and Value Systems

Examples in recent history help clarify the existence of memes and their effect, the spread of ideas: In the West the Beatles were a meme in the 1960s. At the same time *Um Kulthoom* and *Abdel Halim Hafiz* were the musical memes that captivated the Middle East and swept through its culture. Liberal democracy is a meme in Western Europe while the Muslim Brotherhood is a meme in the Arab World. Opera Winfrey is a meme. Al Jazeera television is a meme.

The collective presence of memes and their unique cultural context form into general groupings of larger memes that further define a cul-ture's macro-memetic content. Our framework calls these groupings of large memes "General Category" memes, or ^{G}MEMEs. Categories are wider concepts like philosophy, politics, religion, education, healthcare, architecture, civil society, sports, music, commerce, corporate structures, and governance. The stratified content, or the spectrum of meaning that these larger memes have, form the ^{V}MEME, or value-systems meme that shapes how individuals, organizations and cultures think.

Within the scope of Spiral Dynamics, the term *Value Systems* refers to values as a set of priorities and assumptions that determine the worldview of individuals and societies. Relevant to this discussion, they determine why different groups choose different leaders and different forms of gover-nance. On a cultural level, these value systems have a great impact on what is important to a society, how resources are allocated and distributed, and how decisions are made. Dr. Beck uses the terminology of "^{V}MEMEs" and "levels of existence" described by a culture's value systems interchange-ably. I will use the "value-system levels" and "^{V}MEMEs" interchangeably throughout this book as well.

Theoretically, *value systems* determine almost every aspect of life. Because humans and societies are adaptable, new memes evolve as bio-logical, psychological, and social conditions change, eventually facilitating the emergence of new value systems. It is important to point out that the emergence of new value systems takes many years, decades, or even

ᴳMEME: THE ᵛMEME ATTRACTOR

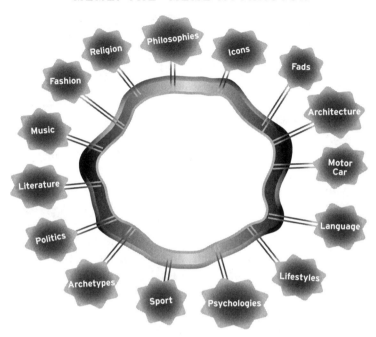

*Each ᵛMEME is an organizing principle, center of gravity, geometric fractal, self-replicating force, and magnetic field that attracts content-rich little ᴳMEMEs.

Adapted from *Spiral Dynamics* by Beck and Cowan and used here with permission.

centuries to happen. Historically there have been only eight value systems to emerge in human society from the days of the cave men and women to the present time. The evolutionary aspect of this theory lies in the emphasis that it places on changes in *life conditions*. This is what makes the Spiral Dynamics approach unique, adaptable, and transformational by nature. By taking into account the ever-changing nature of human needs and values, and formulating a design scheme based on a predictable hierarchy of socio-cultural development, one can create a resilient and sustainable change model that scans the horizon to anticipate signs of change. Change may include regression, emergence, or a system may exhibit signs of being in a closed, paralyzed state.

Think tanks addressing the issues in the Middle East today pay little attention to *life conditions* on the ground and the long-term needs of the people. They do not understand that where people are emerging *from* is systemically tied to where they are *going*. The vital elements of *life conditions* identify the needs of every institution within the culture and offers solutions that fit the *existing* and the *emerging* socio-cultural value systems.

There are characteristics unique to every ᵛMEME—such as a specific preference for a particular type of education, respect for a particular type of authority, perspectives on politics, economics, health care, religious institutions, and expressions reflected in architecture, law enforcement, and so on. The Integral Design Architect (IDA) finds specialists in all these areas within a particular society. These specialists, the *Indigenous Intelligence Experts,* are the primary providers of content and dimension for each of these *life conditions.* Unlike most models that address only the surface manifestation of a problem, change that starts with addressing *life conditions* penetrates through many layers of surface memes in order to recognize culturally-fit solutions that can be lasting and sustainable.

At one point I explained *life conditions* to participants in an executive training program. A participant asked if the concept is like the Chinese Proverb about teaching a man how to fish in order to feed himself for life. My explanation was that we help cultures build the pond (habitat) that will attract the fish. What I meant was that we don't only provide technique or skills or tools for fishing, we provide a means to develop a healthy habitat to sustain the fishery and the fishing industry. In order to create the most resilient habitat we look at the existing needs of a society and help them envision how to take it to next level. These efforts are led by specialists within the culture rather than Westerners unfamiliar with dynamics between existing *life conditions* and the changing belief systems and mindsets of the culture.

The rest of this chapter focuses on detailing the characteristics of the eight levels of human existence identified under this framework. I will introduce many examples from my consulting work and the activities of the CHE-Mideast, all involving the active engagement of Dr. Beck.

THE EIGHT-KNOWN LEVELS OF EXISTENCE AND THE DOUBLE-HELIX NATURE OF THE FRAMEWORK

In the book *Spiral Dynamics*, Beck and Cowan assign a color to each value system or level. The colors have no particular meaning or historic relevance other than to distinguish the placement of each value system within the hierarchy. The colors also make it easy to reference and identify each value system/level of existence/ᵛMEME.

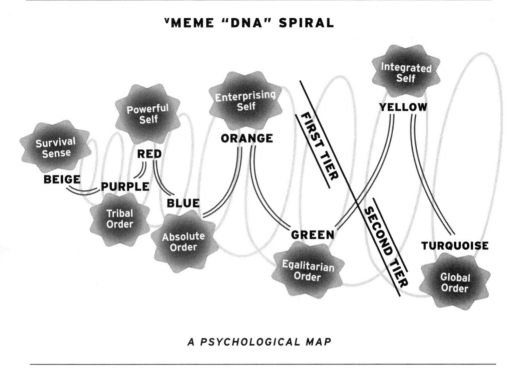

ᵛMEME "DNA" SPIRAL

A PSYCHOLOGICAL MAP

Adapted from *Spiral Dynamics* by Beck and Cowan and used here with permission.

In theory, the number of value systems that might emerge throughout humanity's evolution (the "Spiral" itself) is endless. Our present understanding of the spiral includes two separate tiers. There are only eight known levels of existence within the current spiral. The first six identifiable values systems form the *First Tier*, which Grave calls the *subsistence* levels. On the *Second Tier,* which he called the levels of *being,* there are only two identified levels of human existence so far.[27]

Graves concluded that the six basic themes in every tier repeat with more complexity in the new tier.[28] So the theme in Second Tier comes from the values of *being* not from the values of *subsistence*. As demonstrated in the figure above, the survival level (Beige) in the First Tier repeats in the Integrated Self, Yellow, but the first level of the Second Tier is concerned with the survival of the species not the survival of the individual. Similarly with the tribal order (purple) in First Tier, it repeats in the turquoise global order, but the theme is not limited to the local tribes, it defines Global Tribes or what is refer to today as Global Commons.

Since the different cultures of the world emerge along their own evolutionary time line, less advanced cultures may borrow from more advanced cultures to assist their emergence. The contemporary manifestation of value systems in terms of their memetic profile and style of governance are easiest to visualize in modern countries and regions. Therefore, a description of the system of governance that existed when each ᵛMEME first emerged and dominated societies and organizations is provided herein.

Like biological systems, the *life conditions* of cultures mimic nature in their archetypes and transformational processes. Evolutionary biologist Elisabet Sathouris did grounding-breaking work on biological systems, demonstrating that they alternate between "the survival of the fittest" and "communal activities" in a dance that helps life forms survive and evolve.[29]

Based on Graves' research, the study of the biology, and Beck and Cowan's real life applications, the eight known ᵛMEMEs fall into these two alternating social archetypes. One archetype is individualistic and expressive (survival of the fittest), where individuals break away from the group and seek merit through creative innovation. The other archetype is group-oriented, communal, sharing, and sacrificial.[30]

Since no stages in the hierarchy of eight (existing) value systems can be skipped, a system with preference for either the individualistic or communal archetype makes its way through the alternating type at a faster pace. Both individual humans and our cultures tend to oscillate between one archetype and the other. In the color-coding sequence, the communal archetype is identified by "cool" colors (Purple, Blue, Green on the First Tier, and Turquoise on Second Tier) and the individualistic archetype is identified by the warm colors (Beige, Red, and Orange on First Tier and Yellow on Second Tier).

In human social evolution, with the passage of time, existential problems arise within each value system that cause crises because new problems cannot be solved within the existing context. This is true with regard to both the individualistic and the communal archetypes. The pressure and energy created by the value system's inability to solve its problems eventually leads to the emergence of a system capable of sustaining an increased level of complexity. Thus, humanity, like other natural life forms, spirals forward while alternating between each cultural archetype. Each emerging system seeks to fill gaps left by the previous system, whether they are gaps in innovation and knowledge, or caring for those left behind, endangered or marginalized.

According the Graves/Spiral Dynamics framework, the endless continuing quest for a more and more unifying complex value system has always been the pattern of societal emergence and always will be. This assumption is underpinned by the "double helix" nature of the spiral framework. Beck calls the double helix model a coupling of our human capacities with existential realities. In this regard:

1. ^vMEME Capacities Create New *Life Conditions*: Humans possess the capacities to create value systems which create new *life conditions*. Graves was firmly convinced that the neurological structures within the human brain have the capacity to generate increasingly intricate levels of complexity, which in turn manifest in different levels of psychological development and coping mechanisms. Beck refers to this unique neurological phenomenon as "a software system with latent upgrades just waiting to be turned on." There are three conditions that preclude manifestation of new neurological structures: the brain's ability to contain these systems an individual's DNA, and the dynamic between nature vs. nurture, meaning the human brain's capacity to respond to environmental challenges, i.e., *life conditions*.

2. *Life Conditions* Activate ^vMEME Capacities: The vital role that *life conditions* play in this model is key to the model's uniqueness. The nature of human and societal evolution is its adaptability to *life conditions*. Continuous interaction between the socio-cultural and physical environments and our neurological systems enables us to identify and evaluate potential solutions to problems we encounter. There are four important pillars that define *life conditions* and determine the ^vMemetic patterns of cultural emergence: Time, Place, Problems, and Circumstances.[31]

> *Time* This is the location along the overall line of human development. Graves called them psychological time lines. Before the onset of the Information Age, the psychological time lines in the Middle East moved very slowly. Today, with immediate access to vast amounts of information about *life conditions* elsewhere, the timeline for development moves much faster.

> *Place* This is the geographical location and physical *life conditions* under which individuals and groups exist. The importance of geographical location and physical *life conditions* is best summarized in the book: *The Power of Place: How Our Surroundings Shape Our Thoughts, Emotions, and Actions* (Gallagher, 2007). In this context, depending on where they are born and raised, children can have the means and facilities for great prosperity or face desperate deprivation.[32] Place affects political, historical, and economic aspects of a society.

Problems Human challenges are presented in terms of needs, priorities, concerns, and requirements for a particular individual, group, or culture. These issues are present at every level of existence. Maslow's Hierarchy of Needs addresses these aspects of *life conditions*, which involve survival, safety, belonging, and so on. It was Graves who revealed that when problems overwhelm the existing coping mechanisms they trigger new systems in the brain that can more accurately perceive the problem and deal with it appropriately.[33]

Circumstances Placement within hierarchies of power, status, and social influence are the conditions within a culture that define an individual's circumstances. One's socio-economic class, level of education, race, gender, and family lineage play a crucial role in defining individual *life conditions.* Circumstances act like a set of blinders that can prevent an individual centered in a given ᵛMEME from seeing the contribution of other levels of existence on the spiral. Understanding each aspect of *life conditions* helps a value systems expert design tools that naturally help people in certain circumstances to transcend the values created by those blinders and allows new perspectives to emerge.

The interaction between *human capacities* and *life conditions* define the cyclic and emergent nature of this framework. They describe the transforming mechanisms that define the movement from one value system to the next. For example, *life conditions* play an important role in designing the economic system of the future. The *Memenomics* (Dawlabani, 2013) framework, which describes functional economic structures designed from the Second Tier value systems, is therefore different from any other approach to economics to date. Still, within each value system there are many characteristics that impact how, when, and why cultures emerge that give each culture its unique ᵛMemetic contours.

COMMONALITIES AMONG ALL VALUE SYSTEMS

Just like there are characteristics unique to every level of existence, there are characteristics that are common at all levels. The following are the most relevant to our discussion about the culture of the Arab world. These are the seven critical commonalities that shape the dynamics of governance and the interactions between the citizens, business, and political leaders at the individual, organizational, and societal levels:

1. A Bio-Psycho-Social Model: ᵛMEMEs affect individuals as well as societies. An individual develops through the various value systems in his or her own life as *life conditions* change. The number of levels expressed in an individual depends on the biological, psychological, and social conditions he or she faces as his or her life progresses.[34] Forces affecting *life conditions* at the individual and societal levels play an integral part in determining why and how political leadership styles at any ᵛMemetic level succeed, stagnate, or fail.

2. A Main Center of Gravity (COG): Different people, groups, or whole societies operating from one or another ᵛMEME can co-exist at the same time.[35] For example, an individual might act from one level (perhaps dutiful, compliant, and respectful) when he or she is with family and from a completely different level when at work (perhaps innovative, entrepreneurial, and creative) or with friends. Human nature has the capacity for flexibility. In addition, individuals and societies are often in transition between value systems. Yet, each will have a center of gravity or "default "foundation. No single value system exists on its own; it's the value system *"stack"* (or *meme stack*) on the spiral determines the totality of what's important for an individual or a culture.

3. The Healthy and Unhealthy Expression of a ᵛMEME: Each value system can exhibit both healthy or unhealthy expressions.[36] For example, one could argue that Turkey's style of democracy (order-driven-->-enterprise-driven) is a *healthy* manifestation of a Fourth-to-Fifth Level political system for the country, while Syria's oppressive system (a feudal system) is an *unhealthy* expression of the Third-Level value system. Democracy in the West is a healthy form of expression of the order-driven Fourth-Level system, while other forms of governance, like Iran's theocracy, might be considered an *unhealthy* expression of the same Fourth-Level system.

Healthy and unhealthy expressions of a values system are relative to which culture or which leaders within a culture are interpreting the system. For example, to the West, Iran's current expression of Fourth-Level, Order-Driven values seems unhealthy, and it has been penalized for it through economic sanctions. In spite of these sanctions, Iran's industrial and technological drive is only second to Israel and Turkey in the Middle East. The sanctions that looked to curtail Iran's unhealthy practices didn't prevent it from emerging into the next system.

4. An Open, Arrested, or Closed System: When determining the capacity for change in an individual, organization, or culture, each level of existence or value system can be described as being in one of three conditions: open, arrested, or closed.[37]

- ✦ An open system is a dynamic culture that anticipates and adapts to change.

- ✦ An arrested system has stagnant institutions that may change incrementally but not enough to keep up with internal or external dynamics. The financial crisis was a result of an arrested regulatory system, for example.

- ✦ A closed system is one that doesn't accept even incremental change, and is uninterested in input from the outside. The only change possible is through a crisis of revolution. The Arab Spring is the undeniable result of people living within a closed system.

5. The Ability to Transcend and Include: As a person or a culture evolves to the next level of complexity on the spiral, they transcend and include all the previous value systems in their "meme stack."[38] For example, a person at the Fourth Level (*Law and Order*) who moves to the Fifth-Level system (*Strategic Enterprise)* might no longer identify with the Fourth-Level system as his or her predominant mean of expression, yet this does not mean she or he will break away completely from the constraints of the Fourth-Level system. The Fourth-Level system has become an integral part of his/her mindset, but is now a smaller part of what defines his or her total meme stack. It no longer is a powerful influence upon his or her everyday existence. In later years, Beck added the concept of *"Anticipation"* to describe how an open system can assess risks and predict future trends. Since the publication of Spiral Dynamics this tenet of the theory is known today, as *Transcend, Include, and Anticipate.*

6. Ascension to Greater Levels of Complexity: When a person or culture solves the problems of existence within their value system, they enter a resting state temporarily. However, immediately the problems that will trigger the emergence of the next value system begin to arise. Faced with greater complexity, humans deal with the dissonance and this leads to new insights. Dealing with dissonance activates higher capacities in the brain to solve new problems with new thinking. This exercise requires the development of new coping mechanisms and new tools specific to the new level of existence. These new insights, mechanisms, and tools eventually spread memetically within the culture.

THE SPIRAL OF DEVELOPMENT

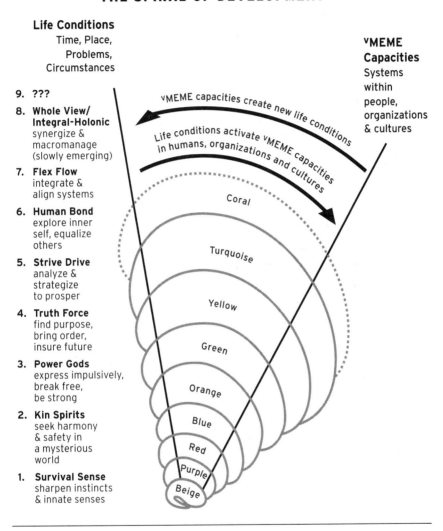

Life Conditions
Time, Place,
Problems,
Circumstances

9. **???**

8. **Whole View/
   Integral-Holonic**
   synergize &
   macromanage
   (slowly emerging)

7. **Flex Flow**
   integrate &
   align systems

6. **Human Bond**
   explore inner
   self, equalize
   others

5. **Strive Drive**
   analyze &
   strategize
   to prosper

4. **Truth Force**
   find purpose,
   bring order,
   insure future

3. **Power Gods**
   express impulsively,
   break free,
   be strong

2. **Kin Spirits**
   seek harmony
   & safety in
   a mysterious
   world

1. **Survival Sense**
   sharpen instincts
   & innate senses

**ᵛMEME
Capacities**
Systems
within
people,
organizations
& cultures

ᵛMEME capacities create new life conditions

Life conditions activate ᵛMEME capacities
in humans, organizations and cultures

Coral

Turquoise

Yellow

Green

Orange

Blue

Red

Purple

Beige

Adapted from *Spiral Dynamics* by Beck and Cowan and used here with permission

7. The Culture's Inability to Skip a Developmental Stage: This is true still in the Age of Technology and the Knowledge Economy. Law and order must precede prosperity and science. Socio-cultural evolution must ratchet between communal and individualistic value systems in order to solve the problems of the previous system. In the age of globalization, the developing world might move through these phases faster than previous cultures, but they still move at their own pace, with their own unique indigenous content. If an outside entity or innovative leader tries to impose a more complex higher-level solution on a less complex culture, the culture experiences extraordinary stress and runs the risk of collapse.

It is important for the reader to understand the common characteristics that all value systems share in order to distinguish the emergent nature of the theory. Next is a description of each of the eight value systems that form the spiral. Both Western and Middle Eastern examples will be given in each ᵛMEME description on these systems within individuals, organizations and societies.

LEVELS OF THE *FIRST TIER*: VALUES OF SUBSISTENCE

Beige: Survival Bands

The First-Level System

This is the first *individualistic* survival system. In Beige, all energy is directed toward survival through innate sensory abilities and instinctual reactions. At this level, humans form loosely organized and herd-like survival bands with little structure.[39] This is the first emergence of humans from their animal nature. Food, water, warmth, sex, and safety are the primary focus of life. This value system level is uncommon today, but is seen in newborns, drug addicts, late-stage Alzheimer's disease, and mentally-ill street people. Beige is an individualistic system where the motto is *"express self now to survive."* At this level the healthy expression of Beige sharpens instincts and innate senses.

The movie *Lord of the Flies* provides a good contemporary illustration of how we regress and activate the survival system when our environment is under stress. In this system, instinct is heightened, for example, in places experiencing war. I experienced this firsthand when I was a child during the civil war in Lebanon. We would sense rockets before we heard them explode. In Beige, individuals live via "the law of the jungle." There is no system of governance under this ᵛMEME. As food becomes scarcer and the habitat for this First Level of existence no longer supports survival, individuals form groups, often families or extended clans, and move to the Second Level system.

Purple: Tribal Kinship

The Second-Level System

This is the first *communal* level survival system consisting of clans and tribes.[40] This is also the first value system with socio-cultural indigenous intelligences. At this level of existence, people seek harmony and safety together in the mysterious world. Nature is magical, powerful, and feared. We must band together and protect each other and our territory to survive. Although the emphasis is on safety, survival is achieved through the togetherness of the tribe. This is still the lifestyle of Bedouins in the desert and the Zulu tribes in Africa. Purple is a sacrificial group-oriented system, in which people sacrifice individual needs for the tribe, the elders, and the ancient ways. Pleasing the gods and spirits, maintaining the tribal traditions, and keeping the tribe's home warm and safe become the highest priority.

In this value system there is no room for individual thinking or action. Purple must sacrifice for, and show allegiance to the tribe, the chief, the elders, and Al-Za'eem (feudal lord). It seeks to preserve sacred objects, places, events, and memories. It observes the traditional rites of passage, the seasonal cycles, and the tribal customs. Ancestral land and territory are sacred to this value system. Tribes have historically waged wars to retain and protect their land. These are agrarian societies that still exist today and rely on cultivating the land as their primary source of economic security. A good depiction of historic *life conditions* under Purple is shown in the 2007 movie *Mongol: The Rise of Genghis Khan.*

THE PURPLE SECOND-LEVEL 'MEME'S LEADERSHIP STRUCTURE

Tribe/Clan

▲ Tribal Leader/Clan Chief (usually the oldest and wisest)
▲ Small Tribal Leader/traditionally responsible for safety, rituals, medicine, etc.)
● Tribal Member/Clan Member

Music in this value system is circular. It is the beat of the drum that rallies the tribe to celebrate: the Dabka in the Middle East, the powwow on Native Indian-American land, and the ecstatic dance of the Shaman in African tribes. They all dance to the beat of *Nature,* some appeasing the gods, others imploring them for rain. In more sophisticated societies today, these traditions continue as folklore without the magical allure. Sadly, many cultures have transcended but not included this form of Purple, as it is a grounding force that sustains our communion with nature. Art, in its historic appearance, was preverbal and relied on symbols like petroglyphs that told the story of the tribe. Many times these images were the only historic records of a culture.

In spite of the move towards globalization, there are still many pockets of the Purple value system around the world today, not just in the Middle East and Africa. Purple is a primary way of life in many parts of Asia, South and Central America, and on Native American land in the United States. Many aspects of Purple are found in First World societies as well, but with far more societal complexity. Beliefs in guardian angels, blood oaths and good luck charms, and family rituals or superstitions are all signs of the Purple ᵛMEME. Rituals in fraternities and sororities, fraternal lodges, teams in professional sports, and certain corporate tribes are all manifestations of Purple. Rituals in religious practices are steeped in Purple undertones especially in the developing world.

On the individual and family level, biological and neurological Purple bonds are created between the newly born and the mother through the hormone oxytocin. This strengthens the familial bond as well as the immune system of the child. Where the traditional immediate family structure is broken, grandparents or other relatives may be a stabilizing Purple force, providing the needed safety for children to thrive, grow, experience their childhood, and lead fairly normal lives.

Decision making in this Second-Level system is based on custom and tradition. Decisions are made by a council of elders. In its historic context, the council may rely on mystical information supplied by a shaman or a high priest. The average tribal member is uninvolved in much of the decision-making process since they trust the tribal leadership to do what is best for the tribe. Attempts to introduce democratic thought into tribal groups do not work, as individual decision making may lead to retribution and exclusion. Tribe members must follow tradition. Wealth is divided in a communal manner, regardless of who may have actually created it. A good example of this practice is how native Indian tribes distribute gambling revenues from their casinos among tribe members.

The Second-Level system is wary of the world outside the tribe. Rules must be obeyed and tribal leaders must be honored along with past generations of leaders. Education is paternalistic, relying heavily on rituals and routines. The learning process is passive, and symbolism helps to make sense of the world outside the tribe. The family includes extended kinships marked by strict role relationships. Protecting bloodlines is of paramount importance. Rites of passage and rituals thrust young men and women into adulthood.

At the organizational level today in the Middle East, most family-run businesses fall into the Purple ᵛMEME. At this level, leaders concentrate on the whole tribe/organization rather than choosing individuals for special awards or compensation. The message within the organization is "we are all one." Declarations such as "job well done" directed at an employee might earn him the wrath of the group and result in alienation. High seniority leaders are honored in similar fashion to the historic tribal leader.

When working in the Middle East, Western managers have a hard time developing sensitivities to the internal dynamics of a Purple group. People living in societies with more complexity tend to overlook the important bonds that this ᵛMEME creates in less complex societies. Individuals coming from greater complexity, who are supposed to have transcended and included the previous levels, tend to dismiss the importance of including less complex systems, which results in misalignment of purpose within the organization.

When the individual self becomes more powerful than the group and develops a dominant ego, he or she has no choice but to break out of the group. Historically it was young men who exited this stage to the next level of existence. They might feel that traditions and rituals had become repressive. In the movie *Mongol*, we see when Genghis Khan triumphs over fear of nature and breaks the myth of safety to become the leader we now remember him to be.

In the contemporary manifestation of this system in the Middle East, both young men and women are rebelling against repressive group and clan beliefs. Historically the means of exiting this value system was through tribal conflicts and the rise of warlords. As *life conditions* exit Purple, the leader who breaks from the grip of group conformity controls the group. Dictators past and present are a good example of individuals who broke through the bonds of the tribe to control the masses. Alternately, with the passage of time, as the Purple meme provides stability and safety, and as *life conditions* change, younger and stronger members of the tribe start to develop individual thinking. There is diminishing fear of the mystery of the universe and a weakening of tribal bonds. As tribes solve the problems of existence at this stage they immediately begin to experience the next set of problems that will nudge them toward the next level of existence.

Red: Feudal, Heroic, and Egocentric

The Third-Level System

Red is the second individualistic level. It is expressive and represents the first emergence of the individual ego. This is the value system of the Big Boss and the Za'eem in the Arab world. Red individuals are interested in personal gain, which can include power and domination. They enforce power over self, others, and nature through creative independent action, which can often be exploitive.[41] The individual is characterized by the need for instant gratification, respect, and reward. He or she is reactive and assertive, and can embody the concept of "express self now impulsively and to hell with others." This value system cannot experience guilt. It could only be shamed into more acceptable behavior. Personal power and personal reward are the ultimate interests of individuals operating at this level. They take what they want compulsively, and manipulate or persuade other charismatically. In terms of societal structures, historically Red is a violent organizing force that creates armies and empires. Examples include the Sumerian Dynasty, the Babylonian Dynasty, the Persian Empire, and the Roman Empire. Both Graves and Beck believe that this is the hardest transition for a culture to overcome.

In its unhealthy manifestation, this is a system where "might makes right" and those in power make their own rules. To Red, the world is a jungle full of threats and predators. It wants to be at the top of the food chain, to break free from domination and any constraint. Pure Red demands respect and needs attention from others. Red has to call the shots. Sacrificing others for the sake of empire, power, wealth, and glory is simply a strategy. Red won't shed a tear. It justifies killing based on ethnicity, religion or nationality, or personal objectives. In its primitive state, conscience is absent from the system and it can justify killing for sport, entertainment, or to obtain a particular prize.

In its healthy manifestation, Red can be courageous, takes risks, can be innovative, idealistic, persuasive and persistent, and even topple dictators. However these actions might be absent the foresight of any long-term consequences or objective. Red lives in the present tense. Red has no interest in personal sacrifice or compromise. In the West, compromise is thought to hold the promise of a win-win outcome, but that is not the case with

Red-centered societies. In Red society compromise is seen as weakness. As described in the book *Getting to Yes: Negotiating Agreements Without Giving In (1992),* when the word "compromise" was used by a Western diplomat trying to negotiate freedom for American hostages at the height of the Islamic revolution in Iran, to the Iranians this meant defeat so the mission became an immediate failure.[42]

On the bio-psycho level, examples of Red include the toddler stage where children say "NO-to-everything," know-it-all teenagers, rap musicians and the content of their lyrics, cultures within prisons, dictators, and gangs who share Purple symbolism as a tribal bond but experience no guilt about instantly killing a traitor or rival. The mob culture depicted in the *Godfather* movie trilogy represents Red in modern Western culture. Educators in this value system view a liberal Western education as dangerous. They would alter the entire educational system to fit their needs for control of the student population. In this Third-Level system, students are considered weak, malleable, and unreliable. Teachers must be ruthless with students and force them to study specific, a narrowly-focused dogmatic curriculum. They don't believe children would be otherwise motivated to succeed.

Historically, music in this value system speaks of conquest. It keeps the tribal beat but climaxes to a euphoric high of heroism and bravery. The lyrics are full of mythic stories of heroes who conquered other tribes and took the spoils. My tribe, the Ghassanids, are forever memorialized in heroic chants of conquest. I was called on by a European Union organization in recent years. They had reached a stalemate with tribal leaders in Syria. After arguing with community leaders all day, I finally invoked the name of my tribe. It was the Syrian leaders' memory of my tribe that broke the ice and brought out the heroic Red self in those leaders, too. They actually broke into song about the glory of Bani Ghassan (Sons of Ghassan).

In its contemporary manifestation, healthy Red music is seen in Frank Sinatra's *My Way* (1968) and in other lyrics that express social discontent. Grunge rock is another Red music expression.

In this feudal ᵛMEME, decisions are made by the Big Boss who stands out from the rest by an act of valor or notoriety. This is a hierarchical structure with primarily top-down communication. The leader forces others to obey through coercion or conviction. A typical feudal leader, such as Gaddafi or Saddam Hussein, never asks for his followers' views, unless they are the most highly-trusted, closed inner circle. That circle is usually formed of two or three people who have been tested for their loyalty many times over. No form of democracy is possible. Feudal lords may be presidents and heads

THE RED THIRD-LEVEL 'MEME'S LEADERSHIP STRUCTURE

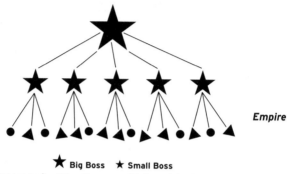

Empire

★ Big Boss ★ Small Boss
▲ Small Tribal Leader/traditionally responsible for safety, rituals, medicine, etc.)
● Tribal Member/Clan Member

of state who manipulate power to ensure the continuity of their bloodline. They may offer their people "fair and just" elections to appease the world community while rigging the vote in every election.

The tactics of Red governance exist throughout the Middle East. Syria is now under the rule of a second generation Assad. Mubarak was grooming his son Gamal to succeed him before being overthrown. Exploitative, self-serving leadership creates dynasties. They believe that humans are lazy and must be dominated. Leaders believe that people generally cannot be trusted and lack focus or discipline. This was typified in 1979 Iraq when Saddam sought to consolidate power over what he perceived to be disloyal members of the Revolutionary Command Council. At a Ba'ath Party gathering in Baghdad he infamously read off a list of names, had his loyalist soldiers escort them to the parking lot and summarily executed them. Guiltless, Saddam went back to smoking his cigar and attending to the scheduled events of the day.

Individuals in this Third Level are always looking for a dragon to slay. If it's not an external dragon, he or she can be fighting their own demons while blaming their plight on everyone else around them. The concept of accountability is not a part of their psychological make up. Historically, Red exploits women, children, and the weak. This phenomenon continues today in Western societies in less pronounced ways as in the rap sub-culture that calls women degrading names, and in parts of Africa and the Middle East where women's participation in the workforce, politics, higher education, and elsewhere is limited. Although women have much to contribute to society, the egocentric Red males who dominate the culture relegate them to second-class citizens.

Organizations at this Third Level are run much like the feudal lords who govern societies from that same level. To the victor belong the spoils. There is one dominant Big Boss at the top and a few enforcers who affirm that employees are by nature lazy and require coercive supervision tactics to keep them on task. Usually the laborers are unskilled and uneducated and find these employment conditions preferable to not having any work at all. There have been many reports over the past few years of the terrible conditions at the factories owned by the giant Chinese company who manufactures 90 percent of Apple's products. Workers who couldn't cope with Big Boss Red might commit suicide by jumping out of the factory window. Several decades ago, before the appearance of unions, poor factory conditions similar to the ones in China today were prevalent in the United States.

In Dubai, workers (in Purple) from Bangladesh and India would have their passports taken away from them by Bangladeshi and Indian Red Agents, forcing them to work in deplorable conditions. As human rights groups and the media exposed these issues, Red eased its grip for the fear of losing profits. External pressures can be a powerful influence in countries where Red work conditions exist, requiring a shift toward new labor laws more palatable to the next system (Blue-Order). Red organizations, if unchecked, create huge disparities between the haves and the have-nots, the CEOs and their employees. Nepotism, regardless of skills or talent or merit, is inherent in Red organizations.

Because of its dominant nature, a Third-Level organization can make indentured servants out of employees. Charismatic leaders attract followers and then take advantage of their hope and need. Companies operating in the developing world may be subsidized by unhealthy Western, enterprising Fifth-Level system corporations (Orange). Sweatshops, child labor, cruelty to animals, and dire circumstances for women workers are all signs of exploitation in a Red organization. The profit margin is the priority, and quality suffers, too.

Like every value system, this Red ᵛMEME can exhibits healthy or unhealthy attributes and attitudes that range in functionality from the heroic to the vastly destructive. At this level, young men and women can be courageous, street smart, and enterprising without the need for long-term planning. Individuals make good salespersons, working on the promise of the immediate reward of commission or other incentives without a thought for organizational capacity for production or delivery to match the promises Red makes.

Red organizations survive in tough times and remain resilient. This ᵛMEME helps societies and individuals break out of the superstition and the safety of the tribe and to be assertive in the face of conflict. Red expects reward for extraordinary valor or merit. It makes individual human potential possible.

A modern day expression of a healthy Red leader in the Middle East is the ruler of Dubai, who is also the UAE vice president and prime minister. He is undertaking one of the bravest social experiments in history as he attempts to move an entire culture up the ladder several stages in what historically seems to be a very short period of time. If it weren't for the raw courage of this value system, Syrian, Egyptian, and Libyan nationals in the opposition of their governance wouldn't have lead street battles and revolutions to liberate their countries.

As the need for accountability and transparency rises in a society, pressure builds on rulers or Big Bosses to surrender personal power. In organizational contexts, this is where the founder is pressured to step back and allow management systems to institutionalize controls. If the founder won't relinquish control, the organization falls into "the family trap." As organizations or cultures attempt to emerge from this type of individualized control, there is likely to be a long and bloody battle to exit this phase. Europe went through this as it transitioned from empire to nation-states. The Arab world is going through the transition now in a quest for patriotism and nation building.

Cultures naturally evolve but cannot skip a stage. Tribal societies in general must move through this feudal empire-driven stage to get to the next level of social development where an indigenous type of democracy (Blue-Order) moves power from the hands of "Big Boss" to "civilized institutions." How to facilitate this transition is one of the biggest challenges facing the Middle East today. This transition represents the most significant leap forward in socio-cultural organization, but often fails in its first few attempts. The transition from a Red feudal stage to a democracy (where everyone is equal under the law) has been the focus of the CHE-Mideast since 2005.

Blue: Orderly, Absolutist, and Authoritarian

The Fourth-Level System

The Fourth Level of Blue is the first system of nation-states. The prevailing institutions are based on the rule of law. At the individual level, according to Swiss developmental psychologist and philosopher, Jean Piaget, this is when children develop abstract reasoning. This is where concepts such as mortality, science, mathematics, classical music, and philosophy of nations began to materialize. Music at this level of existence is represented by sequential rhythms and marching bands like national anthems that evoke feelings of unity, religiosity, and patriotism. The *Battle Hymn of the Republic* and Beethoven's classical music are musical memes of this value system in the West. In the Arab world Um Kulthum's songs that championed the Nasserist brand of Arab Nationalism riled up the Arab street.

The Blue ᵛMEME is often described as "the Truth Force" because it is organized around an absolutist belief in one correct way requiring obedience to authority.[43] There are several segments that make up the total expression of this code around the world, but an important segment is religion. In religion, it is represented by *the one and only truth* of the Catholic Church, Islamic Sharia, and the Jewish Seven Laws of Noah. The trinity of *the son, the father, and the holy spirit* and the firm belief that the body is the *temple of God* in Christianity are parts of the religion's Fourth-Level system. So are the five tenets of Islam that are the *shahada* (Islamic creed), *salat* (daily prayer), *zakat* (alms giving), *sawm* (fasting during Ramadan), *hajj* (pilgrimage to Mecca). Historically, religion has represented the first appearance of the Fourth-level system and has remained a pillar in holding cultures together for centuries. Many societies resort to religious faith, a cornerstone of the Blue Fourth-Level system, in tumultuous times to restore their sense of purpose and the will to pull through during hard times.

Blue is a communal system where individuality is sacrificed as it is in the Purple system, but unlike Purple, the sacrifice is for a transcendent cause and not for the safety of the tribe. The theme is that life has a purpose, whether it is Godly or patriotic. If one stays on the straight and narrow there are rewards that will follow.

The nonreligious expression of this Fourth-Level system is prevalent in ideals, such as the Western adage prioritizing "Mom, Apple Pie, and the American Dream," or the belief in "God and Country." The Communist Party and the Socialist Party are expressions of Fourth-Level systems. The Marine Corps motto is "Semper Fi." The Girls Scouts and Boy Scouts are other examples of an orderly purpose-driven unifying system. Confucianism was the base of Blue in China's centrally-planned economy, which helped tremendously in making that country a great success. A Chinese citizen working in a company in the Gulf region transplants that same code of ethics and hard work to his or her work environment.

At this level of human existence, life itself has true meaning, specific direction, and predetermined outcomes. Unlike Red, where the spoils are the reward for asserting one's might, in Blue systems the rewards come to those who follow the rules obediently.

Governance in Blue is a clear hierarchy. The system revolves around the one true way of the law. Blue imposes law and order after a culture has been exhausted from the lawlessness of Red. Big Boss power gives way to stratified regulatory structures. In the West, the constitution of a nation defines the executive, representative, legislative, and judicial structures to which all citizens must adhere. Governmental or state agencies such as police, trade commissions, tax collection agencies, customs agencies; local zoning authorities that monitor city and municipal codes and building codes; and agencies that monitor environmental pollution, labeling requirements, food processing, social welfare, and social security, all define governance within the Blue Fourth-Level Value System. In this system, citizens elect bureaucrats who closely represent their values and reinforce the one true way. By invoking the name of whoever represents this ^{v}MEME, whether they are the prophets, a specific law, George Washington, Vladimir Lenin, or the Ayatollah, the masses are marshaled to unite.

In the United States the Second Amendment of the Constitution (the right to bear arms), is considered a red line when there is talk about gun control. In Islam, when it comes to discussions about separating religion and state, the issue becomes mute when Muslim scholars demand that lawmakers recognize Islam as a full system for living. Blue believes that righteous living produces stability and is its own reward in the present tense, as well as the only guarantee of future rewards in the hereafter. It seeks to control impulsive behavior through guilt. Everyone has his or her proper place in society. Morality and character are built through discipline. There are no areas of uncertainty in Blue. There is right, and there is wrong.

In Blue, education is a regimented, proven strategy unchanged for decades. Parochial schools exist in many European and North American countries. In places like the Middle East, religious authorities run Blue schools. They prepare pupils for the challenges of life but use rigid, moralistic, and punitive tactics.

Public schools in the Middle East don't do as well as their counterparts in the West because they lack the nationalistic secular mandate of the West. Education in the Middle East is still defined through religion and family structures regardless of whether you're Christian or Muslim. The teaching of moral values and acceptable codes of conduct are criteria institutionalized formally within the Fourth-Level system. It is often a patriarchal responsibility—the father is feared and the mother provides love and nurturing.

Creativity is not encouraged in Fourth-Level schooling, as it has the potential to distract the child from important dogma. In the Middle East, however, learning and reciting poetry are intertwined and encouraged since poetry is a source of tribal heritage. The Maaloufs are a family of poets and authors. My father was proud to let everyone know that his children could write and recite poetry.

Fourth-Level education in the Middle East doesn't place as much emphasis on educating girls as it does on educating the boys. Although educational systems are modernizing, girls are still expected to settle with their husbands and raise children. This is a concept that relates to the religious influence on education in the Middle East (and elsewhere). It undergoes some change as a culture becomes exposed to global value systems through the Internet.

Education, regardless of geography, is an important meme of this Fourth-Level value system and will continue to play a crucial role in shaping societies and nations. In Western cultures, life up until early adulthood is spent in educational systems. The Blue educational context is a factor that contributes to creating the foundations for continuing socio-cultural evolution and future stages of development.

The Blue organization is one of rigid hierarchy. It is bureaucratic with clear channels of communication. Accountability moves up the command chain while responsibility moves down. There are defined horizontal boundaries separating rank. When working with Blue organizations, I often hear employees say: "You don't talk directly to the suits!"

THE BLUE FOURTH-LEVEL ᵛMEME'S LEADERSHIP STRUCTURE

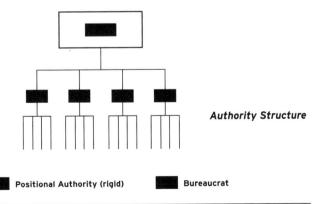

Authority Structure

▬ Positional Authority (rigid)   ■ Bureaucrat

In Fourth-Level organizations, people are sorted by skill-type rather than ability. Power is in the rank of the job, not the personality of the employee—as you would find this in a Red system. The entity is rarely an open system because it places so much emphasis on people being solely in their right and proper places. Job descriptions are set in stone. In theory, hiring practices, especially by government agencies or corporations that bid on government work, have to show transparency and conform to fair employment rules and regulations. However, there is usually an under-pinning social network that assures that only the right people get access. An example of this might be found in the family fortunes that facilitate their children's entry into Ivy League schools, positions of power, fame, or political careers—the political connections that assure the award of contracts to campaign financiers and friends of the family.

Blue organizations in the Middle East tend to hire men, the traditional heads of the household, since jobs are scarce and competition is fierce. Today, Westerners flock to the region to escape the Great Recession in search for work. In the Gulf region, Dubai's government agencies hire many expats for their talents, but their work has to be signed off by a national who is often their boss. This undercurrent of class-consciousness with regard to power and authority is operable through the Red/Blue/Orange ^{v}MEMEs, which is why the emergence of the Sixth Level and subsequent Second Tier value systems can be difficult.

In Blue organization everywhere, obedience and the promise of advancement in the future is obtained through conformity and ethical conduct, whether or not rewards are then actually delivered. Because of its rigid structure, innovation and risk taking are not a part of the orga-nization's core values. Employees are often thought of as a part of a well-oiled machine, important but replaceable cogs in the machine, each with measured input and specified requirements for output. Advancement is based more on seniority and less on meritocracy.

In healthy Blue organizations, the worker expects lifelong employment, and the employer contributes to a retirement account. Promotions, vaca-tions, and retirement are all planned at predetermined times. In an unhealthy Blue organization, workers can be dehumanized, and thus lose their sense of purpose and loyalty. Motivation is usually accomplished through instilling guilt for infractions, and there is an emphasis on tradition and class-con-sciousness. It can become fanatical, intolerant, and authoritarian.

According to cultural economist, Said E. Dawlabani, a Blue economic sys-tem is a necessary stage for a culture to build its infrastructure. In his book, *Memenomics: The Next-Generation Economic System,* Dawlabani describes how central planning and production dominate this system. There's no room for individuality and innovation. A financial system could be well developed, but its purpose is to serve the one true way as determined by its leaders.[44]

After decades or centuries of building Blue institutions, a culture is ready to transition beyond the Fourth Level to a new and more complex individualistic level based on meritocracy. As societies become secure in their Blue foundations, achieved through the development of orderly systems and institutions, they begin to question the constraints of the Fourth-Level Blue value system. Guilt and rigid order become stifling. Now society has far more complexity, so the next individualistic system will not look like Red. The culture has experienced and understood the relevance of the constraints of a Blue Fourth-Level System. The Red system evolved beyond the Purple tribal structure. The Blue system constrained the excesses of Red. The next system will have the strong Blue foundation to build on while it seeks autonomy and opportunity to innovate and be creative.

Life conditions begin to challenge institutions and corporations to produce better results faster, better products, and better scientific, technological, and medical innovations. Organizations compete for market dominance. Individuals begin to ask why wait for future rewards, I want the good life now. Upward mobility and enterprising thinking begin to break away from the rigid structure of society. But because outright Red has been constrained, this will begin a culture's entry into a more complex scientific and strategic Fifth- Level value system.

The Blue system was the hardest one for me to write about since I grew up in the strict confines of a Catholic School where guilt was the order of the day. I'm so thankful for having understanding parents who encouraged my individuality. They helped me realize my dreams even in our family of three overprotective older brothers who tended to categorize objectives for a young girl in a more traditional context than I wished for myself. Learning Spiral Dynamics theory clarified for me my tendencies towards individualistic value systems along my own spiral of personal and professional development.

Orange: Strategic, Enterprising, and Scientific

The Fifth-Level System

When *life conditions* change in a communal, conformist society in such a way that existing methods of dealing with existential conditions no longer work effectively, and when the idea of group sacrifice for the Truth Force loses its influence,[45] once again new ways of addressing the complexities of life must emerge. At this stage of human emergence the culture realizes it is being held back by group conformity. It wants to break out of the shadow of tradition and history to unleash individual potential and try new ideas. At this point in human social emergence, humanity seeks to improve on processes and procedures in corporate management, quality of everyday life, medicine, education, and multiple other systems through technology and innovation.

The Orange Fifth-Level value system tries to uncover the mysteries of the universe through science and mathematical algorithms. The human experience is quantified, categorized, and cataloged. Orange is *the innovative achiever.* The Fifth-Level ᵛMEME is competitive, optimistic, and enthusiastically takes calculated risks.

When in its unhealthy expression, an individual operating at the Fifth Level will not feel guilt if he or she can persuade or manipulate someone into giving up what he's got.[46] After all, this is a more complex form of the competitive Red ᵛMEME. Orange can be just as exploitive as Red, although it has been bound by the constraints of order, and it tends to work within systems. Rather than using force, Orange will use intelligence to create a rationale for what it wants; it will attempt persuasion and look for loopholes in every system that might be exploited.

As much as Orange is a creative knowledge seeker, Orange is individualistic and, thus, self-interested, seeking personal prosperity, recognition, and reward. Life is a strategic game and it is played to win. Unlike Third-Level Red, during negotiations Fifth-Level Orange welcomes compromise if this results in a win-win outcome. Orange achievement and respect does not have to be the result of complete dominance in a conflict, market, or debate, as long as Orange comes away with a recognizable advantageous position or profit.

To differentiate the value systems in the Middle East, when I surveyed Middle-Eastern business executives who attended negotiation trainings in the West, the most common feedback was that win-win thinking does not apply in the region. In the Purple-Red *life conditions* of the Middle East someone has to lose in order for the victor to be respected in his triumph.

Any culture with a dominant Fifth-Level value system will have a prominent middle class. These are the doctors, attorneys, scientists, academics, engineers, economists and other professionals, and the knowledge workers and technical experts that make up more than half of a country's population. Teachers in this value system emphasize science, technology, and math and find new ways of teaching these subjects in concert with the needs of the job market in a society that is on a continual path of innovation. Art, architecture, and music also introduce technologically creative elements.

The educational system in the Arab world had great Orange potential at the end of the Colonial Era, but became complacent in the face of the strength of the existing Blue educational system. Even the oldest and most advanced American Universities in the region, such as AU Beirut and AU Cairo, regressed. They failed to keep up with innovative educational methods that support the increasingly sophisticated needs of the world market. According to the Times Higher Education 2013-2014 World University Rankings, only two Arab institutions of higher education are on the world's list of top 400 Universities.[47]

The Fifth-Level system of values gave us the beginnings of Cubism, Abstract Expressionism, and Surrealism. The West experienced the Fifth-Level Musical Invasion in the form of the Beatles, the Rolling Stones, Led Zeppelin, Elton John, Jimi Hendrix, Janis Joplin, and the Grateful Dead, to name a few. After the genteel conformist Blue of the 1950s, music was a major catalyst that brought the West into the full expression of the innovative Orange ^{V}MEME. Throughout the Arab world today, rock bands are carrying the same social message that 1960s bands brought to the West. They are yet another catalyst pushing the envelope to change the status quo.

At the height of its organizational expression, the Orange ^{V}MEME supplants the Blue Nation-States with Orange Corporate Nations. Corporate boardrooms and shopping malls are the cathedrals of the Fifth-Level system. Orange organizational memes are forever memorialized in the 1976 movie *Network*. Consider the speech where Ned Beatty's character Arthur Jensen explains its highest virtues, which remain true till this day:

> There are no nations! There are no peoples! There are no Russians. There are no Arabs! There are no third worlds! There is no West! There is only one holistic system of systems, one vast and immense, interwoven, interacting, multi-variant, multi-national dominion of dollars! petro-dollars, electro-dollars, multi-dollars!, Reichsmarks, rubles, yen, pounds and shekels! It is the international system of currency that determines the totality of life on this planet! That is the natural order of things today! . . . There is no America. There is no democracy. There is only IBM and ITT and AT&T and Dupont, Dow, Union Carbide, and Exxon. Those are the nations of the world today.[48]

The term "Masters of the Universe" was often used to describe Wall Street bankers during this time. This value system began to emerge because of the mechanization of the Industrial Age, where human productivity increased exponentially in factories and standardized education gave people some time to read and think. It gave us Mm. Currie, the X-Ray, and Louis Pasteur and the germ theory of disease. It gave us Henry Ford's assembly line and mass production. Scientific discoveries popularized the idea that perhaps a human being is the master of his own destiny. Progress is the natural motivational incentive of this level. The good life became accessible through the strategic and efficient manipulation of resources. Enterprising thinking and values advanced Western cultures while leaving the rest of the world behind.

As *life conditions* become more complex in other parts of the world, in part due to the connectivity of global economics and the Internet, the desire for self-reliance and prosperity pushes countries like India, China, Russia, and Brazil (the BRIC countries) to take charge of their destiny and adopt the virtues of the Orange system. Some cultures, in a hurry to attain prosperity, tried to adopt Orange (Enterprising values) from PURPLE–Red (Tribal–Empires) and failed. Since cultures cannot skip a stage of development, emerging countries must spend a considerable amount of time in Blue (Order) before Orange can emerge in a self-sustaining systemic manner.

Prior to the financial crisis of 2008, emirates like Dubai and Abu Dhabi thought they were embracing the Fifth-Level value system. They were in a hurry to become a hub for financial services and the preferred destination for Arab wealth. With little experience in the Fourth-Level system, where institutions have been crafted and tested sufficiently so as to legally protect and sustain long-term prosperity, the region's economy was hit hard with the onset of the financial crisis. Today Dubai finds itself focused on building much of its institutional infrastructure (such as civil laws, laws that protect property rights, and consumer protections laws), and modernizing its commercial regulations before it can resume competition with the BRICs.

THE ORANGE FIFTH-LEVEL 'MEME'S LEADERSHIP STRUCTURE

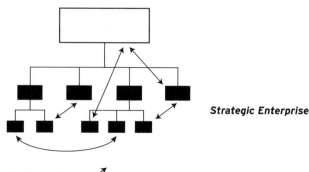

Strategic Enterprise

Positional Authority (flexible)   Leadership resides with the most competent

The organizational structure at the Fifth Level is a reflection of the competitive marketplace. This is where meritocracy supplants the seniority of Blue organizations, sometimes out of a sheer need for innovation and entrepreneurial energy to compete in the accelerating market. A young woman can ascend to the position of corporate vice president if her talents and skills prove superior to those who are older and have been with the corporation longer. At the Fifth Level, *strive-drive* is a function of success.

An Orange organization is an interactive structure where departments and individuals can engage in collaborative projects without worrying about "turfs" or hierarchical protocol. Communication is multi-directional depending on capacities and the needs of the task at hand. Decision-making at this level is based on results and the bottom line, but there is opportunity for risk-taking. Different management styles are tested to see what works best. The focus is on the three P's: profit, process, and people. The ideal corporation at this level is an open system that is both controllable and flexible, and thus able to adapt to the changing challenges of the marketplace. Resilient Orange corporations create ten, fifteen, and twenty-year plans with corresponding strategies on how to implement them. Their R&D departments engage in continual product development that insures the success of an evolving product line for decades to come. Experts rise quickly to leadership positions.

There's very low tolerance for mistakes at this level, as was the case with the Apple engineers who overlooked the simple design of the speaker and the map App on the latest version of the iPhone. They were fired. Maintaining a competitive edge is the primary goal as complacency can spell the end of a corporation within this value system. An example of this was when Apple first ousted Steve Jobs. The company lost its competitive and innovative edge and its spirit—a lesson for many other companies that try to institutionalize Blue ways of thinking in an Orange marketplace. Blue foundations are critical to support and regulate Orange, but Orange leadership is calculatedly entrepreneurial, which is essential in a competitive market today.

Since 2009 I have been working with a mid-size (8,000 employee) corporation in the Middle East to align its organizational structure and make it one of the very first corporations in the region to use a Fifth-Level Orange merit system. Historically, because of the existing oil wealth in the Arab world, corporate structures have remained a reflection of past *life conditions*. Salaries are class conscious and ethnocentrically conscious, based on nationality and ethnicity with secondary attention paid to talent or capacity. Throughout the region, Americans and the British are at the top end of the pay scale, but everyone else is paid much less. I spent an extensive amount of time training top executives in the methodologies of the *Spiral Dynamics Integral* approach. Then we devised a long-term plan for implementing Blue measures, processes, and procedures in every department in an effort to prepare the corporation for emergence into the Fifth-Level Orange system. We spent many hours on addressing meritoc-racy issues, identifying competencies, assessing employee qualifications, and assigning people to positions according to best fit. This continues to be a difficult task for the entire executive team as relationships with suppliers and the majority of customers are centered in the PURPLE–Red ᵛMEMEs. Since practices aren't sophisticated enough to see the benefit of win-win scenarios at the Third and Fourth Level, moving into the Orange Fifth-Level system requires the entire culture to change their "center of gravity."

As we will learn later in the *Natural Design* process, many Western con-sultants have not developed the knowledge or insight to understand the need to design within existing *life conditions* the structures and processes that can take people to the next level. I am fortunate enough to understand the value systems of the region and their content. By being able to trans-late Western Orange to Middle Eastern *life conditions*, I can create unique culturally fit solutions that work to bring success to organizations today. As the world becomes more of a global village, it becomes essential to assess cultural nuances and design for resilient societies in the region beyond the age of oil.

Governance under this value system is geared towards free market economies as societies move from Blue nation-states to Orange corporate nations. Laws, rules, and regulations are revamped to avoid the bureaucratic practices that hold back free trade and competition. *Life conditions* under the Orange ᵛMEME are more concerned with personal net worth than with political, military, and national ideologies. Once a culture is at this level, civil disobedience never descends to destructive levels of PURPLE–Red, as we are witnessing on the Arab street today. At this developmental stage societies have enough regulatory systems in Blue as part of their cultural DNA, so that the common belief is that "obeying the law and paying taxes is for the overall good of society." In the United States this style of governance started with the first Reagan administration, which overhauled the entire regulatory structure and deregulated much of the industrial sector in order to make it more competitive. England went through the same phase of transition under Thatcher's leadership. It's worth noting that much of the world today remains in the Blue governance stage or Red or even Purple. In a nation with unhealthy, predatory, and exploitive business practices, governance can easily be manipulated by big business, as was the case with the recent financial crisis in the United States that rocked the whole world.

Like all other value systems, Orange has a pronounced unhealthy expression. The relentless pursuit of better results, cheaper products, faster production, and bigger markets can come at the cost of damaging professional and personal relationships, *life conditions,* and the environment. With its insatiable appetite for consumption and disposable goods (including selling the concept of wealth and fame and keeping up with the Jones), the Fifth-Level system is responsible for the depletion of global resources and much of the environmental degradation around the world. In its worst form, an Orange system can destroy ecosystems and spread its toxicity—either physical pollution or an economic virus—to the point where it threatens the collapse of national and global economies. This was the case with the "too big to fail" phenomena when banks and insurance companies were bailed out by their governments.

Some economies at this level rely on the import of natural resources, and they will go to war if necessary to protect their supply lines. Wars fought for Orange reasons are far more dangerous due to advanced technologies, as is Orange's calculated exploitation in developing regions where vast tracts of land are deforested by the hour. Orange and Blue values can even mesh in the fostering of self-perpetuating wealth and power. Sadly, the loss of life and the environment become just another part of a calculation that dismisses collateral damage.

In spite of all the criticism of this value system, it is the corporations with global reach that are capable of bringing transformational change to their own practices and to the marketplace where they operate. As consumers demand more socially and environmentally conscious, more transparent, and sustainable production methods (such as organically grown, cage free, renewable, and recyclable resources) force corporations—in order to stay profitable—to alter their ways to answer the demands of the consumer segment of their stakeholders rather than only the stockholders. The sheer size of these corporations with their vast distribution networks makes them de facto change agents in the world.

Corporations also have the financial power to foster helpful innovations. For example, Monsanto was the first to mass-produce visible LEDs[49] and Kodak was the first to patent organic LEDs. LED light bulbs have facilitated massive energy savings. General Electric created the most commonly used sustainable light bulb. Coca-Cola is taking the lead in using stevia, a natural sweetener, to fight obesity; and McDonald's opened its first vegetarian restaurant in India.

Many individuals in this system, after attaining their career goals and material comforts, ask themselves "is this all there is to life?" Others, when faced with a divorce or a life-threatening disease of a loved one, realize that all the wealth they accumulated cannot bring solace. Just as Orange corporations give in to market pressures for sustainability and conscience, Orange individuals who have achieved their objectives and solved the problems of the Fifth Level of existence now begin to emerge from this individualized system and look for something more. This self-introspection, seeking a deeper meaning in life, leads them back to a communal value system. The search for inner peace begins, and some find it in spiritual practices, in nature, or similar pursuits. This is when Orange cultures begin to develop sensitivities to the "have-nots" in their own societies and corporations. As they delve deeper into themselves, they begin to look for ways to right the wrongs of Orange, and that's when they begin to ascend to the next level of existence.

Green: Egalitarian and Humanitarian

The Sixth-Level System

The Green Sixth-Level system is one of communal values again, but unlike Blue, the community is based on equality in a spirit that goes beyond the law or religious guidance. Society has emerged to this point with the solid foundation of Blue systems, which facilitated the emergence of individuals focused on achievement, progress, and material success. At this point, people begin to ask what more there is to life on Earth. Humanity enters the Sixth Level seeking to deepen its understanding of what it means to be a conscious organism.

At the Sixth Level the well-being of all life becomes a very high priority. Like Purple and Blue, Green's tendency is to "sacrifice the self now for the needs of the group."[50] Green often sees its "group" as all human life on Earth, and the ecological diversity that supports all human life.

To resolve the problems caused by unhealthy Orange pathologies, Green experiences a crisis of consciousness. It seeks to deepen a psychospiritual understanding of self, searching for inner peace and embarking on a journey of self-discovery. This Sixth-Level system is sacrificial, but more complex than the previous sacrificial systems. The culture has already integrated the sophistication of Orange and uncovered secrets of the universe through science. Now Green seeks the egalitarian life. A healthy manifestation of this level is apparent in Scandinavian countries where the "cradle to grave" welfare state offers equality to all in education, housing, and healthcare. At the same time, there is a strong work ethic. Everyone's input is valued equally under this system.

At this stage of existence, culture has enough complexity to recognize the importance of the balance between the patriarchy and the wisdom of the feminine. In a culture centered in the Green ᵛMEME women are equal contributors to society with equal pay and access to opportunity. Human existence at this level is a balance of the feminine and the masculine, the yin and the yang.

I often hear employees in organizations say we want consensus, which is a Sixth-Level phenomenon that can only work if all decision makers are at the same level of complex thinking. Since the objective of this level is to create harmony between people and nature, Green seeks to raise the awareness of the group and help with their growth process. A good example is the Human Potential Movement that gave cultures in the West tools to access their untapped potential. The field of humanistic psychology is also rich in Green practices. It looks at the human being as a whole person and proposes that humans are well aware of themselves and their responsibility in the world.

Decision-making at the Sixth Level gives equal importance to all contributors. People do not expect to follow the Chief, as they do in Purple, or follow the Big Boss in Red, or the bureaucrat and the religious authority in Blue, or the most strategic and wealthy in Orange. Green thrives on openness, trust, and sharing. Its values reflect the beginning of man's humanism.[51] This value system however, tends to overlook the hierarchical nature of human development and often misses the synergies between *life conditions* and capacities in humans.

Many young people in this value system live off the hard work and the financial success of Orange parents and Blue grandparents. However, they forget that this is the ladder that helped them ascend to their present level of complexity.

While the Green ᵛMEME sees itself as *world-centric* in its reach and practices, it looks down on other value systems rather than recognizing their contribution and point of view as essential to cultural emergence. Green sees Orange as greedy manipulators who exploit the planet. It despises Blue because of its authoritarianism and religious and patriotic conformity. But it believes that Red and Purple, in their less evolved states, are victims that should be given a chance through dialogue to progress.

Music of the Sixth-Level value-system includes the songs of the Beatles after they visited the Maharishi in India. It is in John Lennon's "Imagine," George Harrison's "My Sweet Lord," and Paul McCartney's "Silly Love

Songs." It is in the Eagles song "Hole in the World," as well as new age music that hopes to heal body and mind. The Monroe Institute uses Green scientific methods including binaural beats of music that alter brain waves and deepen human consciousness.[52] Green music in the Middle East does not exist yet. There, Orange music is just emerging in a few subcultures throughout the region.

In the movies, Green values are symbolized by the defenders of the environment in their fight against the Orange and Blue establishment. We hear Green in the opening lines of Al Gore's *An Inconvenient Truth*, and in the documentaries *Food, Inc.* and *Gasland*. The primary theme is to rally public opinion in support of sustainable practices. It is also seen in the movie *The Contender* (2000) where the president of the United States decides to shatter the glass ceiling for women in politics by nominating a talented female Senator from Ohio to the Vice Presidency and causing much friction with the Blue-Orange political establishment. The television series *Dharma and Greg* captures the essence of the interactions between the Fifth- and Sixth-Level systems. While Greg comes from a wealthy family, fully centered in the Fifth-Level Orange system of values, Dharma's family is well placed in the Sixth-Level Green system. Dharma represents the new generation Green, while Greg represents the transition from Orange to Green. If you can watch reruns of this show, look for these [V]MEMES and all the memetic attractors and the large General Category [G]MEMES that define them.

Leadership under this value system is pursued through providing satisfaction for group needs and desires. Reciprocal participation in decision making is of great importance and the weight of "we're all in this together" carries the heavy burden of reaching consensus. Nonconformists are usually isolated or excluded from the group's social and emotional benefits. If nonconformist behavior persists, individuals are asked to leave the group. Under unhealthy Green leadership, productivity suffers as it diminishes Orange's strategic drive, and Blue's organizational skills. In its aim to avoid hurt feelings, it demands less of its people and forgives mistakes too easily. Since pulling together is one of the hallmarks of the system, Green leadership thrives when everyone is pulling for the same cause, such as in a crisis mode.

Governance under this system is symbolized by the social democracies of Western and Northern Europe. Its goals are to offer economic, political, and social equality to all. It believes in the diversity of views in representative government regardless of ethnicity, creed or social class. Awareness of the environment, the health of the planet, as well as the welfare of each citizen is ideally woven into public sector decisions.

Green taxes Orange activities heavily in order to achieve its desired outcome. The election of France's president Francois Hollande looked to undo Sarkozy's Orange gains by taxing the wealthy at more than 75 percent. This was an indication of how burdensome this form of governance can become. Because of its heavy taxation on the private sector, like the previous communal systems, it discourages innovation and investment in R&D.

In the United States the Green system of governance began to emerge with the first election of Barack Obama. The fact that he was re-elected for a second four-year term is an indication that there's more cultural awareness for the need to spend tax money domestically on social programs, address environmental issues, and rebuild a crumbling infrastructure. Whether or not the president is able to carry out these ideals remains a function of how quickly the values of the Green system are emerging. Since capitalism favors the individualistic systems, the United States isn't likely to spend much time in the Green governance level. Hopefully it will spend enough time in Green to have a sustainable effect. If not, the problems created by the previous systems may not resolve sufficiently.

Foundations, non-profit organizations, community co-ops, and environmental corporations are the kind of organizations that flourish within the Green value system. The knowledge economy has been one of the most successful and profitable forms of Green organization to emerge. Its undeclared goal is to democratize access to information throughout the world. Massive open online courses (MOOCS) being freely offered by collaboration among major U.S. universities to millions of students worldwide exemplify the emerging Green ideal of globally accessible higher education. Of course, this would not be possible without Orange innovation and technology.

Green believes that employees are naturally motivated to perform their tasks, especially when the organizational purpose reaches beyond profit and becomes world centric. The basic organizational unit under this ^vMEME is made up of horizontal relationships among teams with democratic channels of communication. While Orange organizations offer emotional intelligence training to their employees to improve their skills, Green organizations expect their people to have high emotional and interpersonal intelligence. Organizations such as Whole Foods Market use Green practices in their hiring processes, and much of the creative environment around Google's engineers is Green.

It is difficult for an organization to maintain a Green perspective in the face of escalating global challenges and complexity. The Red Cross, whose very neutrality is what enables it to be effective in war zones on both sides of a conflict simultaneously, conducted a survey a few years ago to find out

THE GREEN SIXTH-LEVEL ᵛMEME'S
LEADERSHIP STRUCTURE

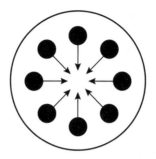

Social Network

● People, organizations and cultures are groupings of equals
coming together to deepen the human bond

whether or not they could offer a statement of opinion in certain circumstances after the fact. Clearly leadership was having difficulty focusing on the primary mission.

Another large Green organization is the United Nations, or Green is what the UN was expected to be ideally. Conservative American politicians, especially in the face of Orange, have accused it of being ineffective and others have accused the organization of bias. A recent example is the mission of UN's special envoy, Kofi Annan, to Syria. He could not convince either side in the civil war to drop their arms and negotiate a peaceful settlement. Seeing the world through an egalitarian lens, it is clear that the UN has no operable understanding of the different value systems around the world. Although its efforts ideally would come from the Sixth Level, its own organizational structure has become a closed bureaucratic system steeped in hierarchy and aristocratic practices.

In the summer of 2007, Dr. Beck and I spoke at a Values Caucus at the UN where we presented a future vision of what the UN could be if they adopted a whole-systems approach. If they use the stratified lenses of Spiral Dynamics to see the world and design for different ᵛMEMES and *life conditions*, they could become more effective. In June of 2013, Dr. Beck and I spoke again at the UN regarding the reforms needed in order for the organization to answer more effectively to increasing global demands. A detailed discussion of our design strategy for a different UN will be detailed in one of the upcoming chapters of this book.

Like all other systems, Green has potential for unhealthy expression of its ideals. Upon reaching consensus everyone in the group must comply. Individual views, regardless how insightful they are, must conform to the group dynamic. Zealot Green leaders often manipulate groups to gain consensus on their own point of view. Leaders might dismiss group members by claiming they are not conscious enough or sensitive enough to contribute or understand the higher purpose of the group. In severe cases, consensus-seeking strategists will wear down those who present of other points of view rather than supporting real open debate and inclusion of all concerns.

By taking the moral high ground on issues and dismissing other input, very little gets accomplished and decisions are less likely to be implemented or sustainable. Because of the lofty goals it sets for itself and for others to follow, Green can become very pessimistic when it fails to save the whales, or shut down the World Bank, or bring peace to Middle East. By failing to see the complexity in the levels below it, Green blames Orange and Blue for the plight of Purple and Red. By making them victims it can undo some good (critical) work that the Orange and Blue systems are engaged in around the world, while enabling Red to take complete advantage of Green's naiveté. Remember, Red wants to win and does not care how.

Once Green begins to realize that not much has changed in its quest for egalitarianism it starts the search for a better, more sophisticated system that can better handle the new levels of complexity it created. It has brought sustainability, social consciousness, and environmental awareness to the fore, but has failed to create an idealistic ascension of humanity. Human warmth and the holding of hands wears thin as *life conditions* begin to require a different set of tools to be used. Individuals with insightful ideas become frustrated with the constraint of communal systems, as always, and with the consensus process in particular. They begin to break out on their own again. First Tier systems are all stuck in terms of seeing the world only from their own point of view, even though each system transcends the prior system. Often the Sixth-Level Green system has to regress to Orange in order to pick up individualistic elements before it can surge to the next tier.

At this point, Green might realize that it must make a profit to forward its ideals and social conscience. Once a culture reconnects with its individualistic values, it can transcend and include Green as it enters the next tier of the spiral. This is where change-agents begin to develop stratified thinking and begin to understand how to handle the coming complexity of multiple value systems co-existing on Earth. Since Green is the final level in the *First Tier*, it takes exceptional vision for the system to transition to the first level of the *Second Tier*. This transition to the Second Tier is what Dr. Graves called a "momentous leap" in the endless quest of the spiral journey.

LEVELS OF THE *SECOND TIER*: VALUES OF THE MAGNIFICENCE OF BEING

Yellow: Flex Flow, Integral, and Functional

The Seventh-Level System

Yellow is the first individualistic level that recognizes the complexity facing the entire world and works to save the spiral from collapse. Based on the seminal research done by Clare W. Graves this level is described in his groundbreaking article in the *Futurist* magazine (April 1974):

> When man is finally able to see himself and the world around him with clear cognition, he finds a picture far more pleasant. Visible in unmistakable clarity and devastating detail is man's failure to be what he might be and his misuse of his world. This revelation causes him to leap out in search of a way of life and system of values which will enable him to be more than a parasite leeching upon the world and all its being. He seeks a foundation of self-respect, which will have a firm base in existential reality. He creates this firm basis through his G-T value system,[53] a value system rooted in knowledge and cosmic reality and not in the delusion caused by animal-like needs. At this level the new thema for existence is: "Express self so that all others, all beings can continue to exist." His values now are of a different order from those at previous levels: They arise not from selfish interest but from the recognition of the magnificence of existence and the desire that it shall continue to be.[54]

This system has a big-picture view and approaches problems from a systemic perspective. While "systems-thinking" has become the latest buzz phrase in the annals of science and academia, complex systems have been a part of the value-systems vernacular for over a half-century. Complexity, when it comes to the Yellow–Integral system is the ability to see the myriad of manifestations of the entire meme stack of the spiral of life with all its levels, expressions, contents, and spectrums. This Seventh-Level Yellow system is compelled to take charge of a shattered world, heal the wounds of every preceding level, and unblock the streams that prevent humanity's continuing emergence.

I often hear Don say, in describing the tenacity of this Seventh Level, that it falls upon the shoulders of this system to transform what political scientist Samuel Huntington termed as "the clash of civilizations" into the "confluence of civilizations." Since society is unable to solve all its problems from the perspective of the First Tier systems that caused these problems, Yellow explores different functional ways to act responsibly in each of these contexts. By recognizing the importance and contribution of each of the different evolutionary stages of the spiral, Yellow is able to employ a different set of strategies than what is available to each specific First Tier stage. At the same time, Yellow is fully conscious of the context of its interaction with each of the other ^vMEMEs.

The *Integral Design Architects* (IDAs) have proficient skills in systemic Seventh-Level Yellow applications. These professionals rely on *Indigenous Intelligence Experts* (IIEs) who know the memetic contours (value-system stack) of their own societies and who can work in a self-organizing manner with Yellow IDAs on the challenges and blockages facing a culture of the First Tier. Through the Natural Design process and principles, the Yellow system teaches culturally-appropriate ways to influence a chief in a tribal society, or an autocrat or a nationalist in an order-seeking society. Yellow also looks for ways from behind the scenes to spread the memes of socially conscious entrepreneurship in an enterprise-driven culture and indigenous humanitarian memes in an egalitarian culture. Actual applications of this systemic design and the "integral toolbox" that provides solutions for every layer of the spiral will be a subject covered in the next few chapters of *Emerge!*

THE YELLOW SEVENTH-LEVEL ^vMEME'S LEADERSHIP STRUCTURE
Integrative/Functional/Natural/Knowledge-Centered/Highly Principled

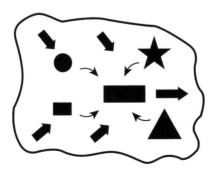

Systemic Flow

Yellow generates a flex-flow perspective as it honors value-system differences and facilitates the movement of people up and down the spiral, which produces a sense of satisfaction, recognition of the layered dynamics of human systems operating within people and societies.[55] This Seventh-Level Yellow system employs "functional analysis" strategy based on intuitive logic. This type of analysis can accommodate a large number of functions and thus have significant relevance for multiple processes of improvement across whole societies.

At a meeting of the Evolutionary Leaders organization, Dr. Beck and I detailed global applications of functional analysis that involve the different segments that exist within every society, including government and religious institutions, educational and health care systems, law enforcement, and civil organizations. Our approach always begins with the question: "What is the change that needs to take place in the world today?" Then as a group we define the pool of talents essential for achieving the goal.

This is a stark contrast to the Western approach of implementing developmental projects in the interest of the so-called modernization of the developing world. Results have shown that funding of development programs falls into the hands of Red leaders, the feudal lords and corrupt officials who squander the money leaving these countries in perpetual debt. There are a few non-profit organizations which intimately study the "memetic lay of the land" to deeply understand the needs of the people and develop unique methods to deliver aid.

The work of the international organization Médecins Sans Frontières (Doctors without Borders) is a functional example of a Seventh-Level approach to humanitarian aid. Médecins Sans Frontières uses differential diagnosis to determine what ails the human body then provides the appropriate medicine. In addition it creates a habitat that supports safe drinking water, providing autonomy to the most remote villages. Yellow values are also seen in actor Brad Pitt's *Make it Right Foundation* where he called upon the top architects in the world to design homes within local environments in New Orleans so that energy efficiency, flood resistance, and cost came together to provide a sustainable solution for the city.[56]

Unlike Green, the Yellow level does not like working in groups. It seeks autonomy and works outside the group once the problems are identified. It performs the "thin slicing" that Malcolm Gladwell describes in his book *Blink.* Thin-slicing means making a conscious effort to make very quick decisions with minimal amounts of information to produce distinct biological and sociocultural effects. Yellow has the capacity to do this for the entire meme stack without being bogged down by the issues that polarize intra-level disputes and inter-level discord.

Yellow music is symbolized by the tension between chaos and order. Jazz with its combined African beat and European classical music is interactive, collaborative, and relies on improvisation to create a new sound that includes the Blues music in Purple, classical music of BLUE–Orange in a collaborative environment of Green. This all crescendos into a smooth flowing sound, with elements of melody and rhythm, as well as dissonance and syncopation that represent musical values from the entire meme stack. Yellow is beautifully depicted in Enya's song *Pilgrim,* where the journey is the endless quest and the pilgrim is the human who is able to see the First Tier levels objectively for the first time. In the arts Yellow is the painter's intention behind his or her art that matters. Alex Gray's transcendentalist art grounds altered states of consciousness within his raw depiction of the human body. This represents Yellow-Level art.

Leadership at the Seventh Level has a big-picture view of living systems. Leaders design for each culture differently, based on recognition of its *life conditions.* Yellow may introduce different ideologies to the mix of solutions. Seventh-Level Yellow leadership bases specific solutions on feedback emanating from the needs of a particular culture, and no other.

Change and tension between ideologies and group dynamics are signs of open systems, those that are capable of change. At the Seventh-Level Yellow of complexity, individuals and groups are comfortable with some uncertainty. The safety of hiding behind an ideology no longer exists. The Seventh Level looks for common goals among people in order to help create a *superordinate goal* informed by the aspirations of a specific society. Yellow is unlikely to be influenced by any political party or a group of people in business or in government who are beholden to their own interest groups. This integrative value system recognizes that each party has its own agenda. Simply put, a superordinate goal is a unifying concept, a future pull that everybody wants, but no individual or group can achieve unilaterally on its own.

Perceptions of a superordinate goal are based on Muzafer and Carolyn Sherif's Social Judgment Theory: an individual weighs every new idea, comparing it with the individual's present point of view to determine where it should be placed on the attitude scale. This construct was further developed by Don Beck by including perspective from within the spectrum of value systems. Dr. Beck applied the concept of a superordinate goal in large-scale systems design in South Africa, and together we applied this concept in Palestine

The superordinate goal is what we call the Third Win (third in the series of a win-win). While the brightest expression of the Fifth-Level system seeks a win-win outcome driven by strategic values, and the Sixth Level is busy seeking consensus, handing out aid or arranging for temporary shelter, the Yellow Seventh-Level system seeks to facilitate the emergence of a resilient society capable of self-sustenance.

The setting of superordinate goals has always played a historical role in moving culture to its next stage of development. During World War II the United States and the British allied with Russia in order to defeat Nazi Germany. The alliance was strategic and intended simply to serve a particular purpose. In this particular case, the objective of the superordinate goal was easily identifiable, but when designing for socio-cultural emergence during a stalemate in relations—such as Arab-Israeli peace negotiations—the superordinate goal has remained vague at best. "Peace" in and of itself is not yet a functional vision, even if it is mutually desirable, because each entity is at a different level of existence. A solution must come from Second Tier, where the *life conditions* and needs of all cultures can be objectively considered in designing functionality for the future.

Yellow always seeks a Third Win. In the case of the many peace accords in the Middle East a reasonable superordinate goal could have been "peace through the people." Yellow leadership could have taken the extra steps and used a layered approach that would have reflected the unique needs coming from the *life conditions* of every culture. A true reflection of "doing the peace people want done" would have reflected more accurately on the existing conditions. It would have also shown the evident asymmetry between the memetic contours of the Israeli and the Palestinian cultures. Chapter five details much of our experience in the use of tools of the Seventh-Level system in Israel and Palestine.

Organizations at the Seventh Level are designed and aligned for functional fit. This is where form follows function and the organizational chart changes according to the desired output. I heard Don many times talk about tossing out the old organizational chart and creating a new one based on the function that people in the organization can fulfill. The organizational authority structure is flexible and tends to favor the most competent individual or group. The diverse mindsets are placed into a functional flow where productivity, happiness and growth are maximized.

In my work in the Middle East I often find this misalignment within corporations where employees with MBAs and a high aptitude for Fifth-Level Orange functions languish in administrative Blue positions. Others with great analytical skills, who should be a part of strategic planning, are assigned routine tasks such as human resource management. One Orange CEO asked me if an employee who was centered in PURPLE–Red should be fired. After seeing this person at work and talking to him, it became clear to me that this person represented the company's connection between the past and the future, a core quality of the *Indigenous Intelligence*. This was a construction conglomerate where hundreds of thousands of Dinars were extended in credit based on this employee's good word. This individual was able to make connections and contribute at a level that the CEO did not really understand. Yellow organizations are always inclusive of healthy practices at every level of the spiral.

The philosophy behind the *Conscious Capitalism* movement of Whole Foods Market is also based on Seventh-Level principles. However, like many ideologies, when it comes to real life applications *Conscious Capitalism* has to meet *life conditions* where they are. This is a system that is emerging from the highest quality Orange entrepreneurship inclusive of sustainable and accountable Green practices. It is bringing prosperity to farmers and suppliers and will eventually emerge into a Seventh-Level Yellow system.

Since *life conditions* in the United States are predominantly in the ORANGE–Green stage, *Conscious Capitalism* is often confused with traditional practices of the Fifth Level, which only seeks to make money. However, this isn't a wolf in sheep's clothing. Yellow organizations identify stakeholders beyond the customer, the employee and the stockholder. While Orange cares about the three P's—*profit, process, and people,* Yellow adds the two P's of *planet and principles* to move the system into fully sustainable practices.

The world only started to experience the Seventh-Level leadership a few decades ago. According to Beck, less than ten percent of leadership in the world today is in Yellow. The problems that this system might resolve or create are only barely visible, mostly in Northern European countries and to a certain extent in U.S. subcultures. Its future expression remains difficult to predict. Theoretically, in order for our planet to fully emerge into the Second Tier, Yellow would have to provide solutions to the major world problems in First Tier before we might begin to witness the start of a transition into the Eighth Level of existence. Today, Dr. Beck is cautiously optimistic about the emergence of Yellow thinkers in the midst of the dysfunction in Washington and elsewhere in the world. Solutions offered by any of the First Tier systems will not result in sustainably integrated outcomes, as is evident in the solutions proposed for the Middle East to date.

I am also cautiously optimistic about the role human evolution will play for the good of our planet. This Seventh-Level system is emerging in young people I meet in the United States, Europe and some parts of Africa and the Middle East. It is empowering healthy practices along the spiral, guided by an army of IDAs that can prevent rogue Red from building another nuclear bomb. It leads Orange away from the continuous destruction of the environment, while moving Green away from its utopian state of mind.

Turquoise: Holistic and Global Commons

The Eighth-Level System

The Eighth Level is anticipated to be a holistic system that looks at Earth as a living organism in order to detect imbalances affecting the entire system. Turquoise works through natural channels to bring the earth and its life forms into an allometric balance. Allometry is a discussion of scale. The term allometry in biological systems, for example, refers to the need for differing density of support structures (like a skeleton) in similar organisms of different size, or with regard to the growth rates of the different parts of a single living organism.[57] Allometry can also describe a number of analogous concepts and mechanisms between cities and biological entities. The field of biomimicry also teaches us about the resilient and adaptive intelligence of nature.

According to Graves' empirical research, there were very few individuals who exhibited Turquoise thinking in the world and they were all above the age of fifty in his time. Today, although I've met some people younger than fifty who have Turquoise thinking, its full manifestation still remains far into the future. Turquoise is not necessarily a spiritual system, as some mistake it to be. Many in the spiritual and integral community believe they are doing the work of the Eighth-Level system when in reality their work is egalitarian. Before the holistic value system becomes a reality, the Seventh Level has to do its work of stitching together the deep wounds of a fragmented world suffering from the damage of First Tier values.

Green often confuses its values with those of the Turquoise *world centric* ᵛMEME. Until egalitarian individuals can respect, assess, and design for each of the First Tier value systems in the world, their efforts are not yet Second Tier. In my conversations with Don about the distinctions of Second Tier, he stated that in First Tier, the individualistic systems are primarily a left-brain function, and the communal systems are a function of the right brain. He went on to explain how in Second Tier, the two hemispheres mesh more closely together. He holds the belief that Yellow is a left-brain function with feelings, and Turquoise is a right brain with data.

We look forward to a fusion in Second Tier where data and feelings are combined in a communal system that encourages individuality. This will make for a balanced and powerful design that can influence global change. This is where the differences between the "we" and the "I" are resolved to form a self-organizing principle that is capable of addressing world problems efficiently. When a significant number of First Tier socio-cultural systems can operate in a healthy and functional manner thanks to the

THE TURQUOISE EIGHTH-LEVEL 'MEME'S LEADERSHIP STRUCTURE
Synergistic/Conscious/Interconnected/Globally Aware

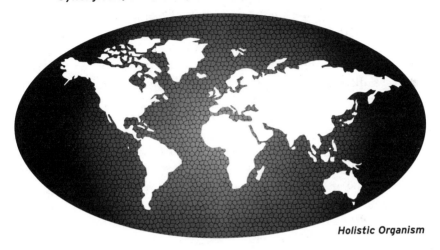

Holistic Organism

Seventh-Level system efforts, then it will become self-actualized. Turquoise, as a Global Governance system can step in to gather its data and diagnose the latest factors that retard evolution, the gaps that Yellow might not be able to fill. It is a system that seeks to create order from the Being Tier of values and not from the Subsistence Tier, so there must be a functioning Seventh-Level Yellow system in order for the Eighth Level to emerge.

In this holistic system, the world is viewed as a single, dynamic organism with its own collective mind. The self is, at the same time, both a distinct and a blended part of a larger, compassionate whole.[58] This Eighth Level is again a communal system in which the motto is "sacrifice self and others as needed for global survival." It shares Yellow's global views and its ability to think systemically. Global Governance tribes emerge as Integrative individuals of the Seventh-Level system step forward as global leaders, rather than working individually. At this stage of development this Eighth-Level system forms "Holarchies," which are a distributed intelligence model that allows Second Tier functions to manifest into what is termed "Global Commons."

Early signs of this phenomenon are manifested in the digital commons as in the website Wikipedia. The term "commons" has origins in the allocation of cultural and natural resources that are accessible to all members of society. The manifestation of these values in the physical realm is not yet possible until we solve the problems the Yellow system leaves behind. As often is the case, technology will act as a future pull that moves emergence forward in adapting the values of the digital commons to the values of culture, thus allowing Turquoise to manifest.

The Second Tier deals with complexity easily and sees patterns and consequences not apparent to the subsistent systems in the First Tier. Turquoise discovers the connections and principles that underlie the diverse spectrum of interwoven living processes on Earth. The principle of self-organization has many parallels within the Turquoise system, similar to how physicist Ilya Prigogine described the Second Law of Thermodynamics. This is what happens after a system reaches entropy and the point of bifurcation and starts reorganizing in a natural way. In value systems studies, Yellow and Turquoise are the stages of culture exiting First Tier values, which were imposed on society. Graves' "momentous leap" can be compared to the point of bifurcation where more natural systems for human existence begin to emerge.

Turquoise is also anticipated to include elements of what Teilhard de Chardin describes as the *noosphere,* the "sphere of human thought" that is a lexical analogy to the atmosphere or biosphere. Vladimir Vernadsky, a contemporary of Chardin, described the noosphere as the third phase of development of the Earth itself, after the geosphere (inanimate matter), and biosphere (biological life). This idea is being researched at the Princeton Global Consciousness Project.

Chardin describes an increase in both material complexity and consciousness, and theorizes that the Earth is being drawn in an updraft towards a higher order point of complexity and consciousness, an *Omega Point.*[59] The Omega Point is, in Chardin's opinion, already existing, unifying, transcendent, autonomous intelligence. Chardin sought to reconcile Christian faith with evolution. Issac Asimov's short story, *The Last Question* (1956), as in *Star Trek: The Motion Picture* (1979), saw human and technological life merging. Bennett, author of *The Dramatic Universe* criticized a perspective of one moment as the culmination of a process separate from the significance of the potentially eternal pattern of the human journey.[60]

The Turquoise system can have spiritual values, but the tenets of its spirituality are to have respect for all religions and spiritual concepts. It recognizes religious Blue as the next healthy stage of emergence for many parts of the world. Unlike Green, which criticizes religion as an instrument of control, Turquoise views it as an essential moralizing stage to facilitate respect for life and continue the emergence of the First Tier systems. Turquoise recognizes that in the absence of a strong Blue presence in the form of societal structures such as educational systems in the developing world, religious institutions fill a crucial role.

The concept of global villages in the Digital Age, where neurosurgeons in a hospital in the United States perform remote brain surgery on a soldier in a military station in the hills of Afghanistan, is an early sign of the potential of Turquoise. The Eighth Level is another order-seeking communal system, but it is the first one that searches for the macro view. Turquoise wants to see everything at once before doing anything specific, and this dominates the thinking process. It recognizes that mutual interdependencies reign supreme.[61]

Since it is a holistic system, Turquoise deals with complexity through Machiavellian paradoxes that might offend the sensitivities of First Tier values that exist today. Life is precious, yet at the same time global resources are precious and limited. Resources must be managed in a prudent way. In this value system, no monopolies, commodity traders, or oligarchs of any kind can manipulate resources against the prevailing ethic.[62]

Eastern traditions often deal with Machiavellian paradoxes as inevitable to human existence. I practice a non-dual meditation where life itself is viewed as a transition on the road to higher consciousness regardless of how we assess our personal accomplishments. These non-dual inspirational states of being (perhaps similar to Zen) are often seen in the poetry of the great Eastern masters like Rumi when he says:

> *Out beyond ideas of wrongdoing and right doing, there is a field.*
> *I'll meet you there.*
> *When the soul lies down in that grass,*
> *the world is too full to talk about.*
> *Ideas, language, even the phrase "each other" doesn't make any sense.*

Governance under this holistic system is expected to be the very definition of the New Global Order where chaos is seamlessly managed and addressing the threats to the survival of the earth itself takes priority. It is highly speculative to describe a governing system under Turquoise since the problems of entering into the Yellow system are just now becoming evident. The pressing question today is not when would Turquoise governance appear, but rather what would Integral Governance in the Yellow system look like to allow for Global Governance in the form of Turquoise leadership to emerge. First Tier systems are still competing fiercely for their subsistence views and resource allocation. This will postpone the manifestation of Second Tier values.

The financial crisis of 2008 exposed many of the structural problems in our presently ineffective Blue governance systems. This will take decades to address before we emerge into the Integral Age. With all the dysfunction in the European Union, few countries seem capable of transitioning into the Seventh-Level system right now. Turquoise regards its goal as the stewardship of planet Earth, and requires the necessary authority and power to get the job done, but current global leadership could be centuries away from the point where such values are a common goal.

At the time the book *Spiral Dynamics* was first published in 1996, there was speculation about the existence of a Ninth-Level system, CORAL. This is shown on the diagram of the original spiral. The debate about the existence of CORAL has created a philosophical difference between the integral philosophy community and the Gravesian school. While followers of integral philosophy believe that this system is manifesting itself, Gravesians contend that in order for a new value system to emerge, problems of existence from the previous system must be solved. As we have stated throughout *Emerge!*, the "life conditions" of the Gravesian framework are not present to support more complex thinking on the spiral yet.

We discuss the emergence of the Seventh-Level Yellow and Eighth-Level Turquoise systems based upon Beck's decades of observations and on-the-ground practical experience of applying these concepts in cultures and organizations around the world. When I asked Beck to address the casual reference to CORAL by the integral community, he acknowledged that there are few individuals around the world with "CORAL thinking." However, CORAL *life conditions* will not be manifested until a time when cultures are ready to solve the problems of the Eighth-Level system and ready to exit that level. This is a phenomenon that remains speculative and far into the future. As previously described, Turquoise is decades or centuries beyond Yellow, which is only beginning to emerge now—in good part thanks to the lifelong work of Dr. Don E. Beck.

THREE

MEMEtocracy:
What Makes Democracy Functional

Many forms of Government have been tried, and will be tried in this world of sin and woe. No one pretends that democracy is perfect or all-wise. Indeed, it has been said that democracy is the worst form of Government except for all those other forms that have been tried from time to time.[63]

Winston Churchill
House of Commons Speech
November 11, 1947

Which form of governance serves as the best model to manage the complexity of human existence? This debate is as old as modern humanity itself. From Aristotle to Lenin, and from liberal social democracy to socialism and Marxism, the West continues to deliberate the issue. The debate has grown even hotter in light of the failure of democratic governments to protect their citizens from financial ruin since the financial crisis of 2008. While Russia and Eastern Europe have abandoned the tenets of communism and central planning, China seems to have made these concepts into powerful, functional tools for prosperity and global economic dominance. It seems that liberal thought leaders in the West want to constrain the free market—a construct that comes with democracy, while in India, the largest democracy in the world, leadership is advocating for the existence of free markets and the democratic institutions that support them. In fact, free markets that are guided by visionary values for governance continue to serve as the most effective tools for spreading prosperity to the masses.

DESIGNING GOVERNANCE THAT FITS

In the Middle East, past Muslim jurists and philosophers shaped many governance philosophies from al-Ghazali and Ibn Rushd (Averroes) to Ataturk. These political philosophies could represent a more native form of leadership, an Arab-style democracy of sorts that is more suited for the region. In the modern history of the Middle East, the few countries that adopted colonial forms of democracy saw their national institutions fall into the hands of competing Za'eems and tribal leaders. Third Level *fiefdoms* competed for resources with little focus on policies that might create the values of the Fourth-Level system (nationalism and equality). Other leaders, like Nasser, ambitiously sought to create one Arab nation spanning the entire region but did not understand that the human capacities required for such a sophisticated level of governance were yet to emerge.

Democracy has to be interpreted through the prism of value systems as it would be seen through a leader's own levels of development and unique *life conditions*. The absence of this type of design is the primary cause of so much modern-day dysfunction in the emerging and developing worlds. Often countries in these regions that haven't built a robust presence in the Fourth Level of Law and Order system tend to use the tenets of democracy as weapons against the opposition political parties within their countries.

While some politicians compete for power as retribution for historic grudges, others draw battle lines and use the democratic institution as their primary means to steal and pillage their nation's resources. Today these examples are rampant in all parts of the world, from the African National Congress (ANC) under the leadership of Jacob Zuma, who is rife with corruption, to the Ukraine's ousted president Viktor Yanukovych. Both leaders are centered in the Egocentric Third-Level system and use democratic institutions of their respective countries to enrich themselves.

Many countries like South Africa and the Ukraine are struggling to reach a political level of development where the leader upholds the abstract concepts of democracy as their highest virtue. I recently interviewed one of Nelson Mandela's closest friends who has political aspirations and wants to revive his long-term vision for South Africa by running for president herself. Dr. Mamphela Ramphele is quite critical of how President Zuma crowned himself as Emperor and enriched himself and his cronies with the people's money.[64] She understands that the post-apartheid era in South Africa hasn't lived up to its promise. Although some of the blacks have prospered, the vast majority of them still live in poverty.

The 2014 presidential candidate is familiar with the value-systems framework from the days of Don Beck's involvement in South Africa. She keenly understands that white South Africans have become arrested in the order-driven Fourth-Level system with little political influence to affect national policy. The name of her party Agang, (A-Khung) means "to build." Dr. Beck and I advised her party to use the election slogan "We've had white rule. We've had black rule. Now it's time for South African rule." No grand ideas from the Fifth Level system or higher but a unifying vision that represents what the new nationalistic fourth-level system would look like for a new, post-post apartheid South Africa.

POLITICIANS OF THE FIRST TIER SYSTEMS

Based on research conducted by our colleague Alan Tonkin at the Global Center for Human Emergence, over 95 percent of political decision making in the world today comes from the values of the First Tier System.[65] In order to define the functionality in MEMEtocracy, which is a concept of the Second Tier, Seventh-Level system, we should describe the political motivations of every First Tier level. This is a stratification of the memetic profiles of that 95 percent and a detailed description of what political leadership represents in each value system of the First Tier:

Second-Level (Purple) Tribal Politician: This politician is primarily concerned with the survival of his tribe and/or clan. Political views are greatly dependent on connection to lineage. What the people of the tribe decide will be done. In contemporary political arenas, this tribal model for politics doesn't exist in its pure form, it's often dominated by Third-Level feudal lords.

Third-Level (Red) Heroic/Egocentric Politician: Strong, expressive self-image, displays raw power and unrestrained by guilt. This politician dictates and the rest listen. The powerful grab the spoils. A Third-Level politician commands respect through fear. Distribution of government services is feudalistic, where the political leader and his or her cronies gain power and wealth and say to hell with others. Under this system societies experience the largest income disparity between the powerful and the powerless, the rich and the poor.

Fourth-Level (Blue) Order-Driven/Nationalist Politician: This politician is ethnocentric, and sacrifices for the greater good of their religion, their party, and the nation. In modern democracies they have stringent party loyalties, where one party rules over control of government. The highest calling is patriotism. Justice is for those who follow the constitution and the rules. Unlike Red politicians, the Blue politician controls his or her impulses to grab power for the promise of higher rewards from religious beliefs or ideals about nationhood. While the need to conform is important to achieve political goals, Blue political systems use guilt to force their members to adhere to the principles and rules of the ideology, regardless of how arrested, or closed the system is. This system is what's next for over 60 percent of the world population from the Middle East to Africa and parts of South America.

Fifth-Level (Orange) Strategic/Enterprising Politician: Many politicians in Western democracies are fully realized in this Fifth-Level system since ambitious individuals seek to leverage their power. Unlike the Fourth-Level politicians, they're not afraid of going out on a limb to advance new ideas. They are pragmatists in their approach and don't take matters personally. Gone unchecked, they strategically and mercilessly manipulate power, even if it borders on the illegal. The unhealthy version of these values is depicted in the highly successful Netflix series *The House of Cards*.

Fifth-Level politicians treat their position as a lifelong career as they accumulate power and block newcomers from entering the system. They are threatened by fresh and new ideas that bring innovation to government practices and dedicate enormous resources toward any efforts that seek to dismantle the status quo. Fifth-Level politicians champion the laws that allow corporate lobbyists to advocate for corporate interest, and they see nothing wrong with loopholes that allow them to buy stocks with insider information. Should they lose an election, they know that they have more lucrative lifetime employment by being political lobbyists. Both Democrats and Republicans in this country are heavily invested in keeping the system the way it is.

Sixth-Level (Green) Egalitarian/Humanitarian Politician: These are the values that we see in mostly homogeneous Western social democracies. This is a political system that views everyone as equal. The government's job is to ensure this equality, even if that means higher tax rates. Northern European countries are leading the way in this political value-system. Social programs don't receive as much scrutiny as they do in our country, as there's little abuse of the system. Green political values are reflected in the level of happiness of the constituents in the system.

A study by *Forbes* magazine shows that six out of the top ten happiest countries in the world are social democracies dominated by the Sixth-Level political values.[66] There are some Democrats in the United States like Vermont Senator Bernie Sanders and Minnesota Senator Al Franken who belong to this value system. Since this is a communal system, the unhealthy aspect can blind leaders from seeing the exploitations of the less complex systems. An example of this manifestation is the failure of the system in Northern Europe to properly integrate immigrants coming from feudal and tribal *life conditions*. European economic integration, although not the subject of this book, is an example of how Green political values failed to assess economic capacities of southern European countries like Portugal, Spain, Italy, and Greece. France and Germany, in their rush to overcome the guilt from WWII, approached European integration from a Green perspective with little regard to ORANGE-Blue political and economic capacities in the southern part of the continent.

These are the dominant values that drive the passions of First Tier politicians. Much of the work that the Yellow Seventh system does, is the alignment of First Tier values on a healthy trajectory, to insure that cultures don't become arrested on their journey toward more sophisticated political systems. The mistake that Western organizations and governments make, is that they presume that the developing and emerging world follows the same modernization trajectory of the first world. They overlook the importance of the memetic profiles of the culture that determine which dominant value system defines that culture's center of gravity. Designing from the Seventh-Level system always moves the less complex levels to their own healthy expression first. This allows each system to have more density as the culture prepares to move to its next natural stage or level. This in turn creates healthy models that fit the unique expression of the culture.

THE HEALTHY MODELS THAT FIT

Interestingly, the three most significant monarchies in the Middle East, Saudi Arabia, Jordan, and Morocco, seem to have escaped the wave of change brought about by the Arab Spring. Benevolent monarchs who seem to be more responsive to their people's needs lead these kingdoms. They have enacted several reform measures to accommodate the evolving changes within their culture and the region around them. A benevolent monarch is a far more compatible fit to govern an emerging Fourth-Level culture than a career politician or a military officer, who may take on the role of a dictator. Monarchs of the region act as caretakers of the land and the people, and they have historical power and recognition which is important to Purple. They are the ideal value systems experts who can transition the PURPLE–Red values that dominate the culture through healthy expressions that enable emergence to the Fourth-Level ᵛMEME.

Examples of these healthy expressions of PURPLE–Red are reflected in the programs that King Abdullah of Saudi Arabia enacted before trouble started brewing in his kingdom. As the Arab Spring was sweeping through the region, he authorized business-lending programs worth tens of billions of dollars to channel the energy of Saudi youth into entrepreneurial pursuits. At the first sign of trouble in Jordan, King Abdullah dissolved the Jordanian parliament and invited the Muslim Brotherhood to participate in the next election.

His actions diffused much of the pressure that was building against the monarchy and served to expose the rhetoric of the Muslim Brotherhood in Jordan. The result was that the Muslim Brotherhood decided not to take part in the elections. King Mohammed VI of Morocco enacted reforms that are helping that country transition to a constitutional monarchy where the Muslim Brotherhood has a mildly Islamist agenda without absolute power.

These are examples of resilient local governance models—those that are congruent with the prevailing value systems of the society. This is what MEMEtocracy embraces as *forms of governance that fits*. Cultures centered in PURPLE–Red, not only in the Middle East, must transition to a Blue system and the values of patriotism, equality, and the rule of law. Absent a monarchy that provides policies leading to this transition, the Muslim Brotherhood in the Middle East and North Africa (MENA) represent the next system.

Blue systems must generally emerge from religion. So, the Muslim Brotherhood will naturally moderate its views, as it must contend with a globalized electorate that seeks modernization. Today, Egypt's Muslim Brotherhood is spread over many levels of the values spectrum, from PURPLE–Red radicals, to BLUE–Orange entrepreneurs who hold the key to Egypt's economic future. While liberal parties in Egypt and other parts of the region want to see Western-style democracies, (ORANGE–Green governance), these ambitions won't be realized until the culture goes through the challenging phases of a uniquely Arab-style Blue that builds the institutions of a nation.

With the military seizing power again in Egypt and outlawing the Muslim Brotherhood, any new leadership must integrate the needs of Egyptians who gravitated to the MB that were being left behind under Mubarak's rule. The new leadership, military or otherwise, must be able to win the hearts and minds of the followers of the MB. It must meet them where they are and provide them with the basic necessities that attracted them to MB in the first place. This has to be a long-term gradual integration program that will diffuse tension and polarization and pull most Egyptian towards a centrist nationalistic Blue.

Where there is a sparse tribal presence, such as in Afghanistan, Pakistan, and remote parts of the Middle East, some form of laissez-faire governance would be a better fit for the nomadic Purple *life conditions*. Safety and tribal conformity is of paramount importance to this value system. Change happens very slowly where there are tribal families run by feudal lords. It will take generations for them to develop alternative ways of thinking and the abstract concepts that lead to nationalistic rather than tribalistic allegiances.

In Lebanon, for example, Red drug lords have a monopoly on heroin and hashish. They have historically controlled the Hermel region in the Bekaa' Valley. No national army or local police force would dare to enter the Hermel. Over the years the area has become a sanctuary for hardened criminals who want to escape the reach of authorities. One of my family members who visited a small town in that region tells the story of how he was offered cocaine served in small silver ashtrays alongside sweets and coffee. This was consistent with Arab tribal customs of hospitality. There is no strong Blue presence to influence or strong-arm the power of these drug warlords. No Lebanese authority can seize the land on which the poppy is grown. No other power can imprison these drug lords. A MEMEtocracy style approach would aim to transition the local farmers to different crops supported by attractive but temporary subsidies.

Another alternative might be for global pharmaceutical companies to buy the opium poppies at prices high enough to compete with the drug smuggling trade. The farmer still might face retribution on the ground locally, as in Mexico where the cartels use scare tactics against the entire civilian population. Still, a number of simultaneous measures might arrest the unhealthy Red drug lords' behavior. Such actions at the local government level could include new, non-punitive Blue measures to educate the youth, to promote national values, and to develop entrepreneurial skills for lucrative careers in the neighboring Gulf region. This memetic template could be used in many parts of the world, including South America, with minor adjustments in messaging relevant to the mindsets and belief systems of the local population.

The presence of any form of nationalism (Blue) has to accommodate the tribal (PURPLE–Red) autonomy that dominates the different regions within each country. This was a hard lesson the Western coalition troops learned in their search for a leadership structure that delivers effective results. Coming from Order-Driven, Strategic (BLUE–Orange) Western value systems, it took them decades to finally realize that the powers that held the key to their success lay in hands of tribal leaders. The success of the Anbar Awakening in Iraq was a clear demonstration of how engaging with the *Indigenous Intelligence* of a culture could significantly alter the outcome of a battle or even influence the emergence of the culture itself. No grand democracy design was needed. The coalition needed a deeper understanding of the memetic lay of land. This explains why the tribal leaders hold the power to restore local order after the rule of a dictatorship collapses.

Many Middle Eastern dictators are being overthrown through revolution, and their countries are left in a free fall. Should new governments and constitutions be designed to best serve the needs of their people, they must take into account factors that reflect each country's level of societal development, its value preferences, and its *life conditions*.

What form of governance can account for all of this and build robust institutions that will care for the future of their citizens? Did the Afghani government installed by the coalition forces survive after Western presence wanes, or are we seeing the Taliban return to dominate tribal life in Afghanistan? Did Iraq naturally transition towards a Federalist system with three semi-autonomous regions or does it continue to exist as one nation? Should Syria be carved into ethnic territories where the predominantly Kurdish northern region is annexed to the semi-autonomous Kurdish part of Iraq, and the rest divided between the Alawite minority and the Sunni majority?

Although much of the oil-rich Gulf region has averted the chaos of the Arab Spring, the future of political leadership in the region faces many challenges. What type of change would these oil-rich countries need to undertake in order to maintain their viability as self-sustaining nations beyond the age of oil? And what would that type of governance look like? The MEMEtocracy framework provides some of the answers to these questions while offering a whole-system approach to geopolitical design.

MEMETOCRACY:
THE MODEL FOR FUNCTIONAL DEMOCRACIES

MEMEtocracy is the design for governance that fits. It takes best political practices that are congruent with a specific culture and places them in a design scheme that meets the societal landscape and prepares the culture for its next stage of emergence. It chooses the mechanisms and functions needed to fulfill the needs of the people. This is based on their value systems and the challenges of the *life conditions* of the culture. MEMEtocracy is the functional operation of democracy that answers the question of why cultures with different memetic profiles require different styles of political leadership and governance. The primary function that MEMEtocracy serves is a memetically-honed, indigenously-informed form of political leadership.

Because of its dynamic nature, the model has pronounced political cycles that mimic natural systems. It represents the widest applications of the Second Tier concepts of *Natural Design* and *Functional Flow*. It is based on decades of academic research in developmental psychology, memetics, complex adaptive systems, and the emerging field of biomimicry. This is what we field-tested as a new governance model in our Build Palestine Initiative that will inform infant Arab democracies about how to sustain healthy indigenous governance.

I will chronicle our experiences in Israel and Palestine through the CHE-Mideast that were based on the application of our theories of the need for the creation of an indigenous type of democracy. This model can also be a catalyst that transforms corporate practices when Blue-Order and Orange-Enterprising values in business can inspire positive change in government.

THE OPERATING SYSTEM

MEMEtocracy is a unifying political theory that answers the question of *why* different people and different cultures need to be governed in different ways. MEMEtocracy provides a new framework on how to structure these governing systems. This is a Second Tier theoretical approach that assesses the memetic contours of the culture in order to uncover the deeper layers of conflict within competing political value systems. It is a whole-governance approach to politics that designs for the needs of a specific society and covers a wide spectrum of global value systems from emerging nations to mature democracies. While democracy defines governance through the power of the people, MEMEtocracy designs a functional flow for an indigenous type of democracy that better serves the needs of the people.

The primary focus of this innovative framework is to place governance on an evolutionary pathway that naturally keeps pace with the changes in culture and selects the proper political form of leadership that fits the memetic composition of that culture. This is a whole-systems approach that addresses the needs of the entire spectrum of a nation's values simultaneously. It embraces the virtues of autocracy where they are needed. It embraces the virtues of liberal democracy where this type of governance serves the needs of the electorate. As long as these systems are congruent with the current needs and the future aspirations of a culture, they serve the functional purpose of MEMEtocracy.

Genesis of MEMEtocracy

Before discussing the applications of MEMEtocracy and the actual case study in Israel and Palestine, it is important for me to share how I came across many of these insights about governance. This was my journey before I uncovered this elegant framework.

The elements of *functional democracy* became apparent to me some time after I began my search for unifying principles of governance. I was looking for constructs that would provide appropriate Blue values rather than a popular system of governance or a system imposed by colonial powers. I spent years researching and studying different political leadership approaches and evaluating the reasons for their success or failure. My journey began after I graduated from law school and set my sights on reforming laws that dealt with women's rights in Lebanon. I quickly realized that a formidable battle lay ahead.

Although Lebanon, a former French colony, had designed its constitution based on the Napoleonic Code, Lebanese democracy looked nothing like French democracy. While the French had a three-decade mandate to try to understand the culture and design appropriate governance for it, something was lost in translation. Lebanon was left with a constitution based on confessionalism, in which the highest offices were proportionately reserved for representatives from certain religious communities. What it needed was a transition from religious Blue to nationalistic Blue. In a place dotted by villages of different ethnicities that rarely trusted each other, this Western experiment was bound to fail. Women's rights were not a constitutional issue; they were an issue of value systems and religion.

Whether these Lebanese sects were Roman Catholic, Maronite, Greek Orthodox, Druze, Shia, or Sunni, for centuries religious courts delivered the rule of law. This was the form that the Fourth-Level Blue systems used to keep order within each of the various sects. This was and still is a flawed system, especially when one compares the resulting level of women's rights in Lebanon with women's rights in other countries in the world today. A national constitution could not eliminate these traditional conduits of power in just a few decades. A deeper understanding of what motivated the PURPLE–Red value systems was needed in order to design appropriate solutions for the culture. This was my first realization of the importance of *life conditions,* the simple term coined by the Graves/Beck framework that animates a "culture." No political system can be designed without the full assessment of where culture lies in its developmental stages. In basing the constitution on sectarianism (in the hope of creating national cohesion) the French carved up the country and destined it for more than seventy years of failure.

Any political system must take into account the prevailing value systems that exist in society before an indigenous form of governance can be designed. This is the Memetics in MEMEtocracy. This framework assesses the memes and the functions they need to perform as they collectively define the governance preferences of a society. Only after the memes are fully understood, will the task of designing the form of leadership for a socio-cultural system begin. We've all heard the phrase that "form follows function." In MEMEtocracy, the form of governance follows the culture's memetic function. This approach represents the continuously evolving (or regressing) dynamics between the people's *life conditions*, value systems, and the political landscape. It is the evolutionary nature of the model that parallels the never-ending quest for balance on the spiral of values.

Recognizing Political Life Cycles

Political philosophies have a life cycle: entry, maturity, and exit. Political systems, regardless of how robust they are, if they are not placed in an evolutionary flow that takes into account the changing dynamics of a culture, become toxic and reach abnormal points of entropy. In complexity models, healthy systems mimic nature and reach entropy as a natural part of the life cycle. Closed systems that fight to survive beyond their normal life cycles are compared to biological systems that become cancerous. Cancer cells, if gone untreated, only die after they kill the host. This is the abnormal entropy of a living system. Similarly, political systems that are not placed into an evolutionary flow will create embedded political practices that are cancerous and toxic. The more they become misaligned with the evolving culture, the higher the toxicity and the effects of abnormal entropy.

An open political system allows entropy in the exit phase to happen naturally, which always leads to a higher level of political sophistication that naturally transcends and includes the lower systems that came before it. The newly emerging system becomes the dominant political philosophy, while the lower, less sophisticated systems convert into informational units that continue to be important to smaller segments of the culture . . . They become an integral but a much smaller part of the whole. This is how the emergence of the entire culture moves to more advanced complex systems. This is the *"transcend, include, and anticipate"* nature of politics based on theories of memetics.

In the Digital Age, socio-political ideas and trends are no longer limited to local or national belief systems. The shape of new governance is influenced by the spread of information globally. Politicians need to integrate this evolutionary process into their thinking. Informed by emerging global memes, MEMEtocracy designs for local and national needs and anticipates global trends to shape its policies. The framework embraces the essential role that information plays in exposing political corruption at every level of the spiral and in different parts of the world. By playing this essential Seventh-Level role in the Digital Age, MEMEtocracy makes the entire spectrum of values transparent. This allows the citizenry to be informed on how well politicians are executing the functions they were elected or appointed to perform. Information spread by the Digital Age in the MEMEtocracy model keeps the open system aligned with the evolving needs of *life conditions*.

Defining the *Indigenous Intelligence*

Indigenous Intelligence is one of the most crucial elements of the MEMEtocracy model. Throughout his career, Beck has emphasized the importance of working with people who know the culture of the country they are working in. It wasn't until I teamed up with him to create the CHE-Mideast that I discovered the need to further define his thinking on this particular subject. For someone who was born in Lebanon, I noticed certain events, behaviors, and phenomena in Middle Eastern cultures that were missed by most of my highly intelligent Western friends. This pattern of things lost or missed in translation kept repeating in higher frequency as our work progressed, making it necessary for me to conduct research into this area.

I began to develop my model after much analysis of field data and assessment of why development problems persist in spite of all the good intentions behind foreign aid and the noble work of non-governmental organizations.

Often the term "indigenous" is associated with native minorities and cultures of the developing world that have been marginalized by progress. In this context, I was looking to redefine the meaning of indigenous to include the "unique value-systems expression" of the complex intelligences within each culture. Those indigenous intelligences can offer their countries, and the world community creative solutions that meet the challenges facing our world today.

As I looked into the field of social sciences, nothing identified the general subject of local cultural knowledge as a separate and distinct field of intelligence or an area worthy of acknowledgment with its own unique characteristics. An Internet search for the term revealed results for a business entity organized to provide Native American veterans with jobs in consulting services.[67] After spending many days in research and failing to find any definitive writings on the subject, I turned to the work of Howard Gardner as a last resort.

Gardner, a Harvard developmental psychologist, had pioneered the field of *multiple intelligences.* In his 1983 book, *Frames of Mind: The Theory of Multiple Intelligences,* he outlined a total of eight types of intelligences that included the original measure of cognitive intelligence.[68] Since then, Gardner has updated his original findings to include many applications, but at the time I conducted my research this pioneer had not included the field of local cultural intelligence as a factor in his influential research the way Beck and I viewed it.

Based on my field experience and the extensive research I conducted in the areas of social psychology and world cultures, I came to define "indigenous intelligence" as follows:

Indigenous Intelligence (II) is the multidimensional capacity of an individual or a group in a specific society to interpret its value-system's complexity to non-natives. It is represented in a cross section of any given society, from the Millennial Generation to women, community leaders and elders of the tribe. Unlike other intelligences, it provides rich and actionable culturally fit answers, to why certain individuals or groups act in certain ways. Why do they have certain preferences, priorities, beliefs and worldviews and why solutions need to be tailored for their specific value-structures.

Indigenous Intelligence informs governance by assessing the *life conditions* of the people and the challenges they face. II paints a more complete picture of the obstacles facing stakeholders in a society, not just the elite and the privileged. It always finds opportunities in the challenges facing a certain society and finds a silver lining through creative thinking. Economic development that is informed by II places the uniqueness of people's capacities into a long-term development scheme that makes the culture move at an accelerated pace while building resilience and self-reliance at every stage.

Indigenous Intelligence Experts (IIEs)

Indigenous Intelligence is manifested in individuals as well as groups that are experts who exhibit the following characteristics:

+ They are most likely natives of the territory who speak the language, know the customs, and understand the culture and the many subcultures within it.

+ Their thinking is an open-system with high cognitive abilities. They can speak with ease to tribal leaders in their same colloquial tongue as well as to a national or Western politician and be fully aware of the value-structure distinctions of what is being said.

+ He/she is shaped by the first-hand experience of his/her own transition from being zealots and flamethrowers. He/she has earned his/her dues in becoming a conciliator and pragmatist who thinks about future generations and their well being, rather than having a need for revenge, instant gratification, and traditional allegiances.

+ IIEs, instinctively discern the complex patterns of their society by identifying developmental gaps and allowing for the process to evolve naturally. This is in stark contrast of how the West paints other societies with broad strokes through their people's own prism of values, missing much of the local nuances.

+ They understand the value-systems meaning of history through first-hand experience and can help Western organizations become more efficient in their fieldwork.

+ They understand the complexity and the uniqueness of the indigenous challenges that brought the culture to its current status of desolation.

+ They're strategic and systemic in their thinking and believe in efforts that can be sustainable and resilient for generations to come.

+ They look at Western organizations' objectives for peace and prosperity and help them channel their efforts in order not to offend local stakeholders with historic grievances, while at the same time providing culturally-honed plans for distributing resources where they're most needed.

+ They are servant leaders who realize that functional alignment with the needs of their society is at the top of their agenda.

IIEs open the door to a culture from the inside in societies that would otherwise be hesitant to disclose any information to outsiders. They can move freely through the various value systems within their culture, knowing how to uncover the challenges facing the culture and repair the expression of every local 'MEME. In parts of the Middle East that have seen war and have gone through the Arab Spring, many IIEs gain respect due to their activism and sacrifice. At times these people served time in jail for their views and actions. The rest of the culture witnessed with admiration their transformation from tribal and feudal lords to pragmatic leaders and conciliators. They live in two worlds and cater to the traditional needs of the tribe while expressing with clarity and vision, the future needs of their nation.

In an intra-conflict they are the ones who most understand the different positions within their own party or clan because they shared that same journey. When it comes to inter-conflict issues, they understand the motivation and value systems of the enemy through pragmatic lenses, and they interpret the actions and decision making of their opponents through strategic thinking.

IIEs become the primary source for information in creating what we call *Indigenous Design*. The concept of Indigenous Design emerged at the same time when I was doing research on the Indigenous Intelligence concept. Because IIEs bring a richer and more resilient perspective to our attention, the nature of what we design has to reflect the uniqueness of the culture. This data becomes the blueprint that informs the design scheme that is specific to each society. It defines the content of each development program based on local need, and made more sustainable by the global knowledge of *Integral Design Architects* (IDAs). Indigenous Design is the fundamental component that makes the MEMEtocracy blueprint actionable.

In creating the blueprint for MEMEtocracy IIEs are the primary source of information for the *Integral Design Architects* who chart the large-scale scheme for the culture. It is only through the data that the IIEs gather from their societies that a large scale design expert can support a Seventh-Level Yellow politician or business leader to design functional solutions and create open systems for Purple, Red, Blue, and Orange. This is the uniqueness of the Indigenous Design approach. Data on local cultural trends collected by IIEs become memes that determine the indigenous content of every 'MEME. This, in turn, determines the meme stack of the entire society for which we are designing a *functional* system for governance. While IDAs can work in any given culture and continue to provide the big picture design, the presence of IIEs is an integral part of the MEMEtocracy framework. They are the only ones who understand the mindsets and belief systems of their own culture.

Defining the *Integral Design Architects* (IDAs)

The *Integral Design Architects* are the experts in the value-systems frame-work and its large-scale designs and applications, which will be discussed in more details in the next chapter. In his earlier work, Beck defined these experts as Integral Design Engineers. The more work we did with NGOs and governmental agencies, the more we noticed the resistance to the term "engineer." To the Green ᵛMEME that dominated these agencies, the word "engineer" was associated with social engineering, which stopped many conversations before they even started. In looking for an alternative word to engineer, the word "architect" seemed to have positive associations and wasn't stigmatized in the field of social science. In 2005 Beck and I adopted the use of architect in the place of engineer.

IDAs are certified practitioners in the applications of Spiral Dynamics Integral Theory and Beck's tools of Large-Scale Psychology (LSP) that are detailed in the chapter on the applications of MEMEtocracy. These are individuals who have committed to the use of both the value-systems framework and Beck's (LSP) as the primary set of tools in their approach to solving problems. Most of them have worked directly with Beck for five to ten years and have played a critical role in successfully designing for cultures during stages of transition. Often times they are the directors of the Centers for Human Emergence in their own region of the world.

IDAs include my colleagues in South Africa, Alan Tonkin and Loraine Laubcsher. They have both worked with Beck since the beginning of his involvement in South Africa. Loraine, who knew Graves personally, and worked with South Africa's tribes during Beck's involvement, continued her work in mapping the PURPLE–Red values within South Africa for the last twenty years. In December 2013 at age 83, she received her PhD from South Africa's Da Vinci Institute for Technology Management. According to Beck who hooded her at her graduation, her thesis entitled "Human Niches-Spiral Dynamics for Africa"[69] represents the widest value-systems account of the inner workings of South Africa's tribes. It explains in detail the indigenous content and the process of how to design for the healthy emergence of cultures with those unique value systems.

Another IDA is our colleague in Iceland, Bjarni Jonsson, who had Beck as one of his PhD advisors at the Adizes Graduate School in Santa Barbara, California. Jonsson earned his PhD in June 2013. His work with transform-ing large-scale social systems took on a new direction after the onset of the financial crisis of 2008 that claimed Iceland as one of its first victim. As a part of his academic research, Jonsson had mapped out the value-systems profiles of Iceland in 2007. Much of the research then pointed to a noticeable change in the direction of the Icelandic way of thinking.[70]

Those value-system profiles were tabulated again in 2009 and both results were shared with Icelandic government officials. After detailing much of the value systems and Beck's LSP approach to government officials, Jonsson was tasked with designing the themes and some of the elements of the 2009 Iceland National Assembly. According to Jonsson, the research that he brought to light through these community meetings became the template that initiated the constitutional process for the 2010 Icelandic National Constitutional Assembly. The proposal for constitutional change referred to Jonsson's work as "a seal of authenticity" and the changes to the constitution were adopted with two-thirds voter approval. [71] A summary of Jonsson's findings and the history of value-systems testing and the different cultural assessments he conducted on Iceland are detailed in Appendix B of this book.

Other examples of the crucial work that IDAs do are shown in Said Dawlabani's book *MEMEnomics, The Next-Generation Economic System*. Before embarking on writing his book, which is an IDA's perspective on the United States economy, Dawlabani played a critical role at the CHE-Mideast in mapping out the economic challenges facing the Palestinians. There are also a number of European CHEs that are headed by IDAs. In Germany, our colleague Dorothea Zimmer works tirelessly on making the value-systems framework accessible to German businesses and government agencies alike.

In the Netherlands, our colleague Peter Merry, heads the CHE-NL that has been working on many global initiatives including the design of a new Hague Center for Global Governance and advising the World Health Organization on a MeshWORKS approach for mother care.[72] Dr. Marilyn Hamilton is the head of the CHE-Canada and the author of the 2008 book *Integral Cities: Evolutionary Intelligence of the Human Hive*. As an IDA, she is bringing eco-regional resilience to cities by incorporating much of the tenets of Beck's work into a whole-systems design scheme for cities and urban regions.[73]

IDAs are the quintessential Second Tier thinkers who approach systems design from Seventh-Level Yellow functionality. They play their crucial roles from behind the scenes as they shape the thinking of Seventh-Level politicians, business leaders, heads of NGOs, and global aid agencies. They are not interested in the visibility their work allots them but in the functionality of what they design. By doing their work from behind the scenes, they insure their recommendations take on the highest form of Indigenous Design resulting in optimum success.

The community of IDAs and the heads of all the CHEs around the world form what Beck calls a global constellation of change agents. Those who are familiar with Beck's framework often refer to IDAs as one of the first-known Turquoise tribes.

Setting Superordinate Goals

In today's global political and economic climate, it seems that the world is divided into two main camps of political thought. The first is liberal and advocates for social programs, fair wages, equal opportunity, and labor rights. In its extreme cases it forces the continued use of social programs out of guilt rather than a measure of effectiveness. The second is more conservative and advocates for meritocracy, fiscal responsibility, and self-reliance. In its extreme cases, it develops religious, racial and gender intolerance. Neither of these two distinct systems serve the full needs of the electorate. In economically stressful times, moderates and independents are left out of the decision-making process. The ideology that has majority rule makes the choice for the entire population. Under these circumstances a governing system cannot articulate a single superordinate goal. As explained earlier, a *superordinate goal* is a value proposition that everybody wants and needs, but no individual or group can achieve unilaterally.

In the past, superordinate goals were created naturally in times of war. Everyone rallied behind the vision of the leader. This was the case when the United States entered WWII and during the first Intifada of the Palestinians, as well as during the 1967 Arab-Israeli war that unified many Arab nations on one side and the politically divided Israelis on the other. The coalition forces' invasion of Afghanistan after 9/11 had a superordinate goal and vision. Patriotism, or an existential threat to the culture, both cause superordinate goals to rise naturally.

But in times of peace how do we define a new superordinate goal without an ominous existential threat? This is a challenge of MEMEtocracy. We need a whole-systems approach to a superordinate vision in times of relative peace to sustain us. John F. Kennedy was able to craft a superordinate goal during the "cold war" between the United States and Russia, inspiring citizens with the vision of a manned mission to the moon.

It's About Value Systems

In the Middle East, political leaders could be monarchs or Za'eem as long as they are advised by *Indigenous Intelligence Experts* (IIEs) and use designs that are formulated with the input of *Integral Design Architects* (IDAs). These leaders will be pioneers and will have the foresight to intentionally move their culture at the same pace as *life conditions* are progressing. This is not to say that if a culture's next system is a RED–Blue stage it calls on a brutal leader like Saddam to oppress the people. Red can be a self-actualized healthy value system within the appropriate constraints of Blue. An IDA would advise those leaders to implement healthy Red measures that call on the bravery and chivalry of the young generation to express itself in other forms of Red, such as sports competitions, and heroic endeavors on behalf of the earth's ecosystem. In a predominantly Red culture, IDAs would also advocate for obligatory service in the military reserves where the hero archetype rises in a contained environment surrounded by Blue structures. This develops patriotism and plants the seeds for a healthy Fourth-Level system. In Arabic this concept is called Al *Mouwattana*.

This new breed of politicians believes in the health of the whole system and of all the people along the entire spectrum of values as they go through different stages of emergence in their lives. These politicians don't just find political solutions; they design memetic master plans that introduce change in order to keep pace with the changing values within a culture as it engages with an increasingly global environment.

MEMEtocracy has elements of all past and present ideologies, yet subscribes to no particular permanent or artificial form of politics. It uses what is appropriate for the stages of development in every level of culture. It places each culture into a functional flow that serves the emergence goal—the superordinate goal of that culture. It takes the bipartisan debate, the dominant form of modern-day deliberative bodies, to the next level of existence—one that is transpartisan. It reframes the targeted outcomes of debates from a win–win or win–lose scenario to a win-win-win scenario where much of the electorate is represented in that third win.

Recognizing the Limitations of Non-Democratic Political Systems

The tools of MEMEtocracy are of little use in nondemocratic closed systems. Closed systems often have a meme stack that appears to have a thin layer of false Blue, which means that the system gives the appearance of ideals that do not really exist functionally. Often a closed political system, which hasn't experienced equality at national Blue level, will disintegrate by force through a coup d'état or a bloody popular uprising. This critical phase is considered a value-systems transitional phase that must play out in order for a culture to find its natural ᵛMemetic center of gravity. MEMEtocracy can help a culture make sense of the crisis, which can help it avoid getting trapped in a regressive cycle.

Closed systems, like North Korea, Iran, and Syria must go through this major dissonance. They might need to regress to a less sophisticated form of governance that fits the natural evolutionary patterns in those societies before an indigenous MEMEtocracy can take shape. In a closed system, higher value systems are prevented from emerging. This causes a buildup of toxic excess energy that eventually explodes in revolution and the disintegration of society.

This is what we are seeing in Syria today. Once the revolution is unleashed, it needs to run its full course until culture reaches its natural ^vMemetic balance. Most, if not all, remnants of the closed system have to disappear before the right (healthy) governance can take hold. Most closed governing systems today are under the control of either a leader or a group of leaders centered in Red, masquerading as a Blue system, with strategic Orange ambition to monopolize regional power. Iran's theocracy provides a good example of how a false Blue system hides behind religion to manipulate the masses and gain strategic power in the region. This is how emergence is arrested today. Red is no longer in its pure pioneering form as it was 10,000 years ago. It borrows from more advanced values to prolong its position of power.

The Essential Value-System's Transition Phase

Both Graves' and Beck's research has repeatedly proven that the most difficult transition for any given culture—past, present, and future—is its exit stage from a Red form of governance and the initial entry phase into Blue. That initial Blue has to be the autocratic kind of governance that instills civil discipline in a citizenry that is just getting acquainted with the abstract concepts of civil institutions for the first time. One of the greatest modern transition success stories is Singapore. Under the watchful eyes of its founding father, Lee Kuan Yew, Singapore was successfully transitioned from an ethnic PURPLE–Red to a nationalistic BLUE–Orange system in less than six decades. It is almost miraculous for a culture to transition within a single human life span.

I often hear Beck speak about the miracle of Singapore by saying "you'd better not spit gum on the sidewalk unless you are ready to pay a big fine or spend a night in jail." This is autocracy done the right way: the Blue "foundation stone" of every resilient nation recognizes the importance of Orange innovation. It creates solid ground, a solid foundation, from which a prosperous society can emerge. Autocratic Blue is a guided form of democracy that has different indigenous content for different parts of the world. Because of its Orange-Enterprising ambition, Blue autocracies, like benevolent monarchies, present a healthy form of governance and emergence for many counties in the Middle East.

Open, Arrested, and Closed Systems in a Democracy

Closed political systems are not the exclusive domain of dictatorships or regions of the world that are dominated by PURPLE–Red values. Western democracies centered on BLUE–Orange, or even ORANGE–Green, can move from an open system to an arrested system and eventually close, if its representatives are beholden to special interests rather than representing the interests of the voter as is their patriotic duty. Today, many constitutional scholars in the United States are bemoaning the corrosive effects that money from the Orange system (Wall Street and corporate lobbyists) has had on the virtues that originally defined American democracy as a government of the people, by the people, and for the people. In its political life cycle, the United States seems to be somewhere between an arrested and a closed system. Because it is unable to transition, this explains much of the dissonance and decay we're experiencing today.

Open System: In a Western democracy like the United States, the actions of elected officials in an *open system* fulfill the needs of the majority of their voters. Although it still has some challenges, the system is closely aligned with *life conditions* and the culture collectively feels that it's charting its future. Under an *open system* collective optimism and the pioneering spirit are the highest they've been in decades. The chaos and hopelessness from the exit phase of the previous system give way to a new order and a hopeful future of the new system. Optimism with new values becomes the dominant meme.

In value-systems evolution the entry phase in an open system is considered a more sophisticated level of political expression. For those who lived in the United States in the mid 1980s this stage was captured in Ronald Reagan's re-election ads with the theme of "It's morning in America again." It was also symbolized by the close relationship between Reagan, a Republican, and the Speaker of The House of Representatives, Tip O'Neill, a Democrat.

Although hindsight today offers much criticism of the Reagan era and its values, the 1980s represented strength in economic and military power after the perceived weakness during the Carter years. Reagan tamed the beast of inflation, the biggest threat to free markets, and something no administration was able to do in the decade before. His influence with the western NATO alliance is credited with bringing an end to the cold war. Many dynamics that represented the chaos of the past decades were replaced in the 1980s by a sense of certainty and a cheerful anticipation of a brighter future. Regardless of how the outcome is viewed today, this was the charting of new frontiers in politics, culture, and economics that set the United States on a healthy trajectory.

Arrested System: The system moves into an arrested stage when politicians misalign the voters' needs and their own purpose. They begin to pursue politics as a lifelong career. This phase is symbolized by the partial loss of independent thinking and the lure of the group dynamic that seduces a politician into established patterns of group behavior and conduct. Legislation is not evaluated upon its merits or its potential for service to the representative's constituency. It is evaluated more on maintaining or obtaining personal political power. Politicians reject transformational models for change and focus instead on Band-Aid solutions within the current system—a system that has become increasingly out of touch with *life conditions.*

Lobbyists have become increasingly a part of the U.S. political process. These special interests introduce wildcards that greatly speed the system towards an arrested state. The initial intent of the lobbying function was to give a Blue voice to all. However, in its current form, it morphed into a tool for Orange Fifth-Level exploitation. In this scenario, a value-systems expert can't help but draw a comparison between the false Blue of Iran's theocracy and the false Blue of lobbying as it hides behind the protection of the First Amendment. The former is designed to serve its Red overlords while the latter its Orange masters. A study done by The Center for Responsible Politics in 2011 shows that 79 percent of members of the U.S. Congress become lobbyists themselves, earning many times their Congressional salaries.[74] Government service in this case becomes a necessary Blue inconvenience for a strategic Orange lobbyists career objective. Exploitation of the Blue system assures that the voices of the most powerful Orange corporations supplant that of the voter. In addition to salaries, a primary component of election strategy is access to funding. Candidates align themselves with national party issues in order to attract funding and party support. Campaign messaging is carefully crafted to sway the voter demographic target.

Party corruption is also evident in the way primaries elections have been managed. For example, on February 9, 2008, the Democratic Party in Washington State decided not to count the ballots cast in the general state-run presidential primary, which included absentee ballots and such. The Democratic Party would only count ballots cast in the local caucuses. A friend of mine attended a local caucus and found that volunteers eagerly endorsed Obama with large banners, and stickers offered to everyone who walked into the voting site. There was no marketing for Clinton. The "ballots" were cast by writing your name and candidate choice on a list in pencil. There was no confidentiality. There was no one checking ID against voter registration records. The pencils had erasers. Lists, when complete with about fifteen names, were tossed into a nearby open box on the floor with no lid and, consequently, no lock.

The caucuses drew around 32,000 voters while the general primary drew over 691,000 voters. In the caucus Clinton got just over 31 percent of the votes and Obama got about 67.5 percent of the votes. In the primary election held by the state, which included all the usual safeguards, Clinton got about 45.5 percent of the votes and Obama got about 51 percent of the votes, a much more realistic indication of voter preference. However, the Democratic Party only counted the caucus votes when allocating 52 of the state's 78 delegates to Obama and 26 to Clinton. A more realistic allocation would have been about 40/35. Iowa, Nevada, and Maine were also caucus states.

In addition, the National Democratic Party penalized Florida and Michigan due to various rules—such as the timing of the primary election—but later let half their delegate votes count. The party only counted half votes in American Samoa, Guam, the U.S. Virgin Islands, and Democrats abroad. In Florida, Clinton had 50 percent of the votes and Obama 33 percent. In Michigan, Clinton was estimated at 46 percent and Obama 35 percent, though the situation was complex. The nomination for president was decided by the delegates, not the popular vote. Federal Election Commission Chairman Michael E. Toner estimated that the 2008 race would be a $1 billion election, and that to be taken seriously, a candidate would have needed to raise at least $100 million by the end of 2007.[75] This is telling in terms of opportunity for leadership in the United States.

As in the example above, in an arrested system there will be consequences for not toeing the party line. Individual thinking continues to diminish and group conformity becomes the requirement. If senior politicians have cozy relationships with lobbyists and other interest groups, new political comers had better fall in line with the prevailing group dynamic or be ostracized and dismissed as disloyal to the party philosophy and values. The more diminished the independent voices become, the closer the system moves to a *closed state*.

Closed System: The system enters a *closed state* when newly elected politicians are incapable of nudging the system forward. Meaningful change becomes impossible. At this stage politics decouple from effective representation, and the system is overrun by special interest groups. In a metaphor describing the political system as a "black hole," political outliers and pioneers of the next system are represented by light and incapable of escaping the far greater forces of the dark matter that constrain the system.

The electorate grows frustrated with extreme levels on all sides of the political arena. Competing political groups become zealots for their causes. Those who present alternative perspectives (from the next system) are vilified and may not make progress on any issue within the current system. As this phase of the political cycle moves forward, politicians become more rigid in their views. They try to fit the new problems arising from *life conditions* into their own outdated set of strategies for managing change from their own point of view. Solutions from within the system, regardless of political party, only add to its toxicity as this creates a dysfunctional cycle. Eventually, the system collapses. This last stage of the political cycle is known as entropy. Nothing changes. It represents the fertile ground, however, from which the next system may emerge. Once all of the same old strategies are proven useless, those who present new alternatives may finally find an audience. This is how it happens:

The culture reaches a tipping point when the majority of the electorate on all sides views the values of their elected representatives as relics of times past. When emerging memes and paradigms start having more explanatory power than all previous meaning-making systems, the culture transitions to higher political values of a new and open political cycle. This transition from political chaos to new and higher order appears impossible while the system is in an arrested or closed state. History demonstrates, however, that political value systems rise and fall, and the best form of democracy in an open system is still in our future, especially when informed by MEMEtocracy.

Defining the Seventh-Level Yellow Politician

In Western applications of this framework, political leaders can belong to the labor party or the conservative party. They can be Democrats or Republicans. MEMEtocracy takes the existing political thinking and adds to it the knowledge of value systems. Thus informed, ordinary political leaders may become Seventh-Level Yellow visionaries. A lifelong political career is a First Tier (subsistence) value. Politicians operating from First Tier systems seem to spend most of their time in the *arrested* and *closed states* of the political cycle. This misalignment becomes the primary source of voter discontent. As culture evolves further on the spiral it begins to create the problems requiring Second Tier thinking and different approaches to governance.

Seventh-Level Yellow political thinking, by nature, produces a functional political system that picks the right politician for the right moment in history. A Seventh-Level Yellow politician can be liberal or conservative, as long as her or his actions serve the superordinate goal. Seventh-Level Yellow leadership function is defined by the ability to align First Tier value systems into a flow to manage the needs of the whole electorate. A Yellow politician sees, with unmistakable clarity, past and current dysfunction.

She or he scans horizons continually for threats to the whole system, assesses the risk of existential problems, and understands that chaos and change are natural part of political cycles. This Seventh-Level Yellow leader is capable of integrating different political views into an evolutionary flow that preserves the integrity of the governance structures in the country and facilitates the healthy expression of each value system. He or she has no fear of thinking outside the group dynamic or party line, as long as actions serve society as a whole.

One can see from the description of the tenets of MEMEtocracy that Seventh-Level Yellow political leadership requires a substantial departure from current political practices. This *Momentous Leap* was characterized by Professor Graves as the difference between First and Second Tier perspectives. Second Tier political values do not arise from *selfish* and *subsistent* interests. Rather, Yellow represents a momentous leap, a conscious evolution that puts their First Tier behavior in perspective. Transitioning into Seventh-Level Yellow political values will not be an easy task, especially when the majority of the world is still transitioning between the First Tier systems.

PLACING DEMOCRACY ON A FUNCTIONAL TRAJECTORY

The concepts and tools that are outlined in this chapter have their origins in the seminal work of the Graves/Beck bio-psycho-social framework. Others were developed as a result of Beck's subsequent experience in South Africa. Additional tools were developed and implemented in our joint work at the CHE-Mideast over the last decade. The overarching methodology grew in complexity as it was applied through an indigenously informed process that Beck and I created. We had many *Indigenous Intelligence Experts* (IIEs) implementing strategies throughout the West Bank and the Arab World. The methods and large-scale design tools outlined in *Emerge!* are detailed through our actual experiences and applications. This represents today's most comprehensive and extensive use of the value system approach to large-scale design for governance.

MEMEtocracy is a *functional* system. Its purpose is to facilitate the healthy emergence of all the different human groupings that make up the spiral of human existence in any given society. In value systems, the term "functional" refers to the "sorting through the noise and dysfunction" of competing First Tier systems. This is necessary in order unlock the natural flows, often blocked by misalignment and toxicity. The purpose of a political system designed under the MEMEtocracy model is different from many prevailing models. The primary purpose of MEMEtocracy is to align

First Tier systems on a trajectory that serves a *superordinate goal.* This goal must speak to all the stakeholders within a culture.

MEMEtocracy does not lean to the left or to the right of any particular political issue. It does not favor liberal views over conservative views or the reverse. At the macro-design level it reexamines the reasoning behind the current configuration of nations, especially in the emerging world, and assesses the compatibility between the prevailing value systems and their form of governance.

A prime example of why all the assessments detailed here are crucial in evaluating the political systems of the Middle East, is the recent history of Iraq. It was the British colonialists who determined the geographic configuration of Iraq in 1932. After the fall of Saddam Hussein, the culture was allowed to find its natural value system's balance. As a result of that process, the nation fractured into three geographically distinct ethnic areas. The Fourth-Level system, designed by the British without the input of *Indigenous Intelligence,* and the use of other critical tools, collapsed and a Third Level system emerged naturally.

Iraq is now made up of three regions where each region takes care of its own people; a healthy PURPLE-Red expression that is congruent with *life conditions.* Each region only sees a need to cooperate with the other regions on the most important issues—such as the allocation of oil revenues and the distribution of raw materials and goods such as food.

At the heart of the MEMEtocracy model is a new form of political leadership that is informed by the values of the Seventh-Level system. In order for the framework to be an effective tool that transforms any given political system, this new breed of politicians must be able to design to the memetic contours of First Tier cultures. To insure that the interest of the people remains their primary concern, their designs must fit into a Seventh-Level functional flow that serves a collectively defined superordinate goal. This is the work that this framework offers. It represents a pioneering sociopolitical frontier for humankind. It is what makes democracy functional.

Don Beck and Elza Maalouf at the Golden Dome in Jerusalem

Safeguarding the future of the Middle East starts by shaping young minds

Our two Palestinian partners who shaped the Build Palestine Initiative (BPI), who are both members of the Third Generation Fatah, Adbel Majid Suwaiti *(next to Dr. Beck)*, and Nafiz Al-Rifae *(next to Elza Maalouf)*

Our three Israeli partners from the Center for Human Emergence-Israel *(from left)* Rafael Nasser, Neri Bar-On, and Oren Entin. Susan Vance with Hearthstone Foundation is standing next to Elza Maalouf.

The Palestinian team of Indigenous Intelligence Experts

The Israeli team of Indigenous Intelligence Experts

Introducing the value systems framework to Salah Al-taamari, Governor of Bethlehem

Introducing the value systems framework to Ahamd Al-Tibi, Deputy Speaker of the Israeli Knesset

Introducing the 5-Deep Model during an IIEs training in Bethlehem

Introducing the framework at The Washington Institute to Special Mideast envoy Dennis Ross

Presenting the framework to Karen Hughes in her office at the US State Department

Discussing the BPI with Gilead Sher, Chief of Staff of former Israeli Prime Minister Ehud Barak

Explaining the model in Daraa, Syria. In 2011 the region became the epicenter of the Syrian revolution.

Introducing the value system framework to the Governor of Daraa' Faysal Kalthoum in 2007. The man on the left, Kassem Khalil, was the mayor of Busra-Alsham. Khalil was killed in February 2013 by sniper fire while delivering medicine to the sick and injured.

February 2, 2008, at the summit for the Build Palestine Initiative organized by the Center for Human Emergence Middle East

February 2, 2008, at the summit for the Build Palestine Initiative organized by the Center for Human Emergence Middle East

FOUR

Mapping the Anatomy of Conflict & Identifying the Spectrum of Values

Great nations are simply the operating fronts of behind-the-scenes, vastly ambitious individuals who had become so effectively powerful because of their ability to remain invisible while operating behind the national scenery.[76]

—R. Buckminster Fuller
From the 1982 book *Critical Path, 2nd edition*

The MEMEtocracy framework provides a theoretical outline on how Seventh-Level Yellow governance can work. More importantly, it helps define the memetic profile of a Second Tier politician. The bigger and more complex question now is how to design for overall political emergence into a systemic Seventh-Level Yellow value system. What elements of a functional political platform resonate with Graves' recognition that we must design a system in order for all life forms to be able to exist and express themselves in a healthy manner?

The quote at the beginning of this chapter summarizes the Seventh-Level Yellow thinking process. Second Tier thinkers work behind the scenes in order to recognize individuals with healthy political and societal capacities. This is not to be confused with individuals from the Orange Fifth-Level system in the United States, such as corporate lobbyists or Wall Street bankers. The Orange system has, for decades, been defining the political landscape from behind the scenes through self-serving manipulations. Second Tier presents integrative systems that align all the First Tier systems on a healthy trajectory. It tames the blind ambitions of the Fifth-Level system through social and organizational conscious responsibility, but also sees the emotional toll that the Green system takes on people in its efforts to spread egalitarian and humanitarian values. Yellow recognizes Green's ineffective attempts to dislodge unhealthy Orange practices. It also detects a diminished or unhealthy Fourth-Level system (Blue), and works on making the presence of law and order quietly more effective rather than militant. In countries where a Third-Level system dominates the meme stack, Yellow Seventh-Level thinking works on containing it and channels its energies towards healthy expressions that lead to a healthy Blue Fourth-Level society.

Leaders at the Seventh Level have a deep memetic understanding of what motivates all the levels that came before, and can easily detect the source of conflict within First Tier ᵛMEMEs. They have the capacity to design natural systems and to assist First Tier in defining mutual superordinate goals. Below is part of a speech Dr. Don Beck presented at a recent gathering of young futurists. He describes the expressions of the "Seventh Code":

> For many of us, the onset of a Seventh-Level Yellow of values will cause a shift from a human-centric system that feels the burden of human suffering to one that is systems-centric. We will seek to improve the human condition through the design of natural systems and arrangements which, as they unfold, will address many human problems in a much more effective manner than the Green views that Europe and the United Nations hold as the highest values. Or the political system in Washington that is beholden to Orange special interest. We will discover a higher level of caring than what is expressed in Green or Orange. We will develop more of a pragmatic versus idealistic approach. We will accept that attempts to push the river with all the toxic practices of First Tier values will only result in frustration and often resistance to what we are trying to accomplish. We will work with Life Conditions, with the structure and texture of ᵛMemetic Codes, and with the content the code has permeated and impacted. A Seventh-Level Yellow political system will accept that life itself is full of paradoxes, mystery, wonderment, sudden surprises, with peaks and valleys of emotions and feelings. Life becomes a journey, not a destination. And, we develop a deep respect and acceptance of the nature of ebb and flow as we experience life and all that it involves.[77]

Don Beck gained attention for describing the theory of Spiral Dynamics, but his work with large-scale systems has gone greatly unnoticed. Working with large-scale systems begins with the analysis of conflict through the prism of value systems and moves through the model of *Natural Design and Functional Flow*, what we call the "design kit" for large-scale system change. This is what operationalizes MEMEtocracy as the tool of choice for future governance.

UNDERSTANDING THE NATURE OF CONFLICTING VIEWS

When dealing with large-scale psychology, one must consider group dynamics of the political parties in power. For someone trying to understand the nature of conflict, different views on politics appear to gravitate towards one side of any given issue, the left or the right. Muzafer Sherif, the modern-day father of social psychology validated a model called Realistic Conflict Theory (RCT)[78] through the Robbers Cave Experiment (1961). The theory accounts for group conflict, negative prejudices, stereotypes, discrimination, and even violence as being the result of competition between the groups for limited resources. An example of this theory in the "real world" would be increasing prejudice in times of high unemployment, but the research itself was not done within a "real world" adult scenario.

Beck was a student of Sherif while working on his PhD at the University of Oklahoma in the 1960s. He always remained an admirer of Muzafer and Carolyn Sherif's work. Beck incorporated two major theories from the Sherif's research into the Graves framework and the resulting model further defined the nature of conflict from the values system perspective.

Into the value-systems framework, Beck integrated the concept that:

a) Differences among members of the same group have limited contribution to intergroup conflict,

b) Hostilities arise between groups when they are competing for the same resources that only one group can attain, and

c) Contact and dialogue do little to reduce friction between groups, while the presence of superordinate goals that promote united cooperative action is a better prescription for reducing intergroup conflict.[79]

Beck's new model was also developed from the work that the Sherif's did with Carl Hovland on Social Judgment Theory (SJT). This work attempted to explain how attitudes are expressed, judged, and modified. Attitude is defined as "the stands the individual upholds and cherishes about objects, issues, persons, groups, or institutions."[80] Beck included much of the construct in his 1966 PhD thesis about the causes of the U.S. civil war. This work is what I consider the first academic articulation of a culture-wide, whole systems framework on the nature of conflict. Beck integrated the field of history, political science, rhetoric, and the behavioral sciences into one platform for understanding human behavior under conditions of conflict.[81]

After uncovering Graves' work and the lessons learned from the first few years into his experience in South Africa, Beck combined the most notable findings from both the Realistic Conflict Theory and the Social Judgment Theory and added to them many elements of the value systems model. Beck redefined what a superordinate goal should represent through the big picture / integral / functional values of the Seventh-Level

Yellow system. He then closely reexamined the underlying assumptions affecting the importance of intra-group dynamics on each side of a conflict. Using Social Judgment Theory, he transformed the assimilation and contrast aspects by providing a far more sophisticated articulation of the different spectrums that represented the different value systems on each side of a conflict. This pioneering model became known as the Value-Systems Assimilation-Contrast Effect model, or the ^{V}ACE model for short. The Assimilation-Contrast Effect model became the basis of Beck's work for the latter years he spent in South Africa and in our work at the CHE-Mideast.

VALUE-SYSTEMS ASSIMILATION-CONTRAST EFFECT MODEL (^{V}ACE)

Beck identified a total of six positions or standings related to beliefs and actions on each side of the spectrum in any given conflict. This model helps to accurately predict the motivation of people, groups, and cultures under conflict conditions. The ^{V}ACE model illustrates graphically the dynamics of polarization, social conflict, and the balance of perspectives in the pursuit of systemic equilibrium (peace, armistice, and nonviolence) between opposing viewpoints or values. Each position has its own value system preferences or mix of value systems.

These are expressed in designations of R-1 through R-6 for positions on one side of the issue, or L-1 through L-6 for positions on the other side. The designation of "right" or "left" side does not indicate any party affiliation or political leanings, although it can be used that way for convenience if a political left and right is being discussed. For example, if one were discussing polarizing forces between two countries like Wales and Iceland, or between two groups competing for water rights, such as Northern and Southern California, rather than having a political context, the "right" or "left" sides would have no specific connotation other than to denote two sides to an issue.

The six positions are based on value-system contexts as follows:

1. **Flamethrowers (R-6 & L-6):** These are the groups that are represented by the Red Third-Level value system. They are aggressive, violent, and predatory with intent to destroy, attack, and eliminate the opposition without the possibility of compromise.

2. **Zealots (R-5 & L-5):** These are groups centered partly in Third-Level Red and partly Fourth-Level Blue. They are highly

directed by doctrine, partisan, and fiercely fervent, tending toward "all or nothing" demands.

3. Ideologues (R-4 & L-4): These are the True Believers represented by the arrested stage of the Blue Fourth-Level system. They are absolutists with firm convictions and rigid boundaries.

4. Moderates (R-3 & L-3): This is where an open Fourth-Level system exhibits softer beliefs. This group recognizes the entry phases of the Orange Fifth-Level system. They are more open to seeing options for compromise and negotiating trade-offs, although they want to come out ahead. Positions can be somewhat intense but have less ego-involved in negotiation.

5. Pragmatists (R-2 & L-2): This position is in the Orange Fifth-Level system. They are very practical and believe in results that work. They advocate the art of the possible, creative and functional solutions, and can be highly skilled at negotiation.

6. Conciliators (R-1 & L-1): This is the position where the Orange Fifth Level meets the Green Sixth-Level system. This position seeks inclusivity, consensus and a place for everyone to feel good about the outcome. They often do not recognize manipulative strategies used by the other First Tier systems to gain sympathy and concessions.

Beck argues that on both sides of the spectrum there are underlying blind spots. This occurs when a person denies or ignores differences between his or her own position and those of others on the same side on the values spectrum. One is likely to imagine that other positions are within his or her zone of acceptance. This is common with R/L-1 or R/L2. This is what is called *Assimilation* on the ^{V}ACE Model. For example, a person centered in the values of R/L-3 will accept others from R/L-4 and R/L-2 because he or she views the values of these nearby systems as if they were aligned or allied more than they actually are.

Contrast, on the other hand, is when the rigid attitudes set in on both sides of the values spectrum and create a "you are either with us or against us" sentiment. This is more common with Flamethrowers, Zealots, and Ideologues and some of the Moderates on both the right and the left. These extreme views consider the others to be "the enemy," thus explain the use of the term *Contrast*.

LEFT-RIGHT SPECTRUMS AND THEIR ᵛMEME CODES

SPECTRUM "Center"			ᵛMEME CODE
L-1 Conciliators R-1			Orange/Green-5th/6th Levels
L-2 Pragmatists R-2			Orange/5th Level
L-3 Moderates R-3			Blue/Orange 5th/4th Levels
L-4 Ideologues R-4			Blue 4th Level
L-5 Zealots R-5			Blue/Red 4th/3rd Level
L-6 Flamethrowers R-6			Red 3rd Level

Figure 4.1. Copyrighted by Don E. Beck, PhD 2003 and used by permission.

The way each value system (each level) perceives the others on the left or right side of an issue determines whether they view the other perspective as one that "assimilates" within their own viewpoint, or is in "contrast" to their viewpoint. *Assimilation* expects that "if you aren't against us, you are with us." Since this isn't really the case, a lot of "internal marketing" might be spent attempting to create stronger converts to the cause. *Contrast* expects that "if you aren't with us, you are against us."

We see examples of the Assimilation Contrast Model in effect in the media today. For example, Rush Limbaugh might be considered an Ideologue with Zealot tendencies. He considers Moderates, Pragmatists and Conciliators on the Republican side to really be in the camp of his political opponents (Democrats) and calls them RINOs (Republicans In Name Only). In his mind, any other position on the values spectrum of the Republican Party is invalidated. On the other side of the spectrum, Rachel Maddow is an Ideologue with Zealot tendencies (with the complexity of Green). By calling conservative Associate Justice of the U.S. Supreme Court Antonin Scalia "a troll,"[82] she positions herself as a far leftist, and considers the Moderates, Pragmatists, and Conciliators of the Democratic Party as leaning to the

Republican side. This has the effect of making the center of the Democrat value spectrum disappear.

As a result of this dynamic, the debate no longer contains six positions on each side of the values spectrum, its the Ideologues, Zealots and Flamethrowers on one side (the rigid "us") vs. the Moderates, Pragmatist and Conciliators on the same side AND the entire other side. As Conciliators, Pragmatists and Moderates on both sides of any issue disappear the remaining positions are those that represent an "us vs. them" ideology, which then becomes the loudest voices being heard. This is extremely important particularly in terms of mass media.

The silencing of the middle spectrums of a debate results in an unbalanced representation of the issues and in further polarization. Ultimately, these dynamics come to define the foundation of historic conflicts.

Unfortunately, in a world that feeds off small sound bites and 24/7 news, the mainstream media only reports the sensationalized polarization of opinions. This creates a broader and more embedded view of the "us vs. them" cultural schism.

THE HEARTS AND MINDS STRATEGY

Beck has designed a four-point strategy on how to drive the hearts and minds of people away from the corrosive effects of the "us vs. them" dynamic. Appropriately, he calls it the "Hearts and Minds Strategy." I have heard him express utter frustration with the status quo. He suggests that this simple model, the value system Assimilation Contrast Effect, is what the United Nations and our State Department should be focusing on—not negotiations with the loudest voices, which have repeatedly resulted in failure. The four "Hearts and Minds" steps for value-spectrum facilitation of Beck's Assimilation–Contrast Model are the following:

1. Create a wedge between the radicals (Flamethrowers, Zealots, and the closed-system Ideologues), and the more Moderate positions on each side of the value spectrum simultaneously.

2. Enhance the capacities of the Pragmatists and the Conciliators so they are able to solve the deep conflict and answer to the needs of the people.

3. Anticipate the radical chitchat among the Flamethrowers and Zealots and depress the polarizing dynamics.

4. Inoculate the masses and the decision makers against "Us vs. Them" rhetoric.[83]

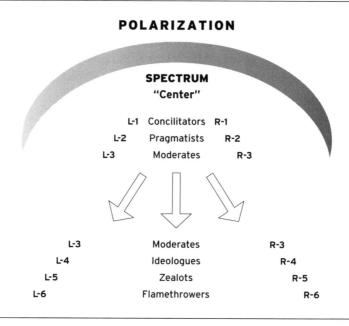

POLARIZATION

SPECTRUM
"Center"

L-1	Concilitators	R-1
L-2	Pragmatists	R-2
L-3	Moderates	R-3

L-3	Moderates	R-3
L-4	Ideologues	R-4
L-5	Zealots	R-5
L-6	Flamethrowers	R-6

Figure 4.2. The hearts and minds strategy. Copyrighted Don E. Beck 2003.
Used by permission.

Of the four steps outlined, the one that takes the highest priority is the first one on the list:

Question: How do we bring the Moderates and Pragmatists on both sides to the table, while empowering them to reject the radical Zealots and Ideologues on their respective side?

The patterns that I observed in Israel and Palestine were more successful in business settings on both sides than they were with politicians. Young Palestinians saw that greater business opportunities could result from a peace treaty with Israel. Beck saw identical patterns in South Africa where apartheid disappeared in the workplace long before it did in politics. The result of this experience is very important:

Answer: If Blue-Orange values can be spread through free enterprise and prosperity, the center of gravity of a culture will tend to move towards more Moderate and Pragmatic positions politically as life conditions change.

ANATOMY OF A CONFLICT

Over the decade-long period of time that Beck and I worked together at the CHE-Mideast, the ᵛACE Model evolved. Early on in our research we noticed that attitudes and positions changed greatly on the values spectrum depending on who's asking the questions and gathering data. An Arab-American asking Israelis about their views on certain issues triggered different answers than if the same questions were asked of Israelis by an Israeli. We noticed the same patterns on the Palestinian side. This is an effect that has long been understood in marketing research and in campaign polling, for example. Although there is always potential for bias, people are generally more likely to be candid and responsive when they trust the interviewer's motivation and sponsor.

Because of how critical it is to be in touch with the hearts and minds of the mid-stream representatives on the ᵛACE model locally, I added a context called "Indigenous Intelligence" as a requirement for value-systems expertise designation. Upon implementation, the resulting new data became more introspective and began to reflect a more realistic spectrum of differences on each side of the issues within each culture.

To illustrate:

I was invited by an EU group that has faced cultural resistance to a historic preservation project in rural Syria. Although the local Mayor was a moderate on the values spectrum and supported the EU group, positions became polarized against him and the Europeans as Flamethrowers and Zealots rose to contrast his position with theirs. They lumped him into the European camp of their enemy. They simply did not understand the complexity of the whole-systems approach the Europeans were undertaking.

Being a native of the region, I first asked to meet with the women of the tribes. I knew they might influence the men. I also met with high school girls and boys separately to understand their aspirations for the future of their own town. This was all in preparation for a town hall meeting. When the meeting day arrived, the women and the high school students were present and we debated the future of the project all day long. At the end of the day I noticed that we hadn't fully neutralized the Flamethrowers or Zealots present at the meeting. To appeal to their hearts and minds, I invoked the rich history of my ancestry and reminded them that I was one of them. I summoned the glorious and proud history of our Ghassanid tribe and expressed how we might bring pride back to Busra el-Sham. The men who objected most throughout the day, suddenly broke into tribal songs about the glory of Bani Ghassan, (the sons of Ghassan), a historic healthy Red Arab tribe. This native-born appeal to the stakeholders' *Indigenous*

Intelligence was an excellent tool. In a matter of hours the three-year stalemate, three years of bickering were over.

Simultaneously, I recommended to the Europeans to create a representative office (something concrete not abstract) for the men. This way, they could tell their wives that they were going to a physical location to meet. Purple tribes and Heroic Red leaders always need something tangible, a location that takes on a local texture and importance. Along with this, I urged the EU group to create a solid Blue structure for the function of this office—meaning specific goals that would bring clarity to the project and its mission.

Understanding the ᵛACE Model and the importance of the *Indigenous Intelligence* in hot spots like Israel and Palestine is essential for determining how to depress the polarizations caused by the "us vs. them" dynamic. More importantly, it becomes an essential tool in *identifying* the Moderates and Pragmatists.

Once that happens a political system designed from the Seventh-Level Yellow can empower exceptional leadership and bring both centers together while pushing the radicalized elements within each culture away from the hearts and minds of people. This will be part of a nationalistic (Blue) campaign with a new superordinate goal.

Before a common superordinate goal can be designed for TWO cultures, one has to be designed for each separately. The Seventh-Level Yellow leadership will recognize the needs of both cultures in designing for each one. It must address the dynamics that were uncovered through the value-systems Assimilation Contrast process in order to depress the destructive elements within each culture, and seamlessly move the power base away from the Flamethrowers and Zealots.

Mideast peace negotiations brokered by the West usually missed the basic anatomy of conflict. To the United States and Europe, the Palestinians have two socio-political value spectrums, Hamas and Fatah. Hamas is labeled as "them" because it refuses to acknowledge the right of Israel to exist. Fatah is of course the "us" because of the "we can work with them" position. By polarizing the conflict, the United States and EU fail to look at the memetic structure of each party to understand the values spectrum within either Hamas or Fatah. Both parties are just as diverse when placed on the ᵛACE Model up to the R-2 and L-2 Pragmatic level. Palestinian *life conditions* don't presently allow for the Conciliator R-1, L-1 positions to exist. The West and Israel presume that the Palestinians should have one Blue position, which only comes when a culture embraces the values of nation- states. When this position is arrested, people negotiate through different means. This explains the Palestinian and Israeli frustration in going directly to the UN after so many negotiation attempts failed.

The Israelis, through their values spectrum still feel they don't have a viable partner on the Palestinian side who can guarantee a sustainable outcome to the negotiations process. From this simple articulation, of the value systems Assimilation Contrast Effect, one can see the importance of assessing each culture from a ᵛMemetic standpoint. This assessment easily points to asymmetry between the cultures and illustrates why traditional negotiations have always failed.

The West could consider Beck's four steps of the Hearts and Minds strategy and work with Moderates and Pragmatist on the Hamas side who want to make a deal with Israel. Not the Mashaals and the Zahars of the Palestinians, but someone like former Minister of Planning Sameer Abu Eisheh, with whom Dr. Beck and I met. The Minister fully appreciated our approach and wanted to work with us. As a Western-educated Pragmatist from Hamas in a Fatah cabinet, Eisheh has a PhD in civil engineering from Penn State and understands many of the tools of MEMEtocracy. He wanted to create a Department of Integration in his Ministry to maximize the benefit of thousands of NGOs engaged in ad-hoc, unsustainable, fragmented activities.

This is one example of the *Indigenous Intelligences* available on the ground locally. The Minister wanted to build capacities on the Palestinian side in order to level the asymmetry between Israelis and Palestinians. This is the kind of leadership, regardless of whether it comes from Fatah or Hamas that is needed for the future of Palestine. The surface manifestation of political affiliation does not matter.

On the Israeli side, one can see the ᵛACE Model and the *Indigenous Intelligence* in play as well. According to our colleague, Neri Bar-On at the Center for Human Emergence-Israel, if we were to reduce the complexity of Israeli politics to left and right positions, we get an interesting model that resembles a European value-systems spectrum. However, unlike Europe, the Israeli political system has a heavy presence in Ideologue Blue. This creates issues related to nationalism (R-4) to which both sides migrate when the culture is under existential threat. The right believes in the increased building of settlements, the Jewish State, and the importance of religion (Zealots and Ideologues, R-5 and R-4). They also believe that Palestine cannot be an independent state (R-4 and R-3). A free market economy and the pursuit of personal wealth are among their highest aspirations (Pragmatists R-2). This is BLUE–Orange.

The left believes in a two-state solution and peace with the Palestinians (Pragmatists and Conciliators, L-2 and L-1). They also advocate for social programs for the poor, a socialist economic system (L-1), and want free-dom from religion (Pragmatists when it comes to religion). This is Blue to Orange to Green. According to Bar-On, in the 2013 Knesset elections, the parties that garnered the most votes were Benjamin Netanyahu's Likud (R-2) followed by Yair Lapid's Yesh Atid (there's a future) party (L-1, L-2). As a common practice in social democracies, the middle made up of posi-tions 1, 2 and 3 on both sides formed a coalition government, effectively arresting any polarization. Although Zealots and Flamethrowers don't appear on the values spectrum in Israeli politics today, the sensitive issue of nationalism arrests the system and prevents a final peace settlement from taking place.

In designing governance that works, understanding the ^{V}ACE Model and the role that the *Indigenous Intelligence* plays is crucial for diagnosing where a country's political positions lie on the values spectrum. ^{V}ACE provides the Seventh-Level Yellow politician or leader with a starting point for the design process. It offers an objective view based on data and identifies what needs to be done to design a functional political system with a resilient outlook on the future. ^{V}ACE also offers an inward look into the changing values of one's own political party. Seeing that spectrum of values is helpful when maneuvering to minimize the loud rigid voices that falsely attempt to represent the values of the whole party or a country.

NATURAL DESIGN AND FUNCTIONAL FLOW

After applying the ^{V}ACE Model informed by the *Indigenous Intelligence Experts*, the next layer in the application of MEMEtocracy is the use of the tools of *Natural Design*. The goal of this concept is to align people, resources, institutions, and processes to serve a Seventh-Level Yellow superordinate goal that speaks to all parties in a conflict. When applied to large-scale political design it is equally effective with first world applica-tions as well as the emerging world. This is the master platform on which all the other Seventh-Level Yellow tools (large-scale psychology and design) get placed. *Natural Design* is always informed by the uniqueness of *life conditions* and not by politicians or policy makers who think they have the answers. They are often beholden to special interests that sup-plant those of the voter.

It seems that when a political cycle is in its arrested or closed state, we elect new politicians and send them to that same dysfunctional system expecting different results. In designs based on value systems, we know the system needs structural changes, not just a mere rearrangement of the chairs on the Titanic. This is when extraordinary measures need to be taken to define the type of change that is needed and where the applications of MEMEtocracy are defined. I often observe Beck describe this structural change by telling political and business leaders, "Getting rid of what you don't want is not the same as getting what you want."

The next appropriate system in political emergence under MEMEtocracy cannot be more than one ^{V}MEME above *life conditions* of that culture, but the new system cannot be designed from that next level. It has to be designed from Second Tier, which is presently operating within the systemic Yellow Seventh-Level Yellow values. Second Tier can anticipate the potential for exploitation by all the First Tier ^{V}MEMEs. It assesses the memetic contours, *life conditions* and belief systems that are unique to each culture to come up with the best solutions.

Our involvement in Iraq is a good example of this. Iraq was a Purple tribal culture whose emergence into a Red heroic-egocentric existence was halted by Saddam Hussein. There were no alternative emergence channels. When Saddam's restraints were removed, the next stage for Iraq was the unhealthy expression of the Red-level system. This neutralized the pent up toxicity from the years of repression. In a sense, the bloody battles for sectarian dominance were an expected repercussion because the system needed to transition to the early stages of the Order-Nation (Blue) state, similar to what happened in Europe in the Middle Ages.

The mistake the United States and its allies made was that they didn't design a form of governance congruent with Iraq's *next* stage of emergence. Such a plan would have channeled the energy of this repressed system, namely the civil unrest in quest for feudal dominance, into memetically-honed channels. The transition needed IIEs who understood how to channel the unhealthy expression of the existing system.

This unique information would have come from the disbanded Iraqi army. A proper plan would have kept the army's command structure in place and replaced Saddam with a benevolent autocrat, someone respected by the generals and who would have won the respect of the people by immediately restoring law and order. A new Iraqi leader with the proper memetic fit would have paid these soldiers well and directed them towards a new sense of heroism endowed by a nationalistic sense of purpose.

Unfortunately with the "you're with us or you're against us" approach to Middle East policy, the Bush administration removed the only remaining institution in Iraq that would have facilitated an infant, healthy expression of a Blue system. If this system had been installed, it would have slowly influenced the culture in a healthy direction while providing the respect needed for the autocratic phase of governance. By disbanding the army, the largest employer in Iraq disappeared overnight creating a new class of poor soldiers who downshifted to Red values. Worse, they had the guns with which to fight against the West, and did so in order to survive.

The value-systems interpretation of these actions is that Western allies created a big Red ideology out of these soldiers. This situation became a catalyst for Al Qaeda and other Red warlords to begin the bloody battle for sectarian dominance. Then, the West added fuel to the Red fire by designing a Western style constitution instead of designing governance that fits the memetic contours of the land. We introduced a non-indigenous, foreign, Fourth-Level Blue democracy with obedience to foreign-imposed order with its own values and perceptions of what represents the rule of law. This immediately disrespected the Red Iraqi system, and Red needs to win without compromise. The Iraqi leaders that were picked by the Western alliance during the transition phase, and for the few years that followed, were all living comfortable lives outside Iraq and had been out of touch with *life conditions* in Iraq for decades. They fit Bush's and Blair's values and belief systems more than they did those of the local culture.

Today, Iraq continues to be a violent place where feudal values of sectarianism continue to play out. The emerging form of governance has three highly autonomous sectarian regions that serve their constituents in a natural process for those people living in those *life conditions* and belief systems. This is just an example how Western superpowers keep projecting their own style of democracy on the emerging world without learning about those worlds, and without learning from their own historical mistakes.

THE NATURAL DESIGN PROCESS

The MEMEtocracy design process begins after identifying where people, groups, and cultures belong on the spectrum of values of the ^{V}ACE Model. *Natural Design* begins with the analysis of the country and its value-system compositions and patterns. With data in hand, we search for ways of identifying the functions to be performed by the new system and how to structure and design the institutions that perform the functions. Finally, we focus on the alignment of modes of thought and decision making to those systems and structures. Because much of this data is gathered by the IIEs with *Indigenous Intelligence*, the population is engaged in a collaborative attempt to create the appropriate system of governance.

As a result of many decades of research and work in political hot spots around the world, Beck has perfected *Natural Design* to a simple formula:

HOW does...
...WHO
lead / teach / manage / design for
...WHOM
...to do WHAT
...for WHICH PEOPLE
...living WHERE and WHEN.[84]

This is precisely the simplicity that lies beyond the complexity of today's polarized political system. It could hold the key to many complex issues that face the world today. The simplicity in *Natural Design* comes from its ability to plug into evidence of healthy First Tier expressions in a political platform before they reach an arrested or closed state. The *Indigenous Intelligence* always informs design. *Natural Design* simply places the genius of those complex First Tier expressions into a platform that serves the health of the entire electorate. This process creates allegiance to a far greater vision. On a *Natural Design* platform, all competing political ideologies become naturally focused on keeping the system sustainably in sync with the needs of *life conditions* while anticipating change and incorporating resilience into the functional flow of the system.

A Seventh-Level Yellow designer always starts by defining these questions in the reverse order. First by acknowledging that this is a dynamic model and that *life conditions* change daily, the "WHEN" is constantly updated to include new changes. At the CHE-Mideast, we discovered that much of the Israeli-Palestinian debate is stuck in the past. We spent a considerable amount of time educating both sides on how to honor the past, respect the present, but design for the future. Cultural progress is often arrested when the WHEN element of the *Natural Design* process is left out of the equation.

The next element to be defined is the "WHERE." In the case of designing a Yellow political platform for the United States, the WHERE would be the *life conditions* in the United States. This is the very diverse landscape where candidates running for political office must get to know the challenges that people are facing at the level they intend to serve (local, district, state, national). They must interpret the mosaic of life painted in the vibrant colors of all the First Tier systems. This could be:

+ the small town that needs to find a solution for its chronic unemployment problem after the major employer closes shop.

+ the college student looking for a first job

+ the small business owner looking to finance the expansion of operations

+ the hourly worker in the service industry struggling to survive on minimum pay

+ the owner of a growing factory looking to add another shift and increase productivity to meet increasing demand

+ the young Green value-system husband and wife with an Ivy League education who decide to settle in Southern California and start an organic winery

+ the streets of the cities from the Rust Belt experiencing poverty and chronic unemployment

+ the geniuses at Google and Apple in Mountain View and the biotech industry in La Jolla creating leading-edge discoveries through scientific and technological breakthroughs ...

MEMEtocracy starts by designing for the needs of all the people and their *life conditions* in a certain locality with the full knowledge of the inventory of resources available to the culture from natural, human, and institutional resources. Of all the elements of the *Natural Design* formula, defining the WHERE (inclusive of WHICH PEOPLE) is by far the most important element that will inform a Second Tier political platform. The geographic, memetic, cultural, and demographic contours of a society must play a crucial role in informing policy makers in order to design policies that are congruent with *life conditions*.

In the Middle East, the WHERE are the streets of Baghdad, Damascus, Cairo, Dubai, Abu Dhabi, Erbil, and Beirut, as well as the rural areas of the respective countries. The most popular WHERE in the Middle East today are the newly emerging cities that are helping cultures discover Orange-Enterprising values. This is happening in oil rich countries much faster than the rest of the Arab world.

Political leaders like Rafik Hariri, the slain Prime Minister of Lebanon, attempted to establish Beirut as the financial hub for the region. In his long-term vision to build a robust society after a devastating civil war, Hariri provided scholarships to young men and women to attend the best schools in the West with a contractual obligation to return and rebuild Lebanese institutions and a robust private sector from the ground up. The one mistake Hariri made is that he did not focus on the rural areas in Lebanon, which remained poor and became resentful of the rapid resurgence of wealth in Beirut. Many young men from southern Lebanon and the Bekaa Valley had to work in oil-rich countries to make a living and send money back home. The WHERE in a small country like Lebanon should have taken into consideration the entire memetic profile of the culture and designed a political system for all to participate in the rising prosperity in the country.

Dubai and Abu Dhabi are emerging as small city-states where people are living in prosperity and reinvesting the oil wealth in infrastructure and institutions that will serve them past the Age of Oil.

The WHERE is also in Erbil, the Kurdish region of Iraq where the Barazanis are distributing the wealth to their people, giving them land to develop and providing them with a sense of self-reliance. These are examples of why the WHERE is an essential source of information for a Second Tier political designer.

The next question that *Natural Design* asks is the WHAT. This is the source of the superordinate goal. We design a superordinate goal for those *life conditions* that the WHERE identified. Since our goal is to design a Second Tier political system, the WHAT is a functional form of democratic MEMEtocracy that is informed by the values of the Seventh-Level Yellow system. It seeks to align all the First Tier ᵛMEMEs and political life cycles into a sustainable and functional flow that serves the long-term viability of the system. Most of the qualities that describe MEMEtocracy and Seventh-Level Yellow political leadership go into defining the WHAT. The lessons learned from past political dysfunction can be reinterpreted through value systems in order to detect the blockages from the past and design the next system for the future of the country. This is the shape that design takes once it has been informed by the needs arising from the WHERE. This is a distributed intelligence model; both the WHERE and WHAT need to take on different regional or local shapes in order to accommodate the local constituencies into the healthy expression of their value systems.

If the WHAT is to design a superordinate goal that serves the needs of the electorate above all else, the goal is declared right away in order to address the remaining elements of *Natural Design.* The WHAT (functional superordinate goal) in today's polarized political climate in the United States would take several forms. It might start by calling on all stakeholders to

+ end unhealthy governance practices that place corporate lobbying interest above the voter, and those that foster political favoritism within the system; and

+ end policies that create a glass ceiling for women in politics and business.

This ambitious declaration requires a wide political and macro memetic perspective that examines many of the long-term issues that threaten the foundation of U.S. democracy. It must examine the value systems that lead dysfunctional politicians to decouple from their patriotic duty. It must place the different perspectives on patriotism into a functional flow that allows politicians to view the entire system and the critical role they play as part of a much greater whole. The superordinate goal that might unify and realign the United States might be: *To rise above differences in order to preserve the Union for future generations.*

The WHAT, for the Middle East and North Africa, especially now when transitioning through the most crucial stage of development, is to build a political platform that empowers each country to build nation-states. One of the essential characteristics of this framework is the acknowledgment that a society cannot skip a developmental stage. In other words, Fifth-Level Orange values will not represent a healthy development unless the culture has spent sufficient time in the Fourth-Level Blue system where both constraints and equal rights are designed into law assure the health of the foundational system.

In the most advanced countries in the Middle East today, there's no equal treatment under the law. Nepotism, favoritism, and feudal dominance define the landscape. In the Middle East, women, minorities, and migrants don't have equal rights, even though in every project I am involved with throughout the region, women step up as natural leaders and take full charge of these projects. Oftentimes it's who you know and which family lineage you belong to that determine how far you advance in life. It is not a system based on meritocracy, which requires far more cultural sophistication. It is these value-system issues that must be addressed first to guarantee long-term political viability in the region, particularly with a culture with an increasingly globalized impact. This is the inescapable Blue stage that every first world country had to go through in order to become a robust society. Any superordinate goal for the Arab world must have declarations comparable to nation-building values where everybody is equal under the law.

The next question in *Natural Design* that must be answered is the WHOM. For WHOM are we designing this system for governance? What are their value-systems priorities? What are their capacities? Are they in an "open, arrested or closed" system? How do their *life conditions* vary from one region of the country to the next? Clearly they are not all entrepreneurs in the fifth-level ʲMEME seeking a better tax policy, or police or firemen and women in a Blue value system living contentedly and trusting that the existing system will take care of all their future needs. They are not all former gang members emerging from Red *life conditions* in inner cities looking for a new life and a job opportunity. They are not only the adults of the Information Age who view the political process as part of an arcane value system that no longer represents who they are. All of these people live in the WHERE.

The WHOM focuses on the value systems of the people who are living in a country, city or a region that were identified by the *life conditions* or the WHERE. It focuses on the bio-psycho makeup of individuals in the culture. It assesses individual capacities and memetic centers of gravity. In the last election, the U.S. Republican Party seemed to miss the WHOM in its efforts to garner votes. The message was more aligned with traditional ORANGE–Blue values and almost completely missed the Green values that the Information Age has created among young voters. It also missed the BLUE–Orange minorities who are becoming stronger, but identify with American values differently than past generations. This misreading of *life conditions* (the WHOM in the *Natural Design* question) cost the Republican Party the U.S. presidential election.

In the United States, the WHOM today is still aligned to the promise of the Obama Administration with regard to the emerging values and the future of the country, more so than the traditional ORANGE–Blue values of the Republican Party. When Senator Obama decided to run for president, most of his speeches pointed to a Yellow-system leader. Don Beck and I had many conversations analyzing the possibilities. As president, however, Obama ran into the systemic dysfunction of Washington and regressed to a pragmatic Orange politician with Green egalitarian ideals. A true Second Tier politician must transcend party politics and understand the long-term ramifications of his decision-making process once he or she ascends to the position of power. Of course, as seen in the case of John F. Kennedy, there is a certain risk from the established infrastructure, if the system is closed or arrested and not ready for change.

Yet, the WHOM for a president must be the entire country complete with its rich mosaic of values. Green egalitarianism cannot be regarded as having the highest value while ignoring the needs of all the other First Tier value systems. By including the WHOM in its design scheme, a Second Tier political system always reflects a true representation of all the needs of the population and its *life conditions*.

In the Middle East today the WHOM are the people in the culture who are primarily centered in the tribal (Purple) and heroic (Red) mindsets with aspirations for enterprising (Orange) values. These masses are being exposed to other values around the globe through the Internet and can no longer accept oppression and tyranny, as became apparent with the uprisings of the Arab Spring. The majority of the people in the region still struggle with literacy and the need to acquire marketable skills.

A Second Tier politician informed by the *Natural Design* process must take these factors into account as they begin to design the long and arduous road towards emergence. They must sift through the memetic deficiencies that plague the region in order to assure a future presence and impact on the global stage. Many young Arabs are becoming impatient with the slow pace of change in Egypt and elsewhere in the region. The WHOM want the same freedoms as the rest of the world. Although I feel for those young people, and I was once in their shoes, they have to understand that the Nation Building stage requires patience and sacrifice in order to assure a strong foundation for a resilient future.

After identifying the WHERE, WHAT, and WHOM we move to identify the WHO. This is a description of the qualifications and the capacities of the people in key positions who will lead and design a Second Tier political system. In his book *MEMEnomics*, IDA and cultural economist Said Dawlabani calls these individuals the designers of *smartBLUE*: a term that implies a functional regulatory structure designed from Seventh-Level Yellow values. These are individuals who are capable of looking beyond the current political chatter. They have a functional vision of the future where a superordinate goal illustrates their highest ideals. Because they're informed by the values of Yellow's big picture, they have no fear of reaction to their decisions from politicians in the First Tier systems.

Staffing key government positions with Second Tier regulators requires these individuals to possess systemic thinking. If it's an industry regulator, that individual must be intimately familiar with how business in that industry gets done. This regulator must overcome the seduction and trappings that come from First Tier self-serving subsistent values. Yellow political leaders always see the complexity of life. Because they recognize when a political system becomes in danger of collapse, they can act and design for sustainability and resilience. They understand that chaos and the need to change are par for the course. A Second Tier regulator designs a Blue system from a functional Yellow perspective. This system will, therefore, be *less bureaucratic and more algorithmic*. The operation of Blue (law and order) becomes a *functional* value that serves the superordinate goal rather than serving the career needs of a bureaucrat or a bureaucracy. In other words, this designer has to recognize what serves the country and the entire culture rather than picking the ideology of one group over another.

A Seventh-Level Yellow political appointee or representative always has one eye on securing the functionality of government many decades down the road, but works behind the scenes. Although he or she will not hesitate to investigate and bring charges against lawbreakers, the primary objective is to inspire all the First Tier ^{V}MEMEs to act in the best interest of the long-term health of the political system. First Tier operators will recognize that this leader has the capacity to anticipate their every move.

Unfortunately, in the United States today, many high level government positions still get filled based on political favoritism with little regard to the talent and proficiencies of the appointees or their potential capacities for Second Tier political thinking. Another issue is the significant amount of personal wealth that is required to run for a political office, and this goes hand-in-hand with the financial strength and coexistent influence of special interests.

The WHO of *natural design* in the United States will be a politician who spends far less time in Washington and more time among the people who elected him in order to fully understand the unique challenges they face. He or she then works on altering the role of all other stakeholders in the political process to serve the concerns of the only beneficiary of the political system who matters: the segmented voter population. This is the nature of the distributed intelligence of Second Tier politics. It strikes a balance between information moving up from the full kaleidoscope of *life conditions* in the population, and designs all government services as function of the voters' values and *life conditions*. This is not to marginalize those who do not "vote," who are also part of the population being served. Immigrants, children, the mentally challenged, the frail elderly, the homeless—all are populations to consider within the memetic contours of the political landscape.

Seventh-Level Yellow politicians and appointees are needed in all three branches of government. They preserve certain command and control structures that are proprietary to issues such as national security, but make transparency and integral leadership the highest values. The judiciary is not immune to ideological practices of First Tier subsistence values. The WHO in a Supreme Court, for example, views the U.S. Constitution in light of the ever-evolving values of a dynamic culture.

If one examines the recent debate over corporate personhood, a Seventh-Level Yellow Supreme Court would have naturally anticipated the predatory nature of an unhealthy Orange system and invited Second Tier legal scholars to present the court with memetically articulated points of view. In order for it to keep up with evolving values, this most intelligent branch of government must be able to see the full consequences of decisions it upholds in a landscape that looks nothing like it did when these high court cases were first tried.

The case that gave corporations the same rights as people was tried in the 1800s and our values have come a long way since then. The Orange knowledge economy and today's financial structures are far more sophisticated than they were in the 1800s. The economic systems are integrated globally, and can manipulate the entire Blue regulatory structure—or fail to act. Yet our First Tier judiciary still uses legal tools that have been out of touch with effective jurisprudence for almost two hundred years.

In the Middle East the WHO are the benevolent monarchs who aim to preserve the long- term health of the monarchy out of ancestral pride, but are fully informed by the changing landscape in the region. They are the value-systems wizards and the IIEs of their culture who are able to anticipate the issues resulting from the Arab Spring. They implement enough reforms to ease the polarization along the spectrum of values within the culture before disputes manifest in physical conflicts.

In a MEMEtocracy, a Second Tier monarch is aware that the majority of youth in the culture are in the Red-heroic value system. The monarch plans to assure the emergence of youth into values that are congruent with national pride and the pursuit of prosperity. Once these young men and women have an investment portfolio to nurture and grow, they naturally gravitate away from any unhealthy Red expression. Now they have something to lose and something to gain, a future to build for. One of the leading examples of the WHO in an Arab MEMEtocracy are the leaders of Dubai, Abu Dhabi, and the Kurdistan region of Iraq. In addition to granting land for development to young men, they are offering government jobs to both young men and women and—importantly—appointing women to be ministers in Cabinet positions. The WHO are visionary leaders who empower women in government and in business and see these values as a natural progression for the whole society.

Nontraditional emergence of political leadership in the Middle East also includes the appearance of values of early nation-states in countries like Lebanon and Kuwait. These are well-educated civil servants born into middle class families. They become activists, then run on a platform that advocates for healthy memes within their respective societies. Ziyad Baroud, who was the former Minister of the Interior for Lebanon, exemplifies the emergence of nation-state values. So does Aseel Al Awadi, a young Kuwaiti woman who is a past member of the Parliament of Kuwait. These young leaders naturally diffuse any sectarian tension as very little in their political agenda is motivated by religion. They are the ambassadors of a promising future for the Middle East.

The next question that the *Natural Design* formula answers is the HOW. Now it is time to describe HOW to connect which memetically-designed system in what memetically-designed way in order to achieve the memetically-designed superordinate goal. HOW points to the political philosophy of political leaders, their capacity to manage the dysfunction in their societies and to rise above it all to lead from the Seventh-Level Yellow system. HOW is the final piece of the puzzle to complete the natural design process and bring it to life. HOW becomes a part of the functional flow of what Beck calls "a MeshWORKS Solution." Because this last step is what places the entire model in motion, it is worthy of close examination.

FUNCTIONAL FLOW AND THE MESHWORKS SOLUTIONS

The MeshWORKs concept is the master plan that puts all the elements of MEMEtocracy together. The name meshworks is derived from brain science and was originally adapted to social models by contemporary Western philosopher Manuel De Landa in a 1995 article in *Mediamatic* as the process of how the brain creates a mind and a mind creates a brain.[85] Beck has developed this concept further and adapted it as a conceptual model for the functional neurology of culture. By articulating how complexity (which arises from *life conditions* that include diverse cultural codes and developmental gaps) can no longer be sufficiently addressed through linear models of development, Beck created a model for mapping connectivity within the global "brain."

Consider that the human brain operates via a mesh of neural connections. A Seventh-Level Yellow leader plays the role of the *Meshweaver*. He or she defines an integrated delivery system that matches memetic structures to the memetic needs of *life conditions* in large-scale design. This is the Functional Flow of Natural Design. It takes inventory of the WHO, WHOM, WHAT, and WHERE and designs the governance system and other essential systems that serves the values best. This process creates synergistic solutions that are resilient and adaptive to more complex *life conditions*, and to emerging *life conditions*, as well. These natural interconnections of the global "MeshWORKs" enable the alignment of values with needs in organizations and in culture. MeshWORKs adapted to governance can detail strategies on how to connect the proper value system functions to achieve the desired value-systems outcome that inform a MEMEtocracy platform. These are the memetic HOWs and management procedures that a systemic Yellow thinker would need to employ in order to best serve the superordinate goal identified by a regulatory structure designed from Second Tier.

Unlike First Tier designs, the MeshWORKS model is informed neither by Industrial Age regulation nor by laissez-faire policies. The HOW seeks the most functional way to connect the elements of *natural design* to answer the cultural challenges of the day. The political HOW is a management system that is the dawn of systems thinking in government. It has the capacity to connect every ^{V}MEME in its stage of evolution to a healthy Second Tier trajectory. It understands what motivates different ^{V}MEMEs and designs controls appropriate to allow each level within the system to function at optimal efficiency. The *Meshweaver* must possess the capacity to realign the resources of the system: financial, human, societal and otherwise, to serve a superordinate goal that—in the case of the United States—aims to preserve the Union for many generations to come. These Seventh-Level Yellow leaders work together according to the principles of self-organization to make sense out of the chaos caused by the misalignment of the First Tier systems.

This can be compared to what Ilya Prigogine, the complex systems scientist, describes as the point of bifurcation when First Tier systems reach maximum entropy and can no longer evolve into something new on their own. The only way forward is for the system to start reorganizing naturally, while adapting to the new complexity forming around it. This new reality in turn creates an open system that has the elements of functionality and resilience that can accommodate emergence into Seventh- and Eighth-Level systems.

Making the MEMEtocracy framework operational through *natural design*, challenges most decision-making processes that dominate political leadership today. MEMEtocracy calls on politicians, and political appointees at every level and branch of government to reframe their way of thinking and decision making through a new prism that answers to the needs of all the value systems that represent *life conditions* in any given country. Unlike current political systems, MEMEtocracy is always aware of the entrapments created by the past motivations of First Tier systems.

The MeshWORKS Solutions process itself calls on IIEs and IDAs to put forth their best thinking and connect everything that has been identified so far to everything else. In order for these efforts to create what Dr. Beck calls Seventh-Level Yellow *critical mass,* they must be integrated and aligned through a process of CAPI, the Coalescence of Authority, Power, and Influence.

Beck's colleague, Dr. Ichak Adizes, introduced the concept of CAPI in his book *Corporate Lifecycles (1988).* In any organization, community, business, or nation (or any human group) there are some people who have the authority, power or influence to assure or disrupt the implementation of a decision (in terms of meeting a goal). CAPI is necessary—meaning the people with authority, power or influence to implement or disrupt a process must be involved in decision making in order to assure implementation. The CAPI team is often temporarily formed to deal with a specific issue. In order for any Seventh-Level Yellow design to succeed, the people that hold power, authority, and influence in any given issue must be included while decisions are being made. This operationalizes the memetic data collected by *Indigenous Intelligence Experts* providing for a resilient and sustainable design.

In a MeshWORK Solution, the CAPI entity introduces new psychological DNA with the capacity to concentrate on both problems and solutions throughout the entire memestack of a culture. The CAPI team scans a culture to assess the value systems of each institution, the private sector and civil society. It defines the policies of a government through the stratified lenses of values. By examining the system the CAPI team will be able to make functional, operational decisions, such as assigning or redesigning the right form of institutions to the right fit in culture.

For example, it defines the educational system into Red, Blue, Orange, and Green and matches those designs to the segments of culture with these values to serve a more effective educational policy that fits those young people living in these specific *life conditions*. It helps address problems specific to that value system and put in place measures that help it transition into that next system. Since this is a MeshWORKS solution; it involves the parents, law enforcement, religious institutions, education policy makers and teachers, and other stakeholders in the society. MeshWORKS does the same with economic policy, foreign policy, and the health care system and every system that is vital to governance. Decision-makers on the CAPI team utilize the data gathered by the IIEs in decision making, which significantly helps assure implementation and acceptance of solutions.

In order to secure the future viability of Seventh-Level Yellow governance, the CAPI team then has to create what Dr. Beck calls a Vital Signs Monitor (VSM). This technology scans the horizon for future threats to the system through analyzing trends, such as the spread of a virus or an increase in crime. Dr. Beck and John Petersen, an IDA with the Arlington Institute, installed such system called RAHS, Risk Assessment and Horizon Scanning in Singapore. The Vital Signs Monitor integrates a state-of-the-art understanding of human nature; i.e., how cultures and countries form, how they experience stresses and strains, and how they go through layers of complexity as *life conditions* warrant, developing boundaries, interacting with other cultures and countries, and dealing internally with the social, political, and technological dynamics that often break out into different forms of conflict.[86]

The vast array of data monitored by the VSM facilitates the detection of the underlying patterns and interrelationships that *mesh* across many domains. This contributes data that is functional to conflict resolution, and facilitates natural human resilience and emergence through evolutionary steps and stages. The VSM data enables the creation of various scenarios in order to anticipate future trends, create predictive models, and influence large-scale, rapid, positive change. It helps IIEs and IDAs identify critical information, analyze its memetic content, and assess the flow of information that connects content to the functions to be performed in support of the superordinate goal(s).

This technology is currently being used by various government agencies as well as the private sector in the United States. With minor adjustments to the system it could be turned into a powerful tool of Seventh-Level Yellow governance. Often times Vital Signs Monitors are the *sources* of conceptual and actionable superordinate goals. For example, the government of Singapore installed this technology after the SARS epidemic threat of 2003.

In our MeshWORKS model, the Meshweaver is the IDA who is proficient in the language of ⱽMEMEs and hires people with the proper value-fit in order to design governance from Second Tier. Political leaders informed by the tenets of MEMEtocracy, whether directly or indirectly, make the superordinate goal known to all the First Tier systems. This dissemination of information keeps First Tier systems functionally aligned in order to facilitate the flow of the system toward its superordinate goal and evolution on the spiral. The same mesh-weaving process would be used to design Second Tier government institutions. By following the MeshWORKS model in hiring practices and in the adoption of new management philosophy, a Second Tier government fulfills a functional and sustainable role in a naturally conscious way. This will in turn provide a leadership model for all stakeholders in the culture.

MEMETOCRACY IN A NUTSHELL

By committing to the use of MEMEtocracy we redefine politics from the Seventh-Level Yellow system. By doing so, we abandon rigid ideologies and commit to the world of continuous change. Seventh-Level Yellow tools are empowered by what Graves calls the "Existence Ethic" rooted in the

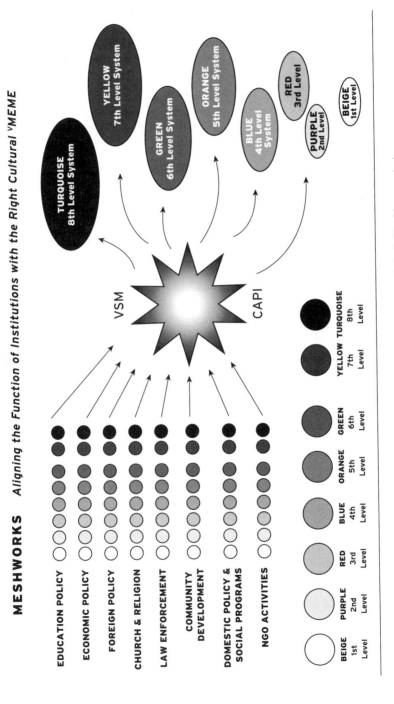

Figure 4.3 The MeshWORKS SOLUTIONS™ flowchart by Don E. Beck. Used by permission.

knowledge of all the different realities of all the First Tier ^{V}MEMEs. Once the challenges of *life conditions* are identified through the ^{V}ACE Model, the formidable task ahead is the alignment of culture to the existence ethic. *Natural design* then proceeds to sequence the elements in identifying new Yellow leaders who know the type of personnel, organizations and institutions needed to design a MEMEtocracy platform that serve the prevailing *life conditions* in the culture. This sequencing process is accomplished through the *functional flow of MeshWORKS.*

Politicians in the world today might know what ails their own political system to an extent; however, very few have the know-how to align the values that place these competing systems onto a functional platform to serve the needs of their citizens.

Yellow political and economic entities are at the base of a society with sustainable institutions. In identifying the different elements for the MEMEtocracy framework, one can see the formidable task that lies ahead—not only for the United States, but also for many emerging democracies in the world. Wise leaders in the Middle East who understand the nature of human and social emergence, naturally seek the help of *Indigenous Intelligence Experts* and *Integral Design Architects* to build a promising future for their people that rests on solid yet resilient ground like a sprung-floor that supports the moves of dancers, softening, absorbing, and minimizing shocks to the system.

The MEMEtocracy framework requires the consciousness of all the stakeholders in a culture. It urgently calls for recognition of the short-sightedness of the past and the need to participate in a sustainable future. The large-scale elements of MEMEtocracy make for a Second Tier political platform that recognizes that the citizens it serves are the most important stakeholders. Period. Full stop. It then designs everything else around them.

FIVE

Uncovering the *Indigenous Intelligence*: A Case Study of Israel & Palestine

The exercise of getting ready for statehood was a concern for some as it represented unilateralism by the Palestinians. I am here to tell everyone it is indeed unilateralism. As it should be. Because it's about building a Palestinian state. It's about getting ready for Palestinian statehood. If we Palestinians don't build it, who's going to build it for us?

—Salam Fayyad
Prime Minister of Palestine
Herzliya Conference on Strategic Governance, Israel
February 3, 2010

THE BIRTH OF NEW INDIGENOUS THINKING

On a moonlit night in late October 2004, two men sat at an outdoor café in the Yemeni Quarter in Tel Aviv engaged in casual conversation over light Middle Eastern fare. Raffi Nasser was a successful securities trader on Wall Street and came from an Arab Jewish family with a long history in the region. For centuries, his ancestors were a part of the cultural fabric of the ancient city of Aleppo, just a few hours drive to the northeast. His family migrated to Europe soon after the creation of the State of Israel. The other man, Neri Bar On, who in later years would become the head of the Center for Human Emergence in Israel, comes from an ancestry of European Jews. He looks deceptively ordinary in his attire, but in reality Neri was a celebrated star in the microchip industry for his contribution to nanotechnology.

A Palestinian coworker and engineer, Mounir Bannoura, had written a technical book about Neri's proprietary technologies and their contribution to Motorola's domination of the cell phone market in the 1990s. Israel is full of bright engineers who are on the cutting edge of the knowledge economy. At any given time, a passer-by can hear conversations in the café's talking enthusiastically about what might be next on the high-tech horizon. Tel Aviv is a technological hub, an oasis of innovation on the Mediterranean shore. It remains a leading source of high-tech inventions in the world, second only to Silicon Valley.

On that October night, sitting in the cafe overlooking the Mediterranean, these two men were not discussing the next big thing in technology or business. They were focused on a different type of value—a product that no amount of money or military might has been able to deliver in the region. They were focused on bringing lasting security and peace to their beloved Israel through new methods. They looked beyond the means that have kept their homeland isolated in its neighborhood for more than sixty years. Developing soft skills in dealing with their neighbors has not been the forte of the Israeli government, but this was exactly the needed shift in thinking that Raffi and Neri anticipated. They were hoping to initiate a movement at a grassroots level where Israelis and Palestinians could talk to each other through a new prism of values, instead of the historic polarized positions on both sides of the ^{V}ACE Model.

Raffi and Neri are two extraordinary men who began pioneering Spiral Dynamics concepts in the region. Neri, along with another Seventh-Level Yellow Israeli, Oren Entin, founded the *Integral Israel Salon*. Raffi joined their activities shortly thereafter. This was a nonpolitical organization made up of ordinary Israeli citizens who wanted to explore alternative approaches to solving complex problems.[87] Based on the framework of *Integral Theory* and the work of Ken Wilber, Integral Cafes were popping up all over the globe at the turn of the 21st Century.

Earlier that evening Raffi and Neri had moderated a deep discussion in the field of conflict resolution based on Don Beck's pioneering work in South Africa. They used the scientific tenets of value systems detailed in the *Spiral Dynamics* (1996) book as a foundation for a fresh discussion on conflict resolution. That evening the words "memetics" and "large-scale psychology" in terms of generating change came together for the first time on Middle Eastern soil. Israel and Palestine's failure to understand each other's cultural value systems was a significant insight to the salon participants. Israelis were getting their first lesson in the scientific differential diagnostic tools for determining what ails a culture, understanding socio-cultural emergence, and remedies for value system conflicts. The two men thought it would be groundbreaking to use a platform, similar to what Beck recommended for the South Africans, to try to resolve the Arab-Israeli conflict.

As they parted ways that evening, both men were convinced that this fresh approach could create a possible shift in thinking. It would certainly represent the first substantive change in the Israeli approach in over three decades. This could be the ultimate tool for facilitating peace, building essential soft skills, and their goal was to place it in the hands of Israelis at all levels of society.

At that time in my life, because of the complicated intricacies and dangers of Arab politics, I had been focusing my work on nonpolitical endeavors. I had been a consultant for Arab businesses for a few years and was forging a pioneering path in the use of the bio-psycho-spiritual dimension of leadership in a culture I knew well. I was mostly engaged in executive leadership training in cultural values for both Western corporations looking to understand the how's and why's of cultures of Middle Eastern businesses, and Middle Eastern corporations looking to develop capacities to understand behaviors of their Western employees.

It is customary for a mid-size enterprise in the Middle East to have its top management team from ten different Western countries, middle management from thirty different countries, and thousands of low-level employees from any of the third world countries in Northern Africa and from the Asian subcontinent. Although I was passionate about the work I was doing, my heart still longed to play a role in Middle Eastern politics. Just like the Israelis were realizing that there might be alternative ways of approaching peace, I had no doubt that a similar understanding can be brought to the Arab world by employing a holistic approach through the Large-Scale Psychology framework. By this time, I had studied many theories that addressed human emergence. I had begun building a repertoire of culturally-sensitive approaches on how to deal with conflict. The Middle East was my birthplace, and Arabic was my mother tongue. Understanding what the region needed in order to emerge had become my lifelong goal.

By 2004 I had known Dr. Beck for a few years and had been following his work. He had known about me and my work with culture in the Middle East, as he would invite me often to speak to his audiences about the cultural sensitivities that the West missed in its dealings with the Middle East. Earlier that same year, he and I had a discussion about the possibility of working together and bringing my years of cultural experience and his Spiral Dynamics framework to the Middle East. We were both excited about the possibility, but didn't give it much thought at the time since we both understood the magnitude of the task at hand and the enormous political barriers that could prevent any meaningful work from taking root. We both knew U.S. Middle East policy makers had been stuck in their thinking for decades and that Washington had become a closed system on this issue.

The possibility of any of our work being sponsored by any government or a Washington establishment was very small or non-existent. Dr. Beck had tried to influence fellow Texan George W. Bush and his aide Karl Rove since Mr. Bush was the Governor of Texas. I, on the other hand, understood how previous Middle East peace treaties were orchestrated by successive administrations purely for political gains. For Washington, the Mideast peace card was always an ace in the hole. To demonstrate how predictable Mideast foreign policy had become, is the following example.

In late summer 2010, after ignoring the Middle East for almost two years, the Obama Administration suddenly decided that a nice photo-op with Prime Minister Netanyahu and President Abbas might go a long way to stem midterm losses for the Democrats. You see, the popularity of President Obama and his programs had hit an all-time low. In a firm, pragmatic voice, President Obama (with Secretary of State Clinton by his side) announced that both sides had a year to sign yet another peace treaty. This would certainly fail, but the strategy served the purpose of improving the Democrats' chances at winning midterm elections. This same pattern of arbitrary and strategic manipulation of Mideast peace is again center stage with Secretary Kerry as its mouthpiece during the 2014 midterm elections. Even the president, who had held the highest promise for hope and change in decades, succumbed to the predictability of politics as usual of the Washington establishment, especially when it comes to Middle East policy.

In early 2005 Raffi Nasser attended a lecture in New York City offered by Dr. Beck on the subject of conflict resolution as seen through the eyes of the *Spiral Dynamics Theory* and the Assimilation Contrast Effect, 'ACE. Raffi met Dr. Beck for the first time after the lecture and was able to share with him the grand vision he and his Israeli colleagues had about the use of cultural value systems as the essential tool for the resolution of the Israeli/ Palestinian conflict. After a few minutes of discussion Dr. Beck accepted Raffi's invitation to come to Israel for an initial assessment of the Israeli/ Palestinian situations. No grand promises were made as to the extent of Dr. Beck's involvement or as to where the first visit might lead.

About a week later Dr. Beck called to ask if I would go with him to Israel to explore the possibility of working on the conflict. My first thought was, "Why would I be needed in Israel when my cultural knowledge was the Arab world?" My skepticism quickly disappeared when I realized that my contribution to the Israelis could be invaluable if they were open to understanding their neighbors from a cultural value-systems approach. To my husband's dismay, I quickly cleared my calendar of consulting engagements and agreed to join Dr. Beck on his first visit. Neri, Raffi, and Orin couldn't have been happier. To them the admixture of a Texan and an Arab advocating jointly for a value-systems view of the Middle East was a powerful combination—breaking every stereotype on both sides.

Preparations to put a framework in place began in earnest. Dr. Beck and I began to guide our Israeli friends on the infrastructure that they needed to prepare prior to our visit. From the get-go, Beck presented the qualities of transparency needed for Seventh-Level Yellow leadership. Meanwhile, I began my search for similarly qualified Palestinians who I might work with—those who understood the culture well and were capable of systemic thinking and can eventually become IIEs. The name Nafiz Rifai kept coming up in various conversations with colleagues. I was then formally introduced to him through Tom Christensen, a fellow IDA from the United States.

Nafiz, a Third Generation Fatah leader, had spent time in Israeli jails for his political views. He was imprisoned with Marwan Barghouti (the Mandela of Palestine) and the two created a learning community similar to Mandela's Robben Island University. Among the intellectual elites within the PLO, Nafiz was highly respected. Young Palestinians serving time in the same jail had no choice but to learn English and Hebrew and engage in intellectual discourse. Some even earned masters degrees while there. Nafiz had written several successful novels and had the personal presence of a deep thinker who commanded respect.

Our other partner on the Palestinian side was Abdel Majid Suwaiti, also a member of the Third Generation Fatah and a man of the people who knew the Palestinian tribal mores and was respected by Palestinians of all ages. Both men were fighters who, after years of struggle, turned to the power of the word rather than the gun to find prudent solutions to the conflict. Both men met many of the qualifications needed to potentially lead a team of IIEs.

Don Beck and I spent months in communication with our newly found partners on both sides to make sure they understood how our initiative was going to address the anatomy of the conflict from the start. We carefully coached both sides on how to find the center positions in each culture separately before we might bring Israelis and Palestinians together. After months of conversations our partners had a good understanding of the shift that needed to take place in both cultures. They began discussions on each side in preparation for our initiative to be sustainable.

To insure against any perceived biases in the conflict, Dr. Beck turned down any Israeli financial sponsorship and chose not to pursue funding from the U.S. State Department for this venture. Instead he turned to business colleagues who had gained a competitive edge through utilizing Beck's management consulting talents in applying the value-systems approach. These were "conscious" CEOs in the United States who fully understood the values of the Seventh-level Yellow system and the superordinate purpose of our project. Many of them also understood Beck's profound involvement in South Africa and were standing by to fund any similar project he wanted to undertake.

PURPLE-RED VILLAGES AND BLUE-ORANGE TOWNS

In February 2006 Don Beck and I made our first trip to the Middle East accompanied by Susan Vance, a former Colonel in the U.S. Air Force representing Hearthstone Global Foundation, the charity that sponsored our work. Hearthstone's founder, John Smith, a businessman who is a conscious business leader, had never visited Israel or Palestine and had no biases to either side of the conflict, but understood the powerful methodologies of Beck's work. Although Dr. Beck, our partners, and I worked on this initiative pro bono for years, John was very generous in making sure everything else was taken care of.

On that day in February, I was the last person to clear Israeli customs after the necessary questioning customary for Arab-Americans. Beck stayed with me through the last interrogation. He later complained about the treatment I received to a journalist from the Israeli daily, *Haaretz*, who was there reporting on the initiative. As we got in our cab I started pointing out to Beck the different Arab villages along the way and how the different architecture defined the simple ancient homes. His only response was "Purple." Then we passed modern Israeli settlements. His only comment was "RED–Blue with Orange architecture." This was my insight on how to keep my focus on the framework—absorbing the culture through the lenses of the spiral.

Many Israelis were gathered in anticipation of our arrival. They wanted to hear about the framework that changed South Africa. For an entire week, we met with influential change agents, academics and politicians in Tel Aviv and Herzliya. At Tel Aviv University, Professor Ephraim Ya'ar, the creator of the Peace Index which tracks highs and lows of the Israeli public sentiment, was happy to meet with us to see how our framework might enhance the predictive measures within his research. The level of Orange sophistication I witnessed in the Israeli academic institutions rivaled that of the best universities in the United States.

Among the politicians we met with were Gilead Sher, the former Chief of Staff for Prime Minister Ehud Barak and one of the chief architects of the Peace Accords with Palestine. During our meeting, Beck made reference to his white paper "*Hard Truths and Fresh Start,*" that he authored in 1991, about why the peace accords cannot succeed and why traditional negotiation methodologies fail to detect the anatomy of the conflict resulting in polarization and alienation on both sides, perpetuating mistrust. Mr. Sher, a seasoned negotiator, understood the approach and remains in contact with Beck to this day.

Later that week, we presented the Spiral Dynamics framework to a group of professors at Bar-Ilan University. One of the professors was so enthusiastic about the framework that he decided to teach the SDi framework his next semester. The new insights these professors uncovered heightened their intellectual passion as they debated the implication of the shift in views and what would be needed in order to reach the "two-state solution. "

Our first week concluded with a public presentation, the first of its kind in Israel, to over two hundred people. We talked about the innovative science of value systems and Beck presented the macro memetic view of his work in global hot spots like South Africa, being careful not to mention the word "apartheid." Beck knew that the Palestinians were highly educated, unlike the majority of blacks in South Africa at the time of his involvement, which made for an entirely different dynamic. My presentation focused on the memetic structures of the different regions of the Arab world, and I updated the attendees on the role that women and the younger generations are playing in shifting business and cultural paradigms.

The following week was our opportunity to work with our Palestinian partners. As our cab drove us through wide roads lined with the Orange architecture of Tel Aviv, we wound our way through bumpy passages in Purple villages and a few Blue checkpoints, and finally made it to the West Bank. Nafiz had arranged for a local news network to meet with us to discuss the purpose of our initiative. After about an hour, the reporter suggested that we film additional interviews by the Wall of Separation that separates Israel from the West Bank to capture what many Palestinians have come to call the "Wall of Injustice."

After we were given a tour of this monstrous concrete barrier, we understood what this young man was talking about. The wall separated families and neighbors. We also saw the opportunity to direct his passion (and that of his viewers) toward proactive efforts at reducing the rhetoric as to why Israel built the wall in the first place. However unjust the Palestinians felt the wall to be, our task was not to judge or justify the rightness or wrongness of its purpose. Our goal was to bring both sides to the center position of moderates, pragmatists, and conciliators who might influence their respective cultures to the point that the wall will disappear on its own like the one in Berlin.

There is no military effort included in this strategy. Military positions can no longer define the two cultures. It is simply a hearts and minds appeal to both populations where memes of self-reliance, respect for insti-tutions, desire for prosperity and, later, peaceful coexistence will come to define the meme stack on both sides.

In an effort to inject these memes through the media, Beck and I pointed to the resilience of Palestinians everywhere in the world. From brilliant professors and philosophers, like Edward Said, who were shaping the minds of future global leaders, to bankers, managers and engineers who made the modern day Middle East so attractive to businesses. We also pointed to the highly educated public in the West Bank and Gaza, and the scientific discoveries at universities in the West Bank. We discovered that the Palestinian youth were flexible, and therein lay an opportunity to shape the thinking of future Palestinian leaders.

In addition to media outlets, we met with influential politicians, including the Governor of Bethlehem. The meeting started with the usual canned speech Palestinian politicians give to Americans. They talk about the occupation and the checkpoints and what the U.S. should do to improve the lives of Palestinians. Half way through the Governor's speech Nafiz re-introduced Beck as a fighter who worked side by side with the Zulus in South Africa to help them claim their freedom. After we introduced the Governor to our approaches and methodologies, the Governor informed Nafiz that he would make available the resources of his office to facilitate our mission.

We also met with a number of Palestinian Parliament members and listened to the concerns their constituents had about the occupation and struggles with Palestinian governmental agencies. The times that we weren't meeting with government officials and organized groups we were doing our own research into the *life conditions* of Palestinians. We visited refugee camps. We talked to people on the streets and in coffee shops. We visited the grounds of a mosque during services held for a young suicide bomber to gain a deeper understanding of the dynamics that created the deadly meme. We used traditional channels of information and readily available research and combined them with our own findings in order to begin to paint a more accurate value-systems view of the Palestinian culture. Our first visit pio-neered new methods for uncovering the dynamics that contribute to conflict, the first macro-memetic picture of the Middle East.

The week with the Palestinians concluded with a town hall meeting at the Palestinian Women's Center. Beck and I delivered a presentation on our framework and engaged many participants, including a group of pro-fessors at Bethlehem University, on how to use the Spiral model to begin a shift toward empowering women and Palestinians youth. At the end of the evening the president of the women's organization presented me with their 50th Anniversary book commemorating the women of Palestine. She pointed to the fact that one of the original, founding women of their organization was a Maalouf. It was a great way to end the week and the first eventful exploratory visit to the region.

EMPATHY AND THE 5-DEEP STRATEGY

To understand what ails a culture is not an easy task. The best one can do is try to understand what keeps it in an arrested state and prevents it from emerging into higher levels of existence. The goal of the first year of our mission was to teach those who were open to the framework, but more so to *listen and learn*. This essential element of the Indigenous Design process informs the alignment of the model to the culture. To an IDA and a Seventh-Level Yellow system designer, there is no higher priority than this first step in large-scale design. *Listening* takes on a completely different dimension at this level than *listening* in the First Tier systems. This a space of deep *empathy* that not only addresses the surface behavior of a culture but employs a specific *five-layer deep strategy* that penetrates to the core of the bio-psycho-social roots of a conflict.

Peace accords are political manipulations not culture-wide solutions, so they become quick fixes that only apply to surface manifestations, the symptoms of a problem. This is essentially the tip of the iceberg in cultural complexity, and navigating through the visible surface ice will not result in a deep or lasting peace. When compared to our center's approach, a traditional conflict assessment barely penetrates the second layer of MEMEtocracy's 5-Deep Assessment Model. Traditional methodologies are as outdated and unscientific as the belief that the world is flat because they do not integrate the wealth of knowledge available today, but we are challenging that assumption.

In our first year of work in Israel and Palestine we intentionally began to look underneath the surface to understand the real-world *life conditions*, fears, and values. Beyond the manifested actions and behaviors, we looked into the systems and structures that contribute to the behavior. Was it random and individual or was it shaped in institutions. With the help of the *Indigenous Intelligence* of our IIEs on both sides, we then looked at the mindsets and ways of thinking: personal, institutional, and societal. It is crucial to understand each culture's worldview, including how it sees itself, its neighbors, its region and the world, and how that affects the design and the culture of its institutions.

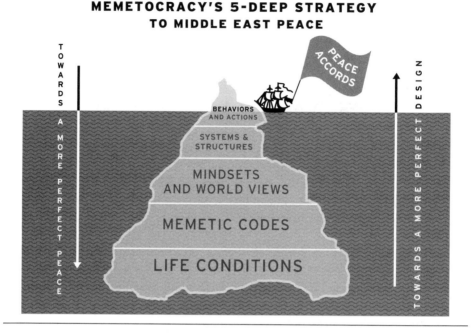

Figure 5.1 The 5-Deep Strategy to peace in the Middle East
(Copyright the Center for Human Emergence Middle East)

Then we examined the memetic codes of each culture in an effort to assess the preference and priorities of the different groups belonging to each value system and what shaped its indigenous content. What or who it held in the highest esteem, and where certain issues ranked on its list of priorities. Finally, we looked at the *life conditions* within each culture. We examined the factors that make ᵛMEMEs surge, emerge, regress, or, in the worst cases, fade and become toxic. We looked to see if solutions that were offered and the ones we intend to offer were aligned with *the times* in which the people live now, or were they relics of times past. Was each progressive peace treaty just another *translation* of previous, failed peace accords, or did it hold the potential to be *transformational* in light of the evolving times? Were either the Israelis or the Palestinians stuck in their views of history to the point that positions on either side of the values spectrum ignored reality? Would those on the ground become naturally polarized because of misalignment with *the times*?

We also examined the importance of *place*, which takes center stage in this conflict as both sides claim one area as their ancestral land. We looked at the internal challenges that faced each culture and the external challenges that might shape any final outcome in a negotiated settlement. Then we examined the *circumstances* that define the socio-economic class, the political class, and educational levels on both sides. In studying *life conditions,* an examination of circumstances must include the external dynamics that influence each side as well the internal dynamics. We had to examine how much military, financial, and international aid played a part in redefining the internal circumstances of each culture, and whether these influences and authorities distorted the views of the various positions on the values ACE spectrum.

We further assessed who or what power mechanism controlled the flow of resources. The diagnostic tools that we have were made available to anyone (on either side) who holds CAPI (authority, power, or influence) allowing them to see how they might make a difference in the future direction of Middle East peace. With the help of many indigenous intelligences (stakeholders) in both the Palestinian and Israeli cultures, we were able to fashion a model of the ᵛMemetic profile of each society that we later used as a general guide for the design aspects of our initiative. These assessments and tests were similar to the ones featured in Appendices A and B that were adjusted for cultural variables and were used to determine the deeper structural layers that defined both Israel and Palestine.

We did not go to the Middle East with preconceived strategies or views to impose on either side. We wanted to examine the existing assumptions for fallacies and deficiencies that were perpetuating the status quo. We introduced a body of knowledge and methodologies that people could use to solve the problems that exist now, and that were based on a more complex system than the one that initially created the problems.

We were careful not to make any grand promises. We provided insightful presentations that addressed the basic commonalities we all share as human beings on our endless quest to create more meaning in our lives. We offered the theoretical model and its applications, which capture that essence. In Israel we listened to politicians, peace negotiators, academics and business leaders, educated women, and young people, who speak passionately about the hopes and dreams for peace and harmony.

On the Palestinian side we listened to parliamentarians, governors, professors, and various leaders of women and youth organizations describe their views and the challenges facing their emerging state. We were educated by both sides on the intricate realities of their daily challenges and heard their vision of what it means to live side by side. We listened to the memes that define a successful Palestine. We captured patterns from the Israelis of what it means to be under constant threat of attack.

By the end of the first year of research we had a better ᵛMemetic picture of the dysfunction. The Israelis, much like the West, expected a partner in peace to be fully developed in the Blue Fourth-Level system. Yet Israel, the West, the Arabs, and the Palestinians themselves have done little to help assure that Palestinian institutions will have the resilience to maintain a prolonged presence at this stage of development. This is what the results of our research kept pointing to, and it was confirmed by our on-the-ground experiences. These findings opened up the space for our participation as a potential partner to inform and assist the designers of the future state of Palestine.

One of most significant factors that Beck and I set out to uncover during the first year of our project was an assessment of whether both cultures were ready for change. Was either side arrested or closed in any part of the memetic structure of their value systems? With the level of interest we generated during our presence, it was clear that both sides actively desired an alternative way to move beyond the failed negotiations of the past. The high level of enthusiasm on both sides came as a surprise to us. I wasn't sure whether the attraction was for learning new perspectives because they wanted to hear about Beck's insights on South Africa, or whether it was because they really wanted a change. Of all the media coverage of our first year activities, Akiva Eldar of the Israeli daily *Haaretz* captured our approach best:

> Beck argues that, any attempt at bridging the gap and negotiating, even if it is done by a side not directly involved in the conflict, cannot be sufficiently neutral. He prefers to look at the different value systems prevailing in the region, and seek bases for technological, economic and environmental growth and progress for each of the societies. "Instead of coexistence, live and let live," he says. "I prefer prosper and let prosper, grow and let grow." He says that in order to reach this goal, it is necessary to map the dominant groups in the two societies, and identify the common denominators in values between them . . . He proposes the following exercise, which has been tried successfully in other conflicts: "Leap to the year 2020 and present yourselves with two mock-up newspapers. In one headline there will be reports about acts of hostility and your grandchildren who are leaving the country. The headline of the other newspaper will be about economic prosperity and a report about your grandchildren's wonderful achievements at school. [88]

CREATING ISRAEL'S MEMETIC PROFILE

The "prosper and grow" strategy is a key driver, a superordinate goal behind large-scale nation-building psychology. It is what defines the functionality behind MEMEtocracy and directs the healthy expressions of countries away from the path of destruction. I previously mentioned Beck's white paper titled "Hard Truths and Fresh Start" where he predicted the failure of every peace accord. It was that paper that got me to believe that an alternative solution for Mideast peace was possible. Since 1991 Beck had hypothesized that at the root of the failed negotiations was the difference in the cultural development stages between the Israelis and the Palestinians. This was at the core of what he believed had prevented lasting peace and prosperity from taking root.

Now that we were on the ground in both countries with a team of competent IDAs, we had the chance to test Beck's hypothesis. We spent much time trying to verify the developmental gaps that have led to the failure of those peace initiatives. Appendix B represents a sample of one of the instruments we used to do culture-wide assessments of both the Israelis and the Palestinians. The questions are modified by input from IIEs and IDAs first in order to capture sensitivities and eliminate biases. Although the questionnaire is called the Global Values Monitor, adjustments were made to capture the deeper memetic profiled of the respective societies. Our data from that first year of engagement and research confirmed that Israel has its center of gravity in BLUE–Orange values with a healthy presence in the Green ᵛMEME.

The founding principles of Israel were born out of the values of Blue political Zionism that emerged during the Industrial Age, Orange values of Europe. This was a state that had been defined by institutions and the belief in the rule of law since its creation in 1948. Blue is the beginning of abstract thinking that replaces personal power with the power of the institution. Respect for these institutions is key to the foundation of every first world country, organization, and human society. Although much criticism continues to be leveled at the treatment of the Palestinians and the bloody history that established the country, Arab Israelis that hold Israeli citizenship today have more individual rights than most Arabs do in their own countries. However limited their power is, they still benefit from the social programs and institutions of Israeli culture.

There is great support for Israel from a highly successful Jewish diaspora around the world, including a strong political lobby in the United States. There is great resilience in the people who believe in a homeland for the Jewish people. While we were laying the groundwork for our research we could not escape the presence of one of the densest Blue memes that define a complex culture. In 2006 Prime Minister Olmert was being investigated for accepting an illegal campaign contribution or bribe which ultimately cost him the leadership of the Kadima Party and lead to his resignation as prime minister.[89]

This was a Blue meme that spoke loud and clear to us. It provided the thin slicing that gave us a forensic look into how well the different branches of government work, and more importantly how the culture held its elected officials accountable. This was a nation of law and order. Mr. Olmert seemed to respect this code in his resignation speech: *"I am proud to be a citizen of a country in which a prime minister can be investigated like any other citizen."*[90] This particular brand of Blue is yet to emerge in many parts of the world.

Some of the other more sensitive memetic profiling, like the culture of the Israeli Defense Ministry and the Knesset, was done by Beck with the help of our Israeli partners. According to Beck, although the Defense Ministry exhibited some of the brightest and most advanced Orange technologies and training, it still lagged behind on reading the memetic profiles of Palestinians crossing checkpoints. With our Israeli partners, Beck offered to train the guards at the checkpoints on how to develop better sensitivities to the values of the Palestinians who were crossing.

Although the military intelligence was superior, their psycho-social skills in understanding the cultural codes of its neighbors and the rest of the region still lagged behind. When Beck asked them to explain this deficiency, high-ranking military officials told him that many in the military sought training in Systemic Design and Leadership, which was a Yellow concept developed in Europe. In addition to dealing with military Blue, the training taught Generals and Commanders how to deal with Orange and Green values, but they failed to communicate these complex principles to soldiers on the front lines who faced Red existential threats from their neighbors. The lack of clear Blue guidelines in the military command and control structure of the IDF was evident in the heavy losses they incurred in their ground invasion of southern Lebanon in the 30-day war of 2006. Most of the damage that was inflicted on Lebanon came from air strikes while the tactical and strategic ground movement suffered the loss of over 160 soldiers in just a few days.

As we continued to construct the Israeli Memetic profile, our Israeli partners arranged for Beck to meet Knesset members from the newly formed Kadima Party. On the Israeli value spectrum, Kadima at the time represented the pragmatist position led by former Prime Minister Ariel

Sharon. It represented the hopes of the Israeli for a unilateral decision to disengage from settlements in Gaza and the northern West Bank. In our view, this represented Israel's entry into the Orange political values of "let's make a deal."

But, with unilateral disengagement, Hamas declared the Israeli actions a victory for themselves and took control over Gaza, undermining the Palestinian Authority and weakening Kadima in the process. To the CHE-Mideast, these dynamics were yet another signal of how much more work needed to be done on the Palestinian side. It also confirmed that when Israel is under an existential threat, all sides shift to a patriotic (hard core) Blue position making any peace efforts or negotiations from other spectrum positions disappear.

Often when an individual or social entity, like a nation or tribe, is confronted by conflict, it will often "hunker down" and exhibit the attributes of a previous value system. Thus the Israeli ORANGE–Green was not in play at the border as much as Blue. Many other memes on the Israeli side came together from other areas to complete our memetic profile of the country. These came to us from many segments of the business community that represents the most innovative Orange in the region. Traditional Orange had the healthiest of all expressions. These were the older entrepreneurs who build modern-day Israel and had working relationships with Palestinian entrepreneurs. They had a sense of patriotic responsibility toward solving the conflict. Because they believe in the two-state solution, they listened intently to Beck and invite us to keep the dialogue open.

The Orange of the knowledge economy, however, was a completely different meme, and to us it was an early indication of disconnect in Israeli culture. The most innovative forms of Orange entering Yellow were totally disconnected from the political process. These young entrepreneurs whose startup ventures crowd the NASDAQ have a personal ambition that enables them to feel that they're in charge of their destiny rather than dominated by cultural tradition and its characterizations. Palestinians, Arabs, and the Israeli political establishment don't exist within their memetic profile of their group. Some of these entrepreneurs had run into Beck's framework as a business management discipline, but when they requested a meeting with us, they showed no interest in what we were doing on the political side.

It was as if Israel's long-term prosperity and safety had nothing to do with what they were engaged in. The only thing they wanted was to know how our methodologies might offer them a more competitive edge in their business practices. They did not want to be bogged down by a slow-moving peace process. Their lives move at the speed of the Internet. As much as the

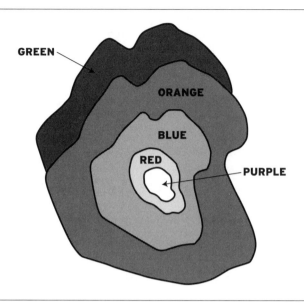

Figure 5.2 Israel's value-system's profile under relative safety.

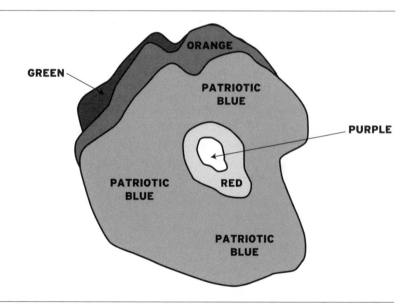

Figure 5.3 Israel's value-system's profile when culture is under existential threat.

values of this group were representative of the future of Israel, they were unfortunately in total disconnect from reality on the ground. In a way, they wanted to live and prosper in denial.

In the mosaic that forms the memetic profile of Israel, the Green values appeared in the mothers and grandmothers helping Palestinians at checkpoints and documenting any abuses by soldiers of the Israeli Defense Forces. Green was also present in some former IDF soldiers who went to India after their military service in order to deepen their understanding of human nature. After achieving "inner peace," they come back to an arrested Blue state and the ongoing realities of the conflict.

Green values were healthiest in the communities that the Israeli *Integral Salon* attracted. These forums draw the interest of individuals from every background that represents Israel's potential to ascend to the Seventh-Level Yellow system. Since they held little political clout, the movement couldn't reach the critical mass it needed to redefine Israeli values. Today, the social movement in Israel has taken on the Green mantle triggered by the global phenomena of the Occupy Movement that exposes the inequality between the rich and poor.

Like all other cultures, Israel has its Red. This value system was represented by defiant Flamethrowers, the settlers who believe that all Judea belongs to the Jews. They are religious Zionists with their own sense of Blue entitlement. They fought the IDF soldiers who came to evict them as a part of the unilateral disengagement plan from Gaza and the northern West Bank. Red is also represented in some of the Orthodox Jews in Jerusalem who refuse to serve in the military on religious grounds, and receive social benefits from the state. They have their own closed-Blue that is not considered patriotic by most Israelis.

MEMETIC PROFILES OF PALESTINE

Much of my responsibilities at the CHE-Mideast during the first year of our mission were focused on the Palestinian side. It was of utmost importance to the success of our mission to create a memetic profile that was indigenously informed in order for our design to be reflective of *life conditions*. Our partners, Nafiz Rifae and Abdel Majid, understood this as we proceeded to construct the Palestinian profile. Just as the dense Israeli Blue spoke loudly to us on the Israeli side, the loudest voices in Palestine came from the NGO activities that were taking place. These were well meaning philanthropic organizations that crowded the streets of Palestine from Ramallah and the refugee camps on the West Bank to the allies of the Gaza

Strip. They numbered 3,200 strong, and they each had their own ideas on how to best serve the Palestinians. Many of them were Europeans dealing with the Green guilt of causing the displacement of the Palestinians in the first place.

Others were well meaning and thought they could enhance the lives of Palestinians by offering weekend sensitivity trainings in the hopes that such arbitrary Green values might somehow take root. Others offered empowerment programs to women who could barely make ends meet. Many could not afford good schools for their kids, and most of their husbands were out of work. Post-modern European values that were steeped in cultivating soft skills, listening and empowerment were all abstract concepts that work extremely well in culture with the postindustrial values of the Orange and Green systems. However, the content of these programs was highly mismatched with the needs of Palestinian society.

One group of conscious Palestinian women told us the story of how their group was turned down by a United States-based NGO for requesting funding to build a community center. The entire project would have cost a fraction of the cost of one week of empowerment training and would have provided a sustained presence in the community for training local women, and out of work youth. Palestinians were resilient people who wanted to be trained in computer skills and other essential trades needed for the local job market. Yet requests were repeatedly denied as the NGO wanted to stay within the "empowerment" parameters defined by their employers.

Our frequent encounter with this phenomenon gave us great insight into how external aid forces were shaping Palestine's memetic profile. Although their intentions were noble, their efforts were not sustainable. By not committing to funding long-term projects that the Palestinians could take charge of, and feel a sense of ownership and pride in, the NGOs were sentencing the Palestinians to a life of dependency.

One model that delivered aid did so effectively by appointing local experts (the *Indigenous Intelligence*) as program directors. Although based in the West, the model these organizations used recognized the importance of what we've been pointing to all along: that the locals understood the needs of their people far better than outsiders.

The activity of the majority of the remaining NGOs, however, were ad hoc, piecemeal, and fragmented, and in desperate need of a unified Blue structure led by conscientious Palestinians themselves. To the members of the CHE-Mideast, this illustrated the absence of a Blue institution to coordinate aid efforts, addressing the inefficiency and waste and delivering essential services that fit the needs of the people.

As our search continued for institutions to deliver appropriate services, an insight came from our Palestinian partners about the political process. Much like the rest of the Arab world, politics had remained Tribalistic Purple—families who have traditionally held political office have the popular vote, with few exceptions. Our *Indigenous Intelligence Experts* kept pointing at the lack of leadership qualified to move their society into a unified Blue under one superordinate goal. Because of the polarized dynamics between Hamas and Fatah, and also within both of these movements, a unified national vision never materialized. When we added the external political and military support of Hamas coming from groups like Hezbollah and from Iran, the Palestinians were further polarized away from a unified vision of statehood and from the middle positions needed by the ^{V}ACE Model for a comprehensive peace with Israel.

As our Palestinian partners completed their research, we all discovered that aside from religion and the presence of some passive institutions, the Blue layer that the West and Israel needed to work with was very thin. They made no effort to hide the prominence of Red observed on both sides of the movements of Hamas and within Fatah.

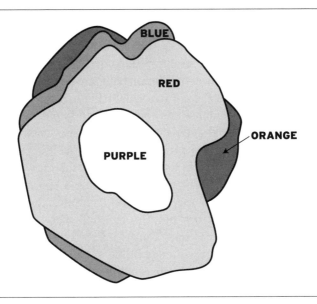

Figure 5.4. A Palestinian value-system profile shown with Red bulge, Purple core, Hamas religious Blue, Fatah transitional Blue, and minimal overall BLUE–Orange emerging in business, academia, women, and the Millennial Generation.

When Nafiz and I presented our model at the Fatah headquarters in Ramallah, they had already lost the 2006 general elections to Hamas and were in desperate search for answers. After we made our way through their parking lot full of luxury cars, passing by Fatah members wearing Rolex watches, we started to question their commitment to the national Blue that served the Palestinian people. When we invoked their past pride, reminding them of the days when they helped Palestinian families with building homes and providing services, they bowed their heads in acknowledgment of how the party had lost its way with the needs of the people.

This was the time when we were able to recognize that Fatah was an open system, willing to grow and learn. They invited Don Beck, Nafiz Rifae, Abdel Majid, and me to train some of the top ranking members of the Third Generation Fatah. The more we were exposed to Fatah and their party members, the more we were able to understand the memetic structure of the Palestinian society. They were honest, self-critical, and candid in depicting their own value structure as well as that of their Hamas adversaries and Palestine in general.

Hamas gained popularity as the new, honest Blue provider of services to most Palestinian living in PURPLE–Red *life conditions*. By painting a picture of the corruption that took place under the leadership of the PLO and convincing their followers that Fatah's treaties with Israel had done little to improve the their lives, Hamas ignited the passions of a grassroots movement. They called for new Palestinian Blue based on Islamic fundamentalism that garnered the support of many Flamethrowers throughout the region. This was the old parochial Islamic Blue. I got to experience a healthier form of Islamic Blue when some of Hamas's moderate members reached out to Nafiz and Abdel Majid because they wanted to meet with Dr. Beck. We were surprised to see that despite the party's perceived closed system, they were open to learning strategies on how to deal with Israel and the West. Beck agreed to offer the group a Spiral Dynamics training session. Nafiz and I provided the Arabic content to the theory.

It is noteworthy at this point to mention that while Dr. Beck wished for his colleagues to call him "Don," I insisted that in Palestine everyone including myself, address him as Dr. Beck. This way he was respected as a professorial presence, as well as being viewed as a freedom fighter who played a major role in changing South Africa. In presenting him in this manner his Blue authority could not be undermined. On the day of the training, the Hamas participants presented themselves in a starkly different way from the Fatah trainees. Dr. Beck commented later that when they walked in to the training room, he felt as if his grandfather walked in. The third-ranking member offered the introductions in ascending order as they all walked in perfect rhythm. The lowest ranking took his seat last. As a reminder of their conservative Islamic values, no one shook my hand.

The Hamas moderates had many grievances and they made sure we knew about them all. The interjections and objections to what we were teaching never stopped. I took this opportunity as a "teachable moment" to show them how their lack of respect represented their Red values. If they wanted to get the attention of decision makers (in other countries) they would have to follow certain polite rules of engagement. I started by limiting their questions to one question per person per hour. Every time someone violated that rule, I stopped him and reminded him of the commitment he gave on his honor to limit himself to just one question.

When the training was over, one of the high-ranking participants approached Dr. Beck and showed him an old key to his ancestral home. With a Red heroic voice he declared that he wouldn't be a man unless he reclaimed his family honor for the future of his children. In an attempt to shift everyone's focus away from perpetuating the old paradigm, Dr. Beck interjected with "What if, for the future of your children, your name was on a school that you built within a civil society?" Then the participant acknowledged what they have known all along: the house probably no longer existed, and it was time to build a new and different house.

These were the type of narratives of a new sense of pride that needed to spread throughout Palestinian society. As we continued to engage with the Palestinians and create their memetic profile, it became more and more apparent to us that the needs of the Palestinians were being overlooked. We reviewed research from every corner of Palestine conducted by the Palestinian team and came to the conclusion that the focus should be on building Blue institutions. *Palestine Times* reporter Maysa Al-Gayyusi captured this best in her interview with Dr. Beck, in which he announced our formation of The Build Palestine Initiative:

> I believe it makes no sense to spend a lot of time attacking the current realities. It is time to create the new models that have in them the complexity that makes the older systems obsolete . . . We will be able to profile Palestine. To identify the underlying currents that erupt in surface level conflicts, and even violence. In doing so, we can construct a methodology and process for calming the frustrated voices, and focus them on constructive activities that can build Palestine .[91]

As we composed these tentative memetic profiles of the Israeli and Palestinian cultures, we were very cognizant of the fact that they only provided a general guide, or an outer parameter that contained our research. Memetic profiles are dynamic and should be used with great caution. A Seventh-Level Yellow designer uses the memetic lay of the land to build a strategy that enables flexibility and accommodation for changes in life conditions. These design elements had been pioneered in part in the book *The Crucible; Forging South Africa's Future,* written by Dr. Beck along with his South African IDA, Graham Linscott. Linscott is a well-known South African journalist. They spent many years compiling the research to derive an accurate memetic profile of the complex socio-cultural strata in South Africa. The book identifies many parallels to what we experienced as we attempted to map the different groups on both sides, with all their memetic complexities along the values spectrum.

THE BIRTH OF THE *BUILD PALESTINE INITIATIVE (BPI)*

Between 2006 and 2008 we supported and guided our IIEs in both Israel and Palestine as they continued to advocate the need for the conflict to be viewed through spiral lenses. On subsequent visits we continued to meet with change agents. Our Palestinian IIEs carried the voices and concerns of the Palestinian people directly to the global community through our CHE-Mideast website, blog and through Israeli and Palestinian media. On the Israeli side, Neri helped disseminate the framework via academic venues and at grassroots levels. Dr. Beck and our Israeli partners continued to meet with the Israeli business community to build further awareness and commitment.

As we continued our cultural assessments of both sides, we came to the realization that the top leaders we were trying to influence on either side represented the arrested stages in the old paradigm. They held the old CAPI, and they would not consider change unless the hearts and minds of the people enforced it. In order for a fresh start to be informed by a new narrative, we had to focus on our own grassroots movement.

Israeli Blue had long been defining Israeli institutions. The same couldn't be said about the Palestinian side, as institutions were in their infancy stages. We looked for ways to build the capacities in Palestine. We began to use our methodologies to balance the asymmetry on the Palestinian side with our sights on the long-term effects this could have on their negotiation positions and capacities in the future.

THE CREATION OF A SUPERORDINATE GOAL

Staying true to our approach, we could not perpetuate past perceptions, but instead of dismissing those past efforts and perspectives, we honored them. On the Palestinian side we used the memetic data that our research had uncovered to decode the message aimed at building Palestinian institutions. Our partners kept telling people from every walk of life that our approach *honored the past, worked with the present, but designed for the future.* The enthusiasm of the Third Generation Fatah members in spreading this message to all corners of the West Bank was extraordinary. They were motivated by the need to re-establish the credibility of their party and redefine it as an organization in tune with the future aspirations of all Palestinians. They felt the personal responsibility for losing to Hamas and for preserving the few Blue institutions they had worked so hard to build.

Moreover they wanted to find ways to communicate a vision of a new Fatah to the powerful Revolutionary Guard, and President Abbas's inner circle. The entire Fatah Party had come to the inevitable realization that corruption, lack of transparency, and denying people the most basic of services were the leading causes of their demise.

Dr. Beck and I started a series of conversations with our Palestinian IIEs about their vision for a prosperous Palestinian state. Together we assessed the internal capacities of Palestinian society and the amount of international aid that poured into Palestine every year. Then, instead of simply asking how they would distribute the aid differently, we asked how they would use it to build the institutions that their society needs. These questions gave our IIEs, and the Palestinian supporters around them, the permission and opportunity to think differently about the future of Palestine. Ideas were exchanged and the level of engagement began to create a real sustainable movement in a new direction.

Then, to prevent a fall into old patterns of political corruption and dysfunction, we helped them create a superordinate goal: one that all Palestinians could get behind but no single group could achieve on its own. A superordinate goal, by its very nature, has to act as a motherboard that provides the means through which the interests and functions of all the competing parties are aligned towards a common purpose. The superordinate goal had to be inspiring enough that it made every Palestinian proud of wanting to pursue it. We were careful not to make premature declarations that might unintentionally exclude meaningful segments of Palestinian society.

Since the time we started our work in Palestine, we had witnessed the optimistic Orange values of the tech-savvy Palestinian Millennial Generation. We examined the possibility of this becoming the primary source of our superordinate goal.

After much discussion with Nafiz and his group, it became apparent that the future pull that we needed towards prosperity was evident in young Palestinians. In order for this to work, the declaration of a superordinate goal could not stop at just creating foundational institutions. The objective had to address leadership and economic and political issues at the regional level. Then, and only then, would a superordinate goal be considered resilient enough that Palestinians and regional and global powers could all support it.

As we vetted our ideas over many months, it became clear to us that Palestinian capacities could definitely accommodate a state as vibrant and as prosperous as the Mumbai region in India. The Palestinian population had one of highest percentage of engineers per capita in the region outside Israel. Many of the youth who join the Intifadas out of frustration and boredom could have employment in high-tech manufacturing and in call centers that cater to 300 million Arabic-speaking customers. Once a culture gets a taste of that individual Orange success, it will be difficult to get its young men to pick up arms or rocks and destroy what they built by their own hands. Or at least that was the premise based on the theoretical framework. Any way we viewed this approach, it had the marking of a successful superordinate goal. Even in the long term it had the potential to become the superordinate goal for both Israel and Palestine. It served as a complimentary match to the Israeli memetic profile and for potential future relationships with the West, and for upward emergence on the spiral.

The future vision will include *Functional Capitalism*, those enterprises and people who are conscientiously implementing practices that benefit humanity and the environment (Orange–Green) designed from the Seventh-Level Yellow. The corporate social responsibility movement is a draw towards Orange innovation in a global and local economic context. With a potential peace treaty the Palestinians can be the ones who bring Israel's— and their own—technological innovations to the region.

We realized that without a working peace, and few Blue Palestinian institutions at the time, our focus should be the Palestinian, not the regional, superordinate goal. The Palestinians needed to focus on building their own institutions first, and that will be a long process on their road to fulfilling the goals of the Build Palestine Initiative. After much deliberation, our Palestinian partners declared that Palestine's superordinate goal for the remainder of the initiative would be: *"To build Palestine as the Mumbai of the Arab World."*

With this declaration as the future pull for Palestine, we brought clarity to the remaining involvement of our mission. Our partners began to spread the word about the need to build resilient institutions. They began to preach the virtues of transparency. They held town meeting on what it means to have good schools in tune with the needs of the job market of the future. They talked about what it means to have good hospitals and good health care.

At the same time they created feedback and feedforward loops that stayed in touch with local *life conditions*, an infant Vital Signs Monitor. They heard from farmers wanting better irrigation technology and knowledge of crop rotation. They got feedback from mothers with regard to the cost of a good education for the future generation destined to lead the Mumbai of the Arab world. Optimism was contagious as Orange talents rose to the surface to address developmental gaps that had been ignored for years. Many conversations ensued about developing a robust tourism sector.

Meanwhile, Dr. Beck and I continued to influence the thinking of political leaders as much as we could. Part of our plan to achieve the superordinate goal was to build the real Vital Signs Monitor, which makes it easier to detect weak signals of change in the fabric of the Palestinian culture. Nafiz arranged for us to meet the Interior Minister who had shown high interest in the project. He promised future cooperation with regard to installing the technology.

Meetings with old guard politicians were tainted with their arrested views about any progress being made. They carried the bitterness from their past failure and had no hesitation in giving us the same canned speech they gave to any Western organization. Many of these politicians were looking in the rearview mirror and missed the rising promise of the Millennial Generation.

Nafiz also arranged for us to meet with Fadwa Barghouti, the wife of the imprisoned "Mandela of Palestine" and Nafiz's prison cellmate in an Israeli jail. This woman witnessed the twenty-year transformation of her husband into a figure that both Hamas and Fatah might embrace as a unifying leader. While Palestinians view him as a freedom fighter, the Israeli continue his detainment based on a violation of their Blue laws. The Israelis had also imprisoned Barghouti's son but now he was being released from prison. Deema Shawa, a Palestinian IIE, extended an invitation for him to attend a training we had arranged for young professional Palestinians. This was the Millennial Generation that held influence, if not immediate power or authority (CAPI) for the future of Palestine.

During the first day of training the young Barghouti demonstrated an uncanny understanding of Palestinian and Israeli value systems. He described how certain prison guards, while having to do their Blue duty, would bring him contraband items, like cigarettes, magazines and newspapers. These guards represent the Orange–Green in Israeli culture—those who just want to move forward and live in peace with the Palestinians. After learning Spiral Dynamics and participating in a simulated enactment of the conflict on the ^{V}ACE values spectrum, the whole group engaged in a discussion about how they might work with the Israeli center positions and specifically the Orange pragmatist positions that want to make a deal.

When we spoke about shifting from seeing geographic maps to seeing memetic maps, Barghouti drew a map that illustrated a memetic profile of Israel. Only an intelligent open system individual who had spent time in Israeli jails could have drawn this map. (See figure 5.5). Barghouti led his team through an exercise that demonstrated how Israel surrounded the West Bank and Gaza with Red settlers as a first line of defense against any Red activity from Palestine. Blue checkpoints and IDF presence was another memetic layer that ran across Jerusalem, and at every entry and exit point from the West Bank. Blue presence was heaviest where it supported the areas around the Red settlers, and at the Lebanese and Syrian borders where they created a buffer zone to protect the Orange business community. Orange itself was in the center of the country, while ORANGE-Green of the knowledge economy occupied the coastal areas from Gaza to the border of Lebanon.

As we continued to expose more and more Palestinians to this new perspective on how to perceive the conflict, a new meme was being created. Nafiz heard from many corners of the West Bank that we were being called *"the spiral people."* The more community meetings Nafiz and our group held, the more people were being inspired by the potential our efforts had. What started as a grassroots effort in 2005 has grown into a movement that could no longer be ignored by the summer of 2007. For the remainder of the year we turned our attention to structuring ways of identifying an effective forum for the Palestinian voices that needed to be heard within Palestine itself and in Israel.

We began to attract the attention of high-ranking politicians on both sides. Suddenly senior members of Fatah wanted to know the nature of the framework from Nafiz, Dr. Beck, and me. Cabinet members and executive committee members from Fatah wanted to know how this theory might translate into more effective governance on the ground. When Nafiz saw the level of interest increasing in Fatah as it was at the grassroots level, he

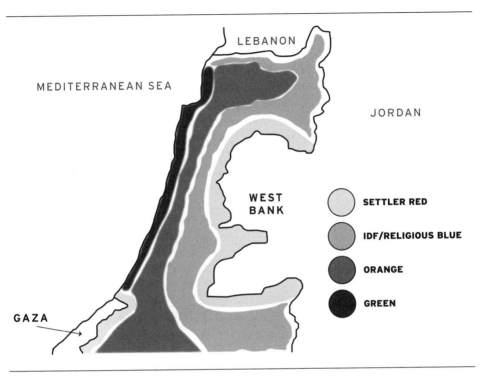

Figure 5.5. Palestinian Millennial Generation view of the map of Israel.

suggested holding a national summit where community leaders from all parts of the West Bank and Gaza could share their ideas on the future of Palestine. He and his colleagues called on the Fatah executive committee to talk to community leaders and canvas the entire West Bank to gather data so that everyone's voice could be heard at the national summit. Our goal was to present an up-to-date profile on Palestinian *life conditions* and to provide the participants with a roadmap of what needed to be done in order to implement the Build Palestine Initiative.

Our activities were now becoming visible to the Israeli leadership as well. At Dr. Beck's request, our partners at the CHE Israel exchanged correspondence with the office of the Israeli Foreign Ministry and the office of the President of Israel, keeping them updated on our activities in Palestine. Dr. Beck and our colleague Neri Bar-On met with Dr. Pundak, the Executive Director of the Peres Peace Center, to explain our model. They explored its possible use within the Center's own efforts at nurturing a culture of peace among the youth on both sides.

These communications simply implemented the lessons learned in South Africa. Whenever Dr. Beck reached a milestone in his work with the African National Congress (ANC), he would inform F.W. de Klerk of the progress he made in balancing the asymmetry on the ANC side. He wanted to stress the importance of continuing to build Blue structures to help the ANC emerge to the next level. (As a sign of the deep commitment to his work in South Africa, Dr. Beck immediately went out to meet with Nelson Mandela upon his release from jail. He wanted to pay tribute to this great freedom fighter.)

Just as he had worked with both sides in South Africa, a similar balance in our Israeli-Palestinian communications was necessary. Our hope was that the Israeli leadership would engage with our Palestinian partners should the summit produce tangible results that might inform future negotiations and contribute to a new roadmap for peace. After all, this was an initiative that reflected the will and aspirations of the people, not the arrested positions of the politicians.

To Dr. Beck the level of interest our mission had garnered by the end of 2007 was a tipping point that he compared to a specific milestone reached in his ten-year experience in South Africa. His first few years there, just as in Israel and Palestine, required work at grassroots levels, and mostly pro bono. By the time his work attracted the attention of the South African business and political leadership, he had exhausted his savings. With three children in college he could no longer work without an income. However, he had anticipated that once the grassroots movement was in place, large South African corporations and national politicians would recognize the change that was taking place in the culture and fund his efforts with a commitment to preserve the integrity of the work.

To Beck it was clear that both the business community and the South African political establishment were committed to overcoming the apartheid system. The first signs of that commitment came from Middleburg Steel and Alloys (MS&A), a large South African mining corporation. This is where he found business partners who were interested in a big picture that transcended and included the bottom line. John C. Hall, who was the managing director of MS&A, knew who held the CAPI within South African white-led businesses. As a show of his commitment to South Africa's transition, he was one of the early adopters of Dr. Beck's value-systems approach and was a catalyst in getting him to meet with FW de Klerk and Nelson Mandela.

While in prison, Mandela had read everything written in the media about Dr. Beck's work. Dr. Beck himself had written a series of articles in several South African newspapers describing his framework. Hall, in later years, became the chairman of the National Peace Committee that managed to get the warring factions to stop fighting each other. He understood the transformational power of the Orange ^vMEME and worked on integrating South African blacks into the business community, making entrepreneurs out of young black men.

One of the key places where Dr. Beck was able to influence the culture of South Africa was through his consulting work with these companies. At the same time, he continued to focus on the political transition. A microcosm of South Africa's future, he thought, was being pioneered in these towns where the motto of *prosper and let prosper* became the catalyst that propelled the country out of its racist past.

Dr. Beck often speaks of programs he designed at MS&A with the Director of Manpower, Alan Tonkin, who later became the Director of South Africa's National Values Center and has remained a member of the global constellation of IDAs till this day. The company focused on large metal production and had little interest in the smaller byproducts of the manufacturing process. Employing value-engineering methods, pioneered by Dr. Beck and his South African clients, MS&A devised a scrap metal program that provided raw materials for a group of young black entrepreneurs. These young men melted the metal scraps to fashion household goods, which they sold door-to-door in the racially integrated mining towns. When Bishop Desmond Tutu heard of this, he wanted to see for himself. Here were young black men working side by side with white men, engaging with each other as equals and partners, while the rest of the country was fighting bloody battles—it brought tears to Bishop Tutu's eyes.[92]

We did not believe that the division between Israel and Palestine was as distanced and institutionalized as the division between people in South Africa. The cultures in the Middle East had a higher level of complexity; i.e., Israel could take a leadership role in making our template a reality. All our Palestinian partners needed from the Israelis was an acknowledgment of their efforts as a starting point to build a state. Israel had no natural resources and its Orange was primarily in information technology.

By the beginning of the fourth year of our project in 2008, we were optimistic that the Israeli business community would understand the vital role that the Orange ^vMEME plays in the emergence of cultures. If Israeli Orange viewed peace as South African Orange viewed it, our mission would be on the right track. Heading into 2008 we thought this could become a sustainable model funded by visionaries from both cultures who saw its transformational nature.

A SUMMIT TO BUILD PALESTINE

On January 2, 2008, one month before the scheduled nation-building summit in Palestine, the Global Center for Human Emergence received a call from the office of the president of Israel expressing regrets about President Peres's inability to attend due to a scheduling conflict. This was followed a few days later by a letter from the Israeli Foreign Minister's office expressing the same regrets. Although this was a confirmation that our work had garnered the right attention, the fact that the Israelis did not offer to engage our Palestinian partners or attempt to make contact with them was a cause for early concern.

The superordinate goal in South Africa was set in stone. It was the "peaceful transition from apartheid," and although it was bloody at times, both parties in the conflict worked towards it. Although the Palestinian superordinate goal was defined, the one between Israel and Palestine required different dynamics and assumptions at the level of the heads of states. After the developmental roadmap of the Build Palestine Initiative was given a chance to succeed, the mutual superordinate goal would have a better chance of becoming a reality.

However, we were worried that there was no clear superordinate goal for a two-state solution to create a new frame of reference. While the Afrikaners under de Klerk's leadership had a clear goal of ending an unfair system and dealt with their own intra-conflict, the Israelis were dealing with far more extremist positions within their own culture. This began to reflect on their ability to commit to our initiative—we could not garner full political support in Israel. The same dynamics were in play in the Palestinian culture on Hamas's side; they wanted no association with a movement that sought national unity based on values that sidelined their extremist position. This was still true five years later.

February 2, 2008, the first day discussed in the first chapter of *Emerge!*, was the day of the Palestinian MeshWORKS, the first conference of its kind in the Middle East. There were only two other MeshWORKS events outside of South Africa:

+ One had been organized in the Netherlands a few years earlier with Dutch IDAs looking to design a new Blue to deal with Muslim extremism in that country.

+ The second MeshWORKS event brought together a national assembly of over one thousand people in Iceland aimed at informing the design of a new future for Iceland after the financial crisis of 2008. This led to revisions of the Icelandic Constitution that were discussed in an earlier part of the book.

All events were research based conferences designed by IDAs certified and personally trained and supervised by Dr. Beck. The MeshWORKS events in Europe were the culmination of many years of work on the ground, first at the grassroots level, and then in coordination with the political leadership. All of the methodologies pioneered by Dr. Beck in South Africa were detailed in the 1991 book *The Crucible* and the 1996 *Spiral Dynamics* book. However, the more up-to-date techniques for large-scale systems design used in Iceland and the Netherlands were parallel in nature to the large-scale design approach we used in Israel and Palestine and are being presented in this book for the first time.

On Feb 2, 2008, the chaotic scene at the Shepherd Hotel in Bethlehem was a result of the energy and enthusiasm that our Palestinian partners had exerted over the preceding three years. Nafiz and Abdel Majid had arranged for many of the community representatives to come and present their input. In a true fashion that captured the Purple soul of the Arab value systems, Nafiz had one thousand Keffiyehs, the traditional Arab headdress, made for the occasion. They were emblazoned with the logo of the Center for Human Emergence and the spiral colors depicting Palestine emerging into the 21st century through the values of the Seventh-Level Yellow system.

While there were many rumors that as many as twelve hundred people would be attending, Dr. Beck and I began to panic when at the scheduled start of the conference very few people had shown up. Nafiz dismissed the tardiness because busloads of Palestinians always received extra scrutiny at Israeli checkpoints. At just fifteen minutes past the start time, buses started rolling in from every part of the West Bank. The last bus arrived, to great applause, after being held by the IDF at a checkpoint for over two hours. Many of its passengers were questioned, but all were allowed to re-board after the IDF verified their passes to the event. There was a sense of order in the midst of all the chaos. Women, who had been essential to the effort from day one, took charge of organizing the speakers, dealing with the media, and delegating responsibilities to the Millennial Generation.

Over seven hundred community leaders and other representatives attended the entire event, with many more coming to hear speeches or to attend specific segments of the event.

With the help of our IIEs, Nafiz organized the attendees into groups with similar abilities, meaning those whose fields of work or knowledge might best serve a particular function needed to inform the design of the future state of Palestine. This could be considered end-user input *feeding forward* into the development of future projects in their field. While the groups were exchanging ideas and the findings of their research, many spoke about "new beginnings." Only a handful of the sixty groups laid any blame on the Israeli occupation. All were focused on the Palestinians' own empowerment and on how to proceed with building their own capacities to build a State.

One of the most moving speeches summarizing the transformational effect of our work came from Nafiz himself. Judea Pearl, the scientist, philosopher, and father of the slain *Wall Street Journal* reporter Daniel Pearl, upon reading a translation of the speech, told his friend Don Beck that it was the most optimistic speech he has heard come out of Palestine in years. It may have been at this moment that our conference became a national summit for change. Below is a partial translation:

> The idea for this convention was born when we asked ourselves the question, "Why haven't we been victorious over the Israeli occupation?" Many in Fatah tried to answer that question and failed. After a rebellion that lasted forty-three years we failed to see any progress. Why? Why were there so few answers to what we were facing? We asked ourselves how did the Zulus manage to bring down the apartheid system in South Africa and become partners in building a nation. Yet we, the people who built the Arabian Gulf, have not been able to build the institutions that will build our nation.
>
> After a lengthy search for answers, we met Dr. Don Beck, the author of the Spiral Dynamics theory. We found that there are reasons for our failures, and for those who have lost hope. I'm telling you all ladies and gentlemen hope is all around you, but you need to know how to find it in order to succeed. We must put Palestine first, and all of us in Fatah, are to serve Palestine. To liberate Palestine. To build Palestine. There have been several attempts at building projects here in the City of Bethlehem, this wonderful city, the birthplace of Jesus, peace be upon him. There was an initiative here called "Bethlehem 2000." Two hundred fifty million dollars was spent on preparations for the festivities for the year 2000. Where is the sustainable development? Where did all the money go? Where is all the job creation?
>
> These are our darkest days. Many of our youth are thinking of leaving this land because there is no opportunity.
>
> Don Beck has opened new windows in our minds. What is our role? We cannot continue complaining about this leadership—what they do and what they spend money on. We have to show them through our actions. Dr. Beck asked us the questions: "The world is going to give you $7 billion in addition to $10 billion already given. Where are

the jobs? Where is the cement factory that employs 10,000 Palestinians so you don't have to depend on the Israelis for jobs?

Do we have the ability, and I'm sure all my brothers and sisters who worked with me on this convention do. That you have the strength and the determination to voice the concerns of the people to the leadership and to the government about the lack of economic opportunities. Victory is perseverance. Building institutions that create opportunities is the answer.

Our image around the world is ugly. They say he's Palestinian, so then he must be a terrorist ready to blow himself up. We must get rid of that image. It must be that they say he's Palestinian, so then he's well educated in every profession possible: psychology, social science, computers, engineering, and medicine. This Palestinian will participate in world emergence, dreams of freedom, and is ready to lead his society in commerce.

From a political perspective, we should ask ourselves, "Are we capable of creating the institutions that practice democracy? Europe did not advance without elections and without political parties that had to evolve. We always speak of the past.

We are a political party that has tremendous capital. From its martyrs to its wounded to its many in prison. Despite that—and I'm a part of this group—we don't know what to do tomorrow. What is our agenda in the Fatah Movement beginning tomorrow . . . so that we'll be back in power . . . so we can build Palestine?

Today, we are at the beginning of the 21st Century and we must arm ourselves with education. In South Africa, the Zulus armed themselves with education. They understood their enemy, but more importantly, they understood themselves. Now comes our turn to apply Dr. Beck's theory.

Please don't speak about the past, because all of us must leave the past behind. Let it be a loud cry and a message carried to our leaders and to the rest of world. We want to talk about our vision for the future. How are we going to shape that future?[93]

Many other speeches followed that day. I spoke about the Palestinians' courage and patience in wanting to try something different by giving our approach a chance. I spoke of how the framework in Palestine fit into our Center's overall work and strategy for the entire Arab region and how we hoped that what we were doing that evening would become a cultural development template to move the Middle East into the 21st Century.

Building human capacities became the focus of the event as it became the tool with which to build the future. Dr. Beck gave a speech that had the Blue content that the Palestinians needed to hear about their patriotic duty toward the future, the Third-Generation Fatah, and their ability to lead real change. Then he turned to the audience and announced that he would like to speak to their future directly: He invited a ten-year old girl to the podium and asked her what she wanted to become when she grew up. She answered by saying she wanted to be a doctor. Dr. Beck then implored all the participants to dedicate their efforts from that day forth to build the institutions that will insure that the ten-year old girl's dream becomes a reality.[94]

Different groups made presentations about what they would like to see in the design of a new Palestinian State. The sixty groups representing broad coverage of the West Bank put together a list of actionable goals that were later presented to the leadership. A woman engineer prepared the list detailed below with her group, and it captured the essence of what Palestine could look like:

> We are Group #40 "The Promising Future." We are mainly formed of professional women from Salfit and Al Khalil. My name is Nasra Zgheil and I'm an engineer. Here is our proposal:
>
> 1. On the economic front: To create the grounds for economic stability through:
>
>> Job Creation (through projects, Industrial parks, strong institutions) that will provide opportunities for women, workers and graduates of universities
>>
>> Opening International markets
>>
>> Supporting the agriculture and tourism sectors and developing the Palestinian rural region
>
> 2. On the Cultural front:
>
>> Focus on programs that help the development of women, children and young people in all aspects (healthcare, psychological and cultural)
>
> 3. On the Educational front:
>
>> Focus on skill training and provide support for innovators
>>
>> Free Public school system
>>
>> Literacy projects
>>
>> Enforce a system of merit for the hiring process based on social justice
>
> 4. On the Political front:
>
>> Put our nation first, not the political movement
>>
>> Electing the right leader

Independence in decision making away from outside influences

Transparency in managing public funds and NO nepotism[95]

Within a few short days after the summit, the effects began reverberating throughout the West Bank. Many high-ranking Fatah party officials called Nafiz to offer their help with the implementation phase for meeting these goals. Our IIEs prepared a booklet with all the recommendations from the summit and made it available to the Palestinian Authority and to Tony Blair's office representing the Middle East Peace Quartet. The findings were also published in many local newspapers. I wrote a summary of our four-year efforts in the *Common Ground* newspaper, which had global readership.[96]

After the summit, Dr. Beck and I began phase two of our initiative in earnest to help our IIEs design the institutions that were to build Palestine. We started a new series of meetings and design sessions with Nafiz and his group. The aim was to consolidate the gains made by the grassroots efforts and to start the design process at the leadership level. Based on the principles of our framework, our Palestinian partners wanted, first and foremost, to create a culture of transparency for anyone wanting to contribute to the future of the movement. Over the next few months we helped our IIEs create a charter for the Build Palestine Initiative (BPI) containing general rules of conduct, covenants, and principles that participants in the design wished to adhere to. This Blue foundation helped assure the sustainability and integrity of the work.

Nafiz suggested the creation of a fifty-member Think Tank representing the diversity of the Palestinian society. Dr. Beck and I made sure that representatives of institutions and segments of society who contributed to the design of the MeshWORKS were included. This was a crucial element to the success of the plan. In order to insure a seamless flow from strategy and planning to implementation on the ground, this phase of our mission needed staffing. Nafiz needed to hire assistants and research associates who could help navigate the political and diplomatic channels of Fatah politics, the NGO community, and the UN agencies.

In the United States, the Global CHE had maintained a volunteer staff for many years and continues to do so till this day. Dr. Beck's inspiration to do work that matters had inspired many capable volunteers around the world. We met with the U.S. State Department in Washington and gave them a rundown on what we had been able to accomplish on a shoestring budget with a volunteer staff over a four-year period.

We met with Dennis Ross, the seasoned Middle East diplomat behind so many of the previous Middle East peace treaties while at the State Department. We had run into Mr. Ross on several occasions in the West Bank and he had been following our work. During one of our meetings with him in Washington he gave me an advance reading copy of his book *Statecraft: And How to Restore America's Standing in the World.* He asked for my opinion of his perspective on Islam. Although Mr. Ross saw the promise of our framework, his views, like many others in the governments of Palestine and Israel, were too influenced by past failures.

We also met with Karen Hughes' right-hand person to explain why the billion-dollar Mideast publicity campaign she had undertaken did little to change the region's opinion of the United States. We presented our framework at many forums in the United States political and otherwise, all in the effort to garner financial support or new sponsorship needed for the implementation phase of the Build Palestine Initiative.

By the summer of 2008 our past sponsors began to feel the effects of the coming financial crisis. In recessionary times, philanthropic causes are the first to suffer. The Hearthstone Foundation, our primary sponsor, went through a major restructuring as homebuilding was going through one of its worst contractions in decades. As the financial crisis took hold of the global economy in the fall of 2008, all funding sources had disappeared. Unlike Beck's experience in South Africa, no one in political leadership on any side stepped forth to sponsor our work. The business community, which played a catalytic role in South Africa, was nowhere to be found in Israel or in Palestine. Nafiz was shocked at the UN's inability to provide funding. One-month's salary for a UN Program Director could fund twelve full-time research associates to help make the Build Palestine Initiative a reality. The UN chose to continue to do weekend empowerment programs instead. These programs certainly did not appear to be a priority to the Palestinians according to our four years of research.

Because of the global financial crisis and lack of interest at the UN, our Palestinian partners couldn't hire the extra help they needed to take our plans to the next phase. This was terribly disappointing, although the memes that our work created had deeply penetrated every segment of Palestinian culture. Building Palestine had become common language on the street of Ramallah, Bethlehem, and everywhere in between by the end of 2009. It gave many Palestinians, young and old, the sense of pride that comes from self-empowerment and self-reliance. It shifted the cultural focus from passive involvement to a people empowered by the capacities for self-determination. The change was most visible at Palestinian universities, where for the first time in ten years, the Third Generation Fatah students had won elections through the student body by painting a picture of a bright future that captured the hearts and minds of their ambitious youth. The "Build Palestine Meme," as Nafiz described it once, became rolling thunder on the ground.

As we continued to seek institutional sponsorship, the Global CHE continued to work on designing the framework for the institutions to inform those capable of building Palestine. Dr. Beck and I helped Nafiz prepare a proposal for implementation of the Vital Signs Monitor, which was to be presented to the Palestinian Ministry of the Interior. Although a non-autocrat had replaced Eisheh, the minister who agreed to implement the VSM initially, Nafiz felt that the new Prime Minister Salam Fayyad was committed to building Palestinian institutions and would support the project.

Our experience throughout Gaza and the West Bank catalyzed the need for central oversight of NGO activity within the *Build Palestine Initiative*. Based on the results of the 2008 summit, we recommended that Palestinian leadership create a cabinet-level Department of Integration. Essential to the MeshWORKS model, this newly created department would align and integrate all NGO activity into one platform serving the needs of Palestinians as determined by the IIEs, meaning Seventh-Level Yellow leadership. The Department of Integration would be able to identify and limit overlapping activities and those without the capacity for sustainability or measurable long-term effects. We needed to develop memetically-honed technology to address past inefficiency and utilize new tools that properly align the good-meaning intentions of NGOs with what life conditions identify about the needs of the Palestinian people.

Our colleague at the Global CHE Kevin Kells holds a PhD in electrical engineering. With his team of volunteers Kells designed testing methods to solve this problem, which had accounted for hundreds of thousands of dollars in inefficiency and misaligned spending. After months of research he presented Dr. Beck and me with a technology similar to that of the barcode. It can measure the memetic profile of an entity in a short period of time and align its values with the segment of Palestinian culture that fits its services. Since its invention, this technology has become an essential part of the large-scale design for the entire constellation of CHEs around the world. Kells described the technology to many of our IIEs and IDAs as follows:

> As part of the Natural Design process, functions are identified that are required to take us from "where we are now" towards the superordinate goal. The functions are characterized according to the 'Meme capacities necessary to carry them out. What capacities are required

to carry out this function effectively, stated in terms of ᵛMemes? This ᵛMeme Barcode Image Generator Tool creates the image for a given function and reflects an immediate visual understanding of this characterization for that function.

Similarly, the Natural Design process identifies resource entities that are available to carry out the functions. Characterize these entities and generate the corresponding barcodes for each.

Once you have the barcodes for the functions that need to be performed and the barcodes for the entities available to your design, you can easily match function to entity, and you can also easily and visually spot mismatches or gaps between functions and entities.[97]

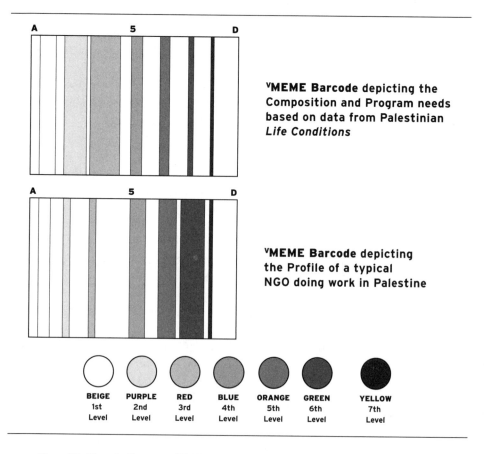

ᵛMEME Barcode depicting the Composition and Program needs based on data from Palestinian *Life Conditions*

ᵛMEME Barcode depicting the Profile of a typical NGO doing work in Palestine

BEIGE	PURPLE	RED	BLUE	ORANGE	GREEN	YELLOW
1st	2nd	3rd	4th	5th	6th	7th
Level	Level	Level	Level	Level	Level	Level

Figure 5.6. The misalignment of NGO activity with *Life Conditions*. Note the oversized need for services to address PURPLE–Red *Life Conditions* compared to NGO capacities that were delivering ORANGE–Green services resulting in non-sustainable efforts.

Although many IIEs and IDAs have developed other psychometric tests with the help of Dr. Beck, the ᵛMEME Barcode was the first of its kind that assessed the memetic profiles of entire institutions. This helps us manage how entire cultures receive services. Our Palestinian partners were the first to apply this technology successfully. As its use became more frequent, we made it a part of the design criteria of specific departments or institutions that the Build Palestine Initiative sought to create.

By 2009 any hopes that we had of institutional sponsorship had faded. The financial crisis had taken its toll on many of our sponsors. Some even sought bankruptcy protection in the face of the harsh economic reality in the United States. My husband, a real estate developer, began to feel the financial pressure from my four years of pro bono work. Meanwhile our Palestinian partners anxiously awaited our return to the West Bank. According to Nafiz, over two hundred thousand Palestinians have shown interest in learning the value-systems approach to conflict resolution. Although, our plans for designing for the BPI had to be shelved, many of its effects continue to be felt everyday.

Prime Minister Fayyad began to build the Palestinian institutions that matter most to Palestinians and have secondary ramifications for Israel and the West. He has focused his efforts on many of the elements that were identified during our presence in Palestine. Before he resigned in June 2013, Mr. Fayyad had created a new Blue layer in the Palestinian culture, which had not been possible under previous leadership. This was a developmental roadmap quite similar in its reach to what we had identified. The only difference is that Fayyad's plan did not include Gaza. Hamas rejected his preconditions to recognize Israel's right to exist.

In an April 2010 article the *Financial Times* identified Prime Minister Fayyad's policies as "Fayyadism." According to the article, Fayyadism rested upon three main tenets for strengthening Palestinian Blue:

1. Strengthening the security forces of the Palestinian Authority,
2. Create the basis for good governance, and
3. Provide economic opportunity.[98]

Fayyad embarked on a detailed two-year working plan for the Palestinian Authority for establishing the fundamental infrastructures and reinforcing the institutions of the future Palestinian State. He called it "Palestine—Ending the Occupation, Establishing the State." This included, among other elements, the development of existing and new infrastructure such as government offices, a stock market, an airport, free markets, and separation of powers.[99]

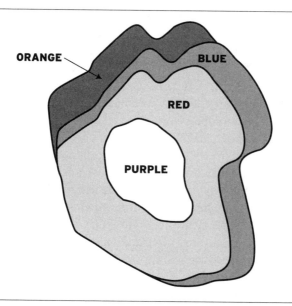

Figure 5.7 Memetic profile of the West Bank at the time of Fayyad's resignation in June 2013.

After witnessing the effects the Blue institutions that Fayyad had put into place, U.S. Secretary of State Hillary Clinton renewed the United State's call for a permanent solution to meet the needs of both sides. In an open letter to President Obama, the CHE-Mideast repeated the call for a design conference to precede any peace negotiations. This continues to be our official position as to how a final settlement can be reached as the facts that we uncovered in our research remain true to this day. Today, as Secretary of State Kerry issues new deadlines for peace negotiations we remain steadfast in our position that before peace can take root, much has to be done to level the asymmetry in capacities between the two cultures.

A very significant development occurred as recently as June of 2013 that was symbolic of the memetic center of gravity for Palestine. The winner of *Arab Idol*, a highly popular show in the Middle East, was Mohammad Assaf a young man from a refugee camp in Gaza. This young man was able to unite more Palestinians behind a nationalistic voice than either Fatah or Hamas have been able to do in decades, especially within the younger generations.

The phenomenon of what Assaf represented was picked up by international news outlets, and he was made into a symbol of unity and hope for Palestine. His sister had to explain to the hardliners in Hamas, who don't watch television, what the program was about and how proud they should

DESIGN CONFERENCE for Palestine/Israel to break the cycle of failed "Peace Negotiations"

The Israeli / Palestinian conflict of a collision of "tectonic plates"—deep values system codes—that have created a logjam. It is this underlying logjam that generates continual surface-level blockages that erupt in conflict.

We propose a problem-solving methodology with the power, precision, and complexity to span over human groupings to construct the unique economic and political structures that overarch the mountains and valleys of those unique human groupings.

We need to see the patterns as if viewing them through a prism—where all the various colors of world views are made visible, each with a different "tint" of perceptions of the world. The goal is to understand the needs of all mind-sets, so as to begin to craft "full spectrum" solutions, which are fundamentally different from those that a single perspective would offer and enable us to achieve the following.

- Have the capacity to uncover the deeper dynamics within each society, as well as between societies.
- Craft decisions and measure priorities, not against the past and not based on *who is responsible for what*.
- Avoid the typical problem-resolution systems, such as *majority rule*, or *rule by the elite* or *rule by the wealthy*, or *rule by the so-called "experts"* or those who have *military strength*.
- Defuse the ideologies that produce "us vs. them."
- Avoid raising expectations that can be faulted.
- Focus on who the people are who live in the region and what their resources are.
- Design a strategy to mesh people, geography, and resources together into a workable solution for all who live in that region.
- Draw upon all of the solutions that are currently available (as well as many that haven't been though of yet). We often call these "scaffoldings of solutions."
- Find solutions that involve the whole region: Israel, Syria, Jordan, and Palestine.

The issue is less about *democracy*; instead, the answer to the question of problem-solving is to design the best structures for meeting the needs of the people as they develop through the stages that are the most natural to them: open, adaptive systems appropriate to their life conditions.

be that a son of Gaza prevailed among thousands of competitors from all over the Middle East and North Africa. Although much of the hype has waned, the Purple memetic undertones and nationalistic Blue messages cannot be underestimated in designing for the future of Palestine and the rest of the region.

POST-INVOLVEMENT ANALYSIS

What ultimately happens between Israel and Palestine will be greatly influenced by what is happening overall in region. It is too early to tell how deeply the Arab Spring will affect a final settlement between the two countries, but it is clear that the change that is sweeping through the Arab world has arrested the movement towards a final settlement at least temporarily.

On the Regional Level

Today, the Israelis have far greater challenges than shaping a negotiation strategy that protects their interests and vision of the future. As the Arab Spring enters maturity, the region will find a memetic center of gravity that is reflective of *life conditions*. That center of gravity may not bode well for how the Arab street views Israel and the United States. Although the Muslim Brotherhood in Egypt honored the peace treaty with Israel, the overthrow of a democratically elected president by the military speaks loudly to where the various regional stages of development are centered.

Today, the liberal Tamarud Party and the Salafist Nour Party, the two zealots R-5 and L-5 on the Egyptian spectrum of values, have refused to meet with the U.S. envoy. They do not wish to bring the parties back to moderate center positions. A functional democracy for the region has to meet the people where they are and design governance that fits their needs. At this time, that place must accommodate the population's transition from PURPLE-Red values to some form of indigenous Blue. This will best serve the people before Israel even appears in its consciousness once again. The Muslim Brotherhood in Egypt will not sit by silently. It will reorganize itself and develop a strategy for reclaiming power. Should a new government fail to incorporate the Muslim Brotherhood into its platform, the MB will flex its organizational muscle and make the voices of the tens of millions of their supporters known.

As a new crucible is forged for Egypt's future, two scenarios could possibly emerge that determine the leadership for the region:

- ✦ The first possibility is that the region could revert to an autocracy with a liberal face that pleases the West, but with similar institutions that were prevalent under Mubarak with the military being the primary power broker.

✦ The second might be an indigenous form of democracy that includes the MB. It would have to rein in the polarization on both sides and move the Egyptians into the middle positions where the right form of Blue will be forged. *A functional democracy* in Egypt will place the Israeli-Palestinian issue further back on its list of priorities while keeping the peace agreement in place.

Existential threats to Israel continue to define its memetic profile for the time being. Iran, under the leadership of President Hassan Rouhani, has shown no sign of giving up its ambition to become a nuclear power. With its powerful Arab ally, Hezbollah, right on Israel's northern border in Lebanon, existential threats remain real. The potential collapse of the Syrian regime and the prospect of Al Qaeda on Israel's border are also real threats to Israel's security. Should the Assad regime survive, its ally Hezbollah will be rewarded with added military and political power for its help against the rebels, thus presenting a greater threat to Israel's security. As Israel deals with these dynamics, its defensive posture is likely to become more rigid and move further towards an arrested Ideologue-Blue on the values spectrum.

The Israeli-Palestinian Dynamic

The Israelis had shown optimism in supporting Prime Minister Fayyad in building the Palestinian infrastructure. Once his development plans were announced, the Obama Administration announced a $20-million grant to back the effort. Congress approved a $200-million deposit into the PA treasury. Fayyad's economic plan included a golden handshake for many of the older PLO leaders in order to stimulate an inflow of leaders from the younger generations with more globally aligned capacities for nation-building.

Israel praised Fayyad's efforts in building capacities within the Palestinian National Security Forces. In 2009 $109-million was committed to finance an expanded training program and all the new personnel were vetted by the Israeli secret security apparatus, the Shin Bet, before being able to join the force. Fayyad's ability to provide needed security for their future state was an essential element of the Oslo accords in order for the two-state solution to move forward. Explicit in Fayyad's economic development program is an emphasis on setting up the West Bank infrastructure for trade with Israel, and Israel then completed construction of six commercial crossings between Israel and the West Bank.[100]

In September 2011, which was at about the same time that Fayyad had envisioned, President Abbas sought to make the dream of a Palestinian state a reality through approaching the UN: He asked for "support for the establishment of the State of Palestine and for its admission to the United Nations as a full member." He reiterated the goal of "the Palestinian Liberation Organization, as the sole legitimate representative of the Palestinian people" to establish the State of Palestine ". . . on all the Palestinian Territory occupied by Israel in 1967" and the "complete cessation of settlement activities." However much Israel had praised Fayyad's creativity and his work in Palestine, there was no agreement on returning to the 1967 borders.

The United States, Canada, Israel, and eight other countries opposed this position. With 1967 conditions on the table, Abbas offered to negotiate the two-state solution, describing the future that everyone wanted to see:

> Our efforts are not aimed at isolating Israel or de-legitimizing it; rather we want to gain legitimacy for the cause of the people of Palestine. I am here to say on behalf of the Palestinian people and the Palestine Liberation Organization: We extend our hands to the Israeli government and the Israeli people for peace-making. I say to them: Let us urgently build together a future for our children where they can enjoy freedom, security and prosperity. Let us build the bridges of dialogue instead of checkpoints and walls of separation, and build cooperative relations based on parity and equity between two neighboring States—Palestine and Israel—instead of policies of occupation, settlement, war and eliminating the other.[101]

Palestine received overwhelming support for an upgraded status in the UN as a "non-member observer state," although Israel restated the need for direct negotiations. At the UN, 138 voted in favor and 41 abstained according to the UN General Assembly report of 29 November 2012.[102] Although many of our Third Generation Fatah colleagues consider Abbas's values a representation of the incompetent and corrupt history of both the PLO and the Palestinian Authority, they still supported his efforts for an independent state. While his speech at the UN was inspirational, his actions on the ground were still shaped by the dynamics of the old system. On the other hand, Fayyad's values were shaped by his pragmatism and the hard work needed to create a modern Palestinian state.

After securing the upgraded status in the UN, Israel withheld the December 2012 tax transfer (more than usual) to pay water and electric debts. Abbas threatened Israel then with criminal court proceedings for withholding the taxes. Part of increasing "fiscal sustainability," according to the World Bank report, was the PA's ability to collect domestic tax revenues for the future Palestinian state. To date, Israel had collected taxes on behalf of the Palestinian Authority and transferred money to the PA regularly. In recent years some taxes had been withheld to pay the debts of the PA for things like power and water, but some additional withholding in 2011-12 seemed to have political basis.

Some considered the Fayyad Plan a normalization mechanism that evades the political and social conditions of the "Occupation" to facilitate building infrastructure and trade. Fayyad's effort to create normal economic life in the West Bank complements the vision of the Israeli state to create a normal economic life. As mentioned earlier, the plan included a golden handshake for many of the PLO old guard in order to facilitate leadership from younger generations who were more globally minded and technologically savvy. From a spiral perspective, this was a positive development in spite of criticism regarding the lack of complete and absolute independence from Israel.

The regional dynamics from the Arab Spring also affected the Palestinian bid for statehood. The oil-rich countries in the region who had brokered deals among Hamas and Fatah and provided financial support, now turned their attention internally. They are busy revitalizing their own political and economic programs in an attempt to prevent the chaos of the Arab Spring from reaching their streets. Since the Qatari Emir handed over power to his son in June 2013, the commitment to Hamas to rebuild Gaza is on hold and may have disappeared. This changes the dynamics within the Hamas political platform, too. The sources of aid that they have gotten used to from the Muslim Brotherhood in Egypt, the oil-rich countries in the Arabian Gulf and Iran under Ahmadinejad seem to have disappeared as well, leaving Gaza without support. All these factors might contribute to the regression of the values in Gaza to the Zealot R-5 position on the Palestinian values spectrum and cause them to become more isolated than before.

Decreased revenue now required the Palestinian Authority to impose other taxes in order to continue to fund its development plans and keep international aid packages flowing. Part of the economic revival plan had included a wage freeze since 2009. President Abbas, in addition, rejected a financial package from the United States at this time. Different perspectives between Abbas and Prime Minister Fayyad, as well as criticism of the economic plan from some sectors, led to the prime minister's unfortunate resignation in April 2013.[103] These, and other factors, dashed many hopes for the creation of the Blue institutions essential to building Palestine's capacities in the region.

After Fayyad's resignation it is likely to be a while before the Palestinians find a new pragmatic prime minister to continue to build healthy Palestinian Blue. Well versed in global finance, Fayyad knew exactly what the World Bank and the International Monetary Fund needed to fund Palestine's development projects. While he proved to the West that Palestinians can build institutions, Fayyad came face to face with the reality that one can't push an Arab culture through the BLUE–Orange stages as quickly as he set out to do.

The conditions imposed by the aid programs that required him to impose property taxes, ran into stiff opposition from Palestinian citizens who weren't receiving any income from these properties. This was a PURPLE–Red culture that barely had Blue institutions with even less Orange density that can withstand the tax burden imposed by international standards. Fayyad couldn't address nagging economic issues that would have produced new revenue streams to overcome the tax payments withheld by the Israelis.

The CHE-Mideast Perspective

For the CHE-Mideast, what started in 2006 as an exploratory visit to the region developed into a large-scale design that still has the potential to transform the conflict between Israel and Palestine. Our work has created a template and a developmental blueprint that would place the region on the road to sustainability and self-reliance. Our center added many tools to an already resilient toolkit, and has honed the applications of value systems to the *Indigenous Intelligence.*

After all is said and done, democracy in the Middle East will be a functional democracy, or a MEMEtocracy based on the needs of the region. This is what the MEMEtocracy theoretical framework provides. No matter where in the world nation-states are built, governance has to be informed by the challenges that face people within their geographic boundaries and within their value-system capacities.

In declaring the superordinate goal for Palestine and Israel, my colleague Don Beck compared it to the same superordinate goal that helped integrate South Africa. This was the motto of "prosper and let prosper" which has in it the mechanisms for building resilient peace. While much of the region begins its long journey towards building Blue institutions and economic viability, the business community must be a partner and a catalyst in making these institutions the pillars on which the future of the region rests. Just as the visionary business leaders in South Africa turned the country's natural resources into an agent of change, business leaders in the Middle East can take the lead in making sure that businesses play a more integral role in defining the future of the region.

SIX

Functional Governance Empowered by *Functional Capitalism*

Today's business and world leaders are faced with unprecedented complexities in rates of social change and in markets. This places extreme pressure on leaders to develop all aspects of themselves to the highest degree possible. Development of their cognitive, emotional, interpersonal, and ethical capacities as well as their fundamental sense of self, and more, are all required. In my opinion, only those who develop to this level, will be successfully equipped to manage a profitable and sustainable growth business or run an effective organization, or lead an effective government.[104]

—Ken Wilber
Integral philosopher
*A Theory of Everything: An Integral Vision for Business,
Politics, Science, and Spirituality*

THE MEMES OF PROSPERITY AT THE ORGANIZATIONAL LEVEL

Most of what has been discussed so far has been geared to answer the question of how to make governance functional with specific emphasis on the Middle East. What hasn't been addressed are the things that are working in the region and from which leadership lessons can be drawn.

In the Middle East commerce has survived many dynasties and has been part of the culture's DNA for centuries. Today many lessons could be adapted from modern business practices in the region and used as a catalyst to propel the culture toward greater and greater capacities for emergence. Generally, this is what we call half-steps and here is how they're introduced:

+ An IDA searches for sectors of society that are working well and designs systems that empower them to spill over into the culture. Once emboldened by a MeshWORKS Solution, the approach naturally creates an ecosystem that is a self-sustaining meme acting as a catalyst for positive change. This strategy has the Indigenous Design already built into it. This is what we

197

call a half step; leveraging what works to enable emergence of a whole culture.

+ In many emerging cultures, commerce seems to be an area that's working well, and by empowering it through this framework, we create a model for long-term sustainability and political stability. This is how capitalism empowers whole societies; what we call functional capitalism.

+ In a Large-scale MeshWORKS design, functional forms of governance come with functional forms of capitalism. This is a Seventh-Level Yellow concept that has a big-picture view on how to adapt the principles of capitalism to the needs of society taking into consideration its existing capacities and resources. *Functional Capitalism* doesn't copy any model blindly, but chooses the right system for the appropriate societal flow. It scans the horizon for many decades into the future in order to inform the designers of a Seventh-Level Yellow economy in regard to potential threats. Since the framework I work with applies to the Macro, Meso, and Micro levels of development, it is important to discuss *Functional Capitalism* practices that I've been implementing at the individual and organizational levels. I've been bringing this type of Seventh-Level Yellow leadership awareness to corporations throughout the region for more than a decade. It is my belief that the more Middle Eastern business engages in this form of Seventh-Level Yellow capitalism, the more positive influence it can have on other sectors in society.

Similar to the whole-systems societal work at the CHE-Mideast and the Build Palestine Initiative, the value-systems framework can be adapted to institutional advisory work. I have been a management consultant to medium and large-size enterprises in the Middle East region for over a decade. It is my belief that by further developing the memes of prosperity in corporations to fit the needs of people, a long and lasting change will follow. As a consultant who specializes in the cultural ᵛMEMEs in the Middle East, I have met many Western consultants who have worked with many companies and governments there. I've had long and fruitful conversations with representatives of the largest consultancies in the world about the future of oil and the Middle East. Ernst & Young, KPMG, they all seem to be the brightest talents that the Enterprising value system has to offer. These consultancies are known for corporate audits, accounting, and finance. They universally standardized corporate functions, forecasts, inefficiencies and rates of returns. But when it came to affecting corporate culture for the better—the leadership skills in corporate efficiency and effectiveness— they left much to be desired. They simply lack the proficiency to interpret the Indigenous Intelligence. In the majority of companies I have consulted with, even when Western style leadership was taught to top executives, the knowledge couldn't be actualized on the ground and would quickly be lost soon after the consultants went home.

This phenomenon of Western leadership skills training was char- acterized by the belief that what works for a Western corporation, one that employs cutting-edge advances in management science, could work for corporations anywhere else in the world. My peers were introducing Orange and Green systems to corporations in cultures that were PURPLE– Red with little regard to the memetic profiles of each country. Their advice came from two values systems above the culture and had no long- term ability or even a beginning point of reference from which to bridge the gap.

My colleagues in the consulting business had the latest behavioral psy- chology buzz phrases and research results. They could present a week-long training workshop complete with motivational pep rallies and leave with the expectation that the knowledge they provided would become a part of the organizational culture. Many Middle Eastern companies allocate training budgets for their upper and middle management employees to go to the West and hear motivational speakers promise the impossible. They hope to change the behavior of management teams, rally their depart- ments around those big ideas, but they eventually come to the realization that the *life conditions* in the company and/or in the region can't provide the sustainable support needed for these grand ideas to take hold.

In our whole-systems approach, the corporate culture, like social cul- ture, has to be assessed with the *5-Deep* approach. Western consultants do not seem to value the importance of assessing the depth and breadth of leadership problems by going beyond the surface manifestation of behav- ior. The *5-Deep* approach in a culturally diverse corporation represents a microcosm of the same *5-Deep* approach for a culture discussed earlier in the book. In order to get to the root of surface problem(s) we must diag- nose *life conditions*. We dig deep into the layers of the corporate culture in order to perform a full memetic analysis of the company.

This is the whole systems *industrial psychology* view of leadership diagnostics. It is the only way to understand the challenges and identify opportunities that will be effective in reaching superordinate leadership goals. This is one of the few methodologies that can lead to long-term solutions. The predominant view among consultants was that teaching the best business processes, the brightest form of strategic Orange, inclusive of some egalitarianism Green in the workplace, will provide the best solutions regardless whether the corporation has the capacities to sustain the changes advised.

These shortcomings became clear to me over a decade ago when I was training a group of executives at a mid-size energy company. The corporation had diversified holdings in the Arabian Gulf.[105] Turnover seemed to be a chronic problem. Consultants brought in from the most prestigious firms had been unable to remedy that particular challenge. My primary goal was to listen through the language of value systems from a Seventh-Level Yellow place of empathy.

The British executives complained about punctuality and missed deadlines. Indian and Arab middle managers complained about not getting enough respect from Western managers. Line managers in the factories come from different parts of the developing world and they also expressed their views on the problems. What emerged was a much fuller picture of the competing values within the company.

We then proceeded to design communication strategies to bridge the value-systems divide. We gave ownership of each problem to each department. This empowered everyone to come up with creative solutions and areas of opportunity. If line managers were Red, we specified respectful language and tapped into their heroic nature. If they were Blue, we empowered their sense of duty and purpose and rewarded loyalty. For Orange, bonuses were tied to two main factors: achieving targeted sales and their ability to successfully manage diversity.

For high-achieving British and American (or Arab-American) executives who needed to maintain big-picture perspectives, we created steering committees that focused on designing strategic expansion plans for the company's future. Over time, the values-based communication systems became a part of the company's standard infrastructure and training processes for all employees. Managers at all levels were trained in how to use communications from a values perspective to overcome deficiencies. This resolved what had seemed to be irreconcilable issues within many previous management systems.

Normally, within a midsize or large corporation in the Gulf region, there are no less than thirty different nationalities at the corporate headquarters. These individuals are in these countries on work visas. They are not residents who feel the urge to assimilate into the culture as permanent residents. This creates a challenge for managing diversity since these employees are mostly attracted to generous pay packages, pure and simple. Although many may aspire to operate using cutting-edge globally recognized Orange practices, they fail to realize their vision due to *life conditions*.

Integrating value-system language into corporate culture enables several things to begin to happen. First, by using colors and levels, we remove the debate from a preconceived national and ethnic prejudice to one that sees the essential function that each manager with his or her own unique ᵛMEME stack can contribute to making the company more profitable in the long-term. Empowering Red and directing its energy towards heroic achievements in operations not only improves productivity; it aligns Blue functions to do a better job. It also inspires Orange to seek more opportunity and pursue bigger more strategic plans knowing that a system is in place that has its own checks and balances. For example, Orange and Red—when closing a deal—can tend to over-promise what a factory has the capacity to deliver.

By integrating value-based strategies, alignment with Blue realities becomes relevant to meeting personal and departmental objectives. ORANGE–Green in human resources departments is freer to recruit, develop, and retain capable, talented, and enthusiastic personnel. Corporations that use the value-systems approach know that this is not just about using the language of memes at the workplace. Using this approach develops sustainable practices that facilitate effectiveness and efficiency while enabling the company to predict and flex with changes affecting its market.

When I consult with Middle Eastern corporations, I always present the "Big Picture" view of the Second Tier Seventh- and Eighth-Level value systems that see the region in terms of "holons." The word "holon" comes from the Greek and means something that is simultaneously a whole and a part. In value systems, this is a concept of the Eighth-Level Turquoise system. Although we are hundreds of years from having *life conditions* identified by Turquoise, any system that seeks that trajectory must be informed by these holistic values today.

Turquoise sees everything as part of a holistic, interdependent organism with complexity and deep intelligence within each part that makes up the entire organism we call Earth. Under this system, the smallest holon, the human being who possesses cognition and consciousness, must possess the same complexity as the largest holon, the global brain. Each part is a complex organism that must be appreciated for its own indigenous intelligence and made resilient in order for the entire ecosystem to survive, adapt, change, and thrive. In an integral approach to corporate practices, a design from the Seventh- and Eighth-level systems, is a reflection of the complexity within the individual and the team structure, which is in turn a reflection of the complexity of the organizations and institutions that define the town, country, and the region as holons within holons. This is what defines the interdependent nature of a holonic organism called Earth.

Before *life conditions* can begin to see the Turquoise system, much still needs to be done from the Yellow Seventh-Level system to fix the damage that the entire First Tier systems have caused. This is called the functional alignment of the First Tier as described before. When I consult with Middle Eastern corporations, I assess the region as a holon, the country as another holon, and the industry in which the company operates as yet another holon. These are the concentric circles that reflect the leadership, the culture, the systems, and the type of technical training that is needed in order to align practices on to a functional platform to serve the entire planet.

THE HOLONIC ECOSYSTEMS APPROACH
of the
Integral Insights Consulting Group, LLC

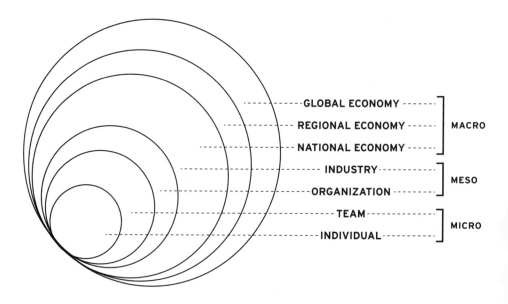

Figure 6.1 The Holonic Model of the Integral Insights Consulting Group, LLC

A WHOLE-SYSTEMS APPROACH TO MIDEAST CORPORATE PRACTICES

The Integral Insights Consulting Group was the first to bring this unique whole-systems approach to corporate practices in the Middle East. This comprehensive model emerged from the collaboration of Ken Wilber with some of the brightest minds in the consciousness movement today, including Don Beck. The AQAL model (All Quadrant All Levels) brings the best of the Integral Theory and Spiral Dynamics Integral Theory together. The model, at its basic construct places all holonic ecosystems into the eight-known levels of the spiral and places each level into the framework of the Four Quadrants that make up Integral Theory.

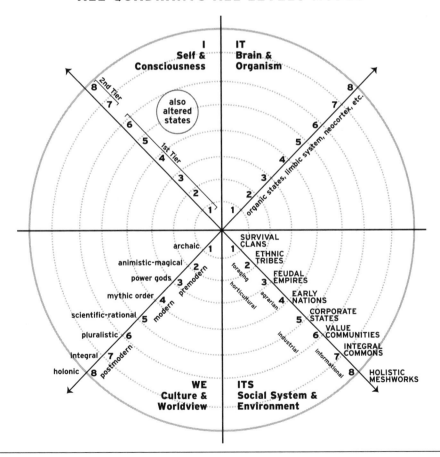

ALL QUADRANTS ALL LEVELS MODEL

Fig 6.2 Adapted from *The Theory of Everything* by Ken Wilber and used here by permission.

In addition to Quadrants and Levels, the AQAL model includes the evaluation of different intelligences, different states of consciousness, and the unique gender-approach to solving problems. In general, the framework sees the feminine as relational while the masculine is agentic.

When working at the micro and meso levels, multiple factors must be assessed to diagnose organizational capacities before deciding how to move forward in consulting. Our approach to consulting provides sustainability that goes beyond the quarterly and yearly financial results. It focuses on the long-term resilience that naturally becomes a tool of the Seventh-Level Yellow system.

What is Integral Consulting?

When it comes to corporate consulting the term *"integral"* refers to a comprehensive map of human capacities. The integral approach contrasts with other methods that exclusively employ psychological, behavioral, rational-scientific, or pluralistic approaches that consider other methodologies inferior. In other words, it is not a one-type-fits all methodology.

Other methodologies tend to generate partial analysis and incomplete solutions to problems. Integral leadership adopts a situational perspective recognizing and integrating the need for different approaches and different psycho-social language in different situations at the micro, meso and macro level. Integral consulting draws together existing paradigms from different theories, meta-theories, philosophies, and approaches to social and organizational management that are mutually enriching.

Using the values-system theory as its primary foundation, the consultant operationalizes different value systems within each social and organizational culture. For example, it could be forceful to channel Red's energy, conventional in handing Blue responsibilities, merit-based so that Orange can lead strategically, and could enable *servant leadership* to deepen the human connection in the workplace. This is how Seventh-Level Yellow leadership is deployed, and it is how Seventh-Level Yellow leadership capacities are developed in an organization or society. At its core, integral consulting is an *authentic* form of leadership that can speak the language of the less complex systems while continuing to empower the organization's long-term goals

The Model Both Transcends and Includes Previous Tools

By nature the integral model *transcends* the previous modes of operation and outdated perspectives. Unlike Orange-Enterprising consultants anxious to embrace the newest practices and abandon previous tools, this methodology recognizes where previous tools might still be beneficial in the developing world, so integral consulting *includes* them all. This is where Seventh-Level Yellow empathy is at work. What was abandoned in the 1980s in places where Green values emerged, is a very effective tool in a world that is just emerging into Orange.

The Model Also Anticipates Future Trends

As described earlier, the Risk Assessment and Horizon Scanning system used in Singapore is a localized version of the Vital Signs Monitor. This is the system we wanted to install with the Minister of Interior in Palestine during our work on the Build Palestine Initiative. By understanding how integral consulting is applied to a given corporate culture, the *anticipatory instinct* becomes second nature. It helps a society or organization capitalize on markets and limits exposure to wild cards.

The AQAL approach identifies the four areas, or quadrants of the Integral Theory as equally essential parts of a whole-systems approach to providing sustainable solutions. These four quadrants are worthy of closer examinations, as a designer of a Seventh-Level Yellow system must be aware of the capacities in the entire system and the environment in which the system operates before effective solutions can be designed. This holds true whether it is with organizations or at the culture-wide scale.

For businesses, the four quadrants give the four "environments" in which people, products, and services must thrive. The levels give us a value-systems insight on who the producer, the service provider, and the consumer are. In the AQAL model, the combination of levels and quadrants gives a multidimensional map of the market place, physical and virtual. The upper two quadrants are singular or individual and the lower two quadrants are plural or collective. The two left hand quadrants are interior and subjective, and the two right hand quadrants are exterior and objective.[106]

1. The Upper-Left Quadrant: This is the "I" Individual/Interior quadrant, that answers the question "Who am I?" This is the interior/intentional quadrant within a person. It deals with the individual and his or her levels of development along the eight stages outlined as the "psycho" in the bio-psycho-social approach of the Beck-Graves framework. From magical Purple and Egocentric Red, all the way to the emergence of some "integral-self" Yellow individuals. This quadrant also includes Howard Gardner's *Theory of Multiple Intelligences.*

2. The Upper-Right Quadrant: This is the individual/exterior quadrant within a person, "IT." This is the quadrant that deals with the brain and the biology of the individual and answers the question "what are my capacities?" In this quadrant the individual expresses the behavior that is motivated by his or her value system, or the psycho-spiritual aspect of his or her Upper-Left quadrant. This is the quadrant where we determine the type of technical training needed for an executive or an employee.

3. The Lower-Left Quadrant: This is the Interior/Collective quadrant of an organization or an institution, the "WE" space. It deals with the intangibles and the unspoken norms that develop the unique expression of a company or an institution. It spans from Purple rumors and the scientific/rational Orange to the whole system approach of Yellow in corporate and institutional practices. Once the corporation or institution embraces higher values and beliefs, it will naturally eject an individual who's a closed system as an improper fit.

4. The Lower-Right Quadrant: This is the Exterior/Collective quadrant of an organization or institution and is identified by the "ITS" space. This deals with the social systems outside the environment in which an organization operates. This includes the tribes who control resources, the nations that lead their peoples' destinies, and the corporate nations that make global commerce go round. In this quadrant fall systems and complexity theories, macroeconomics, geo-political systems, and global environmental and industrial policies.

In my work with corporations, I always start with the Upper-Left Quadrant. In this part of the model we look to evaluate the intelligence capacities of individuals, their value systems, and their ability to manage others. Most of the methodologies we use in these quadrants are based on the theories of multiple intelligences as they relate to value systems.

Among the first academic researchers to uncover the field of multiple intelligences was Harvard developmental psychologist Howard Gardner who outlined this pioneering framework in his 1983 book *Frames of Mind: Theory of Multiple Intelligences.* In this book Gardner claims that intelligence is not just a measure of cognition. There is scientific proof that intelligence can fall into many categories, such as linguistic, logical–mathematical, moral, verbal–bodily–kinesthetic, interpersonal, intrapersonal, visual–spatial, musical–rhythmic, and naturalistic.[107]

A prime example of understanding multiple intelligences is someone who has spacial intelligence who can be moved from an administrative job and become a vital part of a design team. I met many employees who had degrees in design, marketing, and psychology who have been in secretarial

ALL QUADRANTS
At the Organizational Level

	INTERIOR	EXTERIOR
INDIVIDUAL	**UPPER LEFT (I)** **Intentional** Emotional Intelligence Motivation Theory Y	**(UPPER RIGHT) (IT)** **Behavioral** Products, Services Individual Performance Theory X
COLLECTIVE	**LOWER LEFT (WE)** **Cultural** Shared Values & Beliefs "What really matters in this organization"	**(LOWER LEFT) (ITS)** **Systems** Systems Theory, TQM/Six Sigma, Reengineering, Balanced scorecard

Fig 6.3. Adapted from *The Theory of Everything* by Ken Wilber and used here by permission.

positions where their potential was greatly underutilized. By assessing employees' capacities with the multi-intelligence model, we can unleash their potential for growth by moving them to departments that fit their type of intelligence, whether in HR, marketing, the design division in a company's real estate department, or whatever they seem to be passionate about and can prove they have the type of intelligence to excel in.

In short, knowing how to assess the nature of what a person possesses can place him or her in the right function where they are happier and more productive. These types of assessments align the talent of the management team with the goals of the company, with an eye always on cultural sensitivities.

Of the different intelligence training models I offer as a part of this quadrant, the Emotional Intelligence training seems to be the most popular with most of my clients' employees. This is an integral approach to emotional intelligence that I call EQ*i*. It is an essential model that provides employees with tools to recognize and acknowledge their own feelings, and how to manage those feelings and know what triggers their reaction to a stimulus.

Once this is mastered, the person can learn how to recognize other people's emotions and be able to appreciate what the other person in a professional or personal relationship is dealing with. I have seen EQi training create a culture of common bonds in an organization where such camaraderie was not apparent before. This awareness becomes a trigger to address corporate culture as whole departments, individuals, markets, customers, and suppliers.

As a whole-systems approach, all four quadrants in an organization have to be evaluated and addressed at once. Without upgrading the operating systems in the Lower-Right quadrant, efforts often fall short of reaching the goals the management wants to achieve. This is where we work with the finance department on cutting cost, with the operations division on implementing Total Quality Management, and with Human Resources on making sure the benefit packages are competitive enough to attract and retain talent.

Because of the *life conditions* in the region Red-Heroic leaders initially ran most companies I worked with. These corporate leaders bring their own personal style of leadership—largely experiential and less complex than the capacities of some of the executives in the company. In a company that deals in franchises, for example, Heroic values tend to thrive on acquiring the largest number of franchises, regardless of the quality of the product or whether that brand is sustainable in the marketplace. This value system builds the tallest building, the largest mall, and the Five-Star hotel without the market intelligence needed to determine the long-term viability of the project. This is Red-Heroic capitalism at its best.

Several companies called on my services to contain the damage caused by the lack of long-term planning. In many of these cases the culture was so embedded in the unhealthy practices of Red expansionism, and seeking prestige and personal reward, that often a structural change was required at the core of how the corporation did its business.

As previously stated when describing the Beck-Graves model, the transition from the Red Third-Level system is the hardest transition in culture. It is also the most difficult transition in organizations. Depending on the leadership's commitment to the change and how far they can look into the future, the transformation of management practices can take as long as five years to achieve. With the support of the senior management, in many cases the maturing visionary families that own these businesses, together we purge the unhealthy aspects of the Red culture, including the individuals who are resistant to change.

An example of unhealthy Red behavior in the corporate culture would be an executive who paints an image of the profitability of an acquisition target without providing real data and feasibility studies. He or she then convinces the owners to buy the enterprise at an astronomical price, collecting commissions on both ends. One might be surprised at how widespread these practices are. Western executives indulge in these types of practices just as much as anywhere else I've consulted. Such predatory behaviors take advantage of family values in a region or organization. We see Red unethical practices at every level of an organization and must sometimes purge those employees in order for the organization to move up the spiral.

INTRODUCING ORDER-DRIVEN STRUCTURES TO MIDDLE EASTERN CORPORATIONS

In almost all my experiences with Middle Eastern corporations, we had to implement a multi-year program aimed at realigning corporate practices. This is the difficult shift from the intuitive, egocentric operation of a Red system to the power of institutionalized constructs within a Blue system. We always start with a strategy to steer the corporation back on a course based on universal ideals that are at the foundation of Blue structures. Much like our approach within a culture, we begin by defining a superordinate vision of what the future of the organization looks like in the long term. This is the future pull—the superordinate goal—that we design in visioning sessions with corporate leaders.

Often we have to revisit much of the initial core values that created the Vision of the company, its superordinate goal, and adjust it in accordance with the internal capacities of the executives and the external challenges of the marketplace. With a RED–Blue starting structure, the noble past becomes a part of the future pull that enables us to set new goals for improving employee morale, efficiency, and productivity. This places everyone in the company on a clear career path that defines the core values anew. Every employee must become familiar with these core values as they identify the way the company approaches internal communications, processes and procedures. Any employee from the retail clerk or the factory worker all the way to the senior executive must take pride in saying "This is how we do things here at XYZ Company." Or "This is the XYZ Way."

This strategy is very similar to the order-driven phase of IBM that proclaimed the superiority of "the IBM way." This alignment of people with vision helped IBM dominate the mainframe computer market. Once the goals of this phase are achieved, we begin to implement strategies that can align human and financial resources in order to meet the newly declared superordinate goal.

The commitment to this Order-Driven Blue stage of corporate realignment is to redefine the company's core business both vertically and horizontally. Generally this is a multi-year effort where the first phase is the focus on righting the ship by aligning it with best practices that are also informed by the *Indigenous Intelligence*. This almost always involves cutting waste, tightening accounting procedures, and closely scrutinizing costs. Rigorous key performance indicators are introduced in every department to assure alignment toward the company's future pull.

Business expansion through acquisition of other companies is often expected to either revitalize an aging organization that has lost its entrepreneurial spirit, or in a growing organization like many in the Middle East, the entrepreneurial leadership feels so successful in its enterprise that it seeks to diversify impulsively. These patterns are exemplified in the Adizes Corporate Lifecycle mentioned earlier. The Integral Consulting exercise at either stage moves the organization away from misalignment with the appropriate future pull and the reality on the ground. Instead, we move a growing organization toward a disciplined approach and conscientious corporate culture that keeps its eye on both long-term profitability prospects, the right fit of an acquisition, and the right type of leadership for each organization. This requires careful evaluation on multiple levels, rather than impulsivity. The acquisitions memetic structure must be diagnosed just as carefully as the parent firm.

This is the whole-systems integral approach that is functional with organizations at any stage of their lifecycle and when facing any *life conditions* either internally or externally. The Integral Consulting approach facilitates strategic and tactical methods in all systems, including operations, marketing, and finance, and must be informed by a due diligence process administered by resilient and motivated team of managers.

With regard to the organizations of the Middle East, a superordinate goal pulls people forward, creating an element of engagement and a sense of ownership that calls on the people's best qualities to participate in the design of a new and sustainable Fourth-Level Blue platform. This is particularly critical for growing organizations. This is the important stage where evolutionary change will determine the long-term sustainability of the corporation and its ability to expand organically with a robust corporate infrastructure. Processes and procedures become the structure through which new employees are initiated into the system and grounded in a solid Blue foundation.

BUILDING ENTERPRISING CORPORATE VALUES WITH COMPLEXITY

Much like advanced cultures in the ORANGE–Green value systems that are built on solid Blue foundations, Middle Eastern corporations can take the lead in regional emergence by pursuing strategic Enterprising goals, and moving the corporate culture from the Heroic-Red values to the Order-Driven Blue values.

I begin exploring, with the owners and the senior management, how to benchmark and implement best corporate practices. These are Strategic-Enterprising values that have resilience built into them. Expansion, diversification, and capturing larger market share all become part of the lexicon at the weekly meetings in corporate boardrooms. By nature, the Enterprise Fifth-Level Orange system is optimistic and seeks to uncover the mysteries of the universe through objective observation and scientific rigor. New management teams ascend to leadership positions after transforming the culture of a company to one empowered by its adaptability to the ever-evolving marketplace. Many of the companies I have worked with are now being run like Fortune 500 companies. Considering they are family-owned businesses, they're capable of preserving the warmth of Purple, the Heroic Red, and institutionalizing Blue, while being on the cutting-edge of global business practices in operationalized Orange, and this includes the huge market demographic focused on corporate social responsibility in Green.

This whole-systems approach must be guided intentionally to bring about incremental but sustainable change to Middle Eastern corporate practices with an eye on a new era that goes beyond the Age of Oil. My goal is to support Arab businesses to focus on their most valuable resources: the Millennial Generation and women. The next stage of development for the corporate world in the Middle East is self-reliance, gender equality, and non-discriminatory practices against the young generation.

These are the types of integral skills that the region needs to develop in order to compete with emerging markets. A recent conference in Doha, Qatar, highlighted the urgent need for the region to start to focus on its resources beyond the Age of Oil.

The most precious resource is the human resource. The development of human capacities has always been the key that transitioned cultures to advanced economic capacities. This transition starts with the commitment to transform existing practices at the organizational and personal levels so that they will eventually lead to national and regional transformation.

Don Beck focused his efforts on transforming businesses in the extractive industries in South Africa as a strategy to help the country transition from apartheid. In the Middle East it starts with visionary CEOs and government agents, such as former Palestinian Prime Minister Fayyad, who can strategize for decades into the future. As that ethic spreads throughout the culture, these practices will reach a tipping point where the entire region can be transformed.

A whole-systems approach to corporate practices has proven to me that transformation of the Middle East is possible. We have seen the essential changes in people and institutions, in organizations and in government as the region continues to attempt to realign its objectives. The necessary imperatives are taking hold in the hearts and minds of the people where the value-system approach has been used just as they would in the rest of the region if they're designed from a whole system, culture wide approach. It has been proven that the cutting-edge Orange meme represents the future of the Middle East, and organizational management is the core that could turn the entire region towards a prosperous future.

An integral consulting approach combines best practices and integrates them into a whole-systems approach that emphasizes resilience. This type of transformation is rarely achieved without the coalescence of power, authority, and influence of all the stakeholders within the society or organization. This is precisely the kind of bravery the region needs to become a serious contender in a highly competitive global economy.

SEVEN

The Arab Memome Project: Designing for the 21st Century Arab Renaissance

I always ask: How can I help? What can I do for people? How can I improve people's lives? That's part of my value system. It's too late for me to change that system, but it isn't too early for me to say to the world that the Dubai narrative is all about changing people's lives for the better through smart capitalism, willpower and positive energy.[108]

—Sheikh Mohammed bin Rashid Al Maktoum
Ruler of Dubai
Wall Street Journal
January 12, 2008

While oil wealth has brought Orange memes to the region, it hasn't been able to attract the complex Orange entrenched in science, medicine, and technology. Because of this unique value-system interpretation of wealth, the culture has remained primarily centered in Purple kinship values. Business ownership and leadership succession plans in the Middle East look a lot like business values that dominated the economic landscape of the United States from the late 1800s to the early 1900s. While corporate practices in the region can look Orange, the corporations exist in PURPLE–Red *life conditions.*

These are businesses run by families with immense wealth. While historic Orange prides itself on scientific discoveries and continues to improve on human capacities as an expression of modernity, the Middle East has remained on the outskirts having the trappings of the Orange ᵛMEME without the substance. The next frontier for the region is not how to get better management consultants to improve on the Orange memes already there, but how to get leaders to create the habitats that will naturally encourage the culture to emerge into more complex Orange expressions that can sustain their countries beyond the Age of Oil.

GENESIS OF THE ARAB MEMOME PROJECT

Don Beck advocates for the pioneering view that human cultural memes mimic human biological genes. Beck continues his alignment with the most advanced scientific research regarding the function of human DNA. The Human Genome Project is one of the largest collaborative international scientific research efforts ever undertaken. Its primary goal is determining the sequence of chemical base pairs that make up the human DNA. The project intends to identify and map the genes of the human genome from both a physical and functional standpoint.[109]

While the Human Genome Project aims to decode human DNA in order to better understand the building blocks and evolution of our species, the Memome Project aims to decode human cultural DNA in order to better understand human sociocultural structures and the evolution of human groupings. Because of the double-helix nature of the value-systems framework that couples the "base pairs" of *life conditions* with *adaptive intelligence,* there is a physical and functional definition to memes. Beck will address these parallels in his upcoming book, *Humanity's Hidden Code.*

The idea for creating the Arab Memome Project came to us at the Center for Human Emergence Middle East while Dr. Beck and I were in the midst of our work on the Build Palestine Initiative. More precisely, it came to us after years of research and work diagnosing *life conditions* that exposed weak spots in the fabric of the development of the region. This is when we came to realize that far greater institutional complexity in the region needs to emerge in an indigenous way in order to accommodate the confluence of several factors that will profoundly impact the future of Middle-Eastern culture.

+ The first factor was the deluge of global memes influencing cultural emergence and change through the World Wide Web. The Information Age knocked down the walls supporting traditional values, exposing the culture to numerous wildcards and scenarios. The density and rapidity of the information coming through in the last couple of decades has been so significant that it has the potential to accelerate the collapse of the existing socio-cultural constructs in the region.

+ The second factor was the failure of development models, throughout the region to recognize the importance of building human capacities within the culture to deal with the rate and type of change.

+ The third concern was, whether the Age of Oil ended in twenty years or forty years, there was no contingency plan to employ the culture of the Millennials who account for 60 percent of Arab society. This was and still is quite disturbing.

+ The fourth concern was the marginalization of 50 percent of the culture—the women. To us, this represents the pivotal force for moving the culture to the next stage of emergence. Although there are subcultures of women in the middle and upper class who are leading businesses, the majority of women are excluded from the process.

+ Our fifth and final main concern was, once we identified these threats to the future of the region, how do we move forward with funding the implementation of the Arab Memome Project?

No leadership outside the region or a single ally in the world could undertake this massive initiative regardless of their interests. This is an undertaking that has to come from within the culture and has to be a reflection of the indigenous will to emerge. This is the challenge that will define the shape of regional leadership for decades to come. The Center for Human Emergence can only act as a catalyst that informs business and political leadership on the trajectory of the stages of human and cultural development. We will design what we think is an effective and comprehensive cultural emergence plan that helps leaders navigating the road ahead. Most think tanks can only inform Middle Eastern leaders of the ominous challenges they face, but unless these leaders start to think from the future, emergence will continue to be arrested. The CHE-Mideast proposes to design a region-wide Mesh-WORKS, with culture specific needs to initiate the transformational process. This is where we call on the Heroic archetypes in the region to rise to this challenge and create a new Arab Renaissance.

This is the New Frontier in Arab cultural emergence. What we aim to do is to memetically map out the entire Middle East. We have a global network of *Integral Design Architects* (IDAs) who are ready to support the CHE-Mideast and are proficient in the value-systems approach. Many hold advanced degrees in social and industrial psychology with decades of experience in organizational and cultural work based on the value-systems approach. All have had close work relationships with the founders of this innovative school of thought. They have developed proprietary technologies and can identify the functions that need to be performed. Unlike the linear plans that developed the physical infrastructure of the region, our memetically-honed strategies will be informed by local *Indigenous Intelligence Experts (IIEs)* that have the knowledge of the economic, political and religious construct of their unique culture. They will be trained in the value-systems approach relevant to their areas of specialty.

As we did in Palestine, we will conduct full assessments of *life conditions* within every country. Once this extensive data is collected, the same MeshWORKS approach that was used in South Africa, Iceland, the Netherlands, and Palestine will be used to design a resilient plan for overall Middle Eastern emergence. This is not a one-size-fits-all approach as we only design strategies after exhaustive assessment of the needs of an individual culture. We support the specialized experts in their field in shaping and implementing their strategies to support the sustainable movement of the culture to its next stage. This is where Seventh-Level Yellow leadership in the Middle East will be able to see the big picture with our help and be able to navigate to it successfully and plan for a bright future accordingly.

We know from our experience in South Africa and Palestine that a systemic transition of a culture from the Purple Kinship and Red Heroic value systems to their next level of development involves the spreading of the memes of *prosper and let prosper*. While the Gulf Cooperation Council has experienced an entry level into the Enterprising value system through oil wealth, other parts of the region still struggle with the disparities between the haves and have-nots. The solutions for both parts of the region are to begin building institutions and laws to which all citizens subscribe, which also support the Millennials and women. These are the values on which a prosperous culture rests. A Seventh-Level Yellow leadership in the region will regard the design of institutions as a functional necessity for the emergence of their countries.

GOALS OF THE ARAB MEMOME PROJECT

Based on our decade of experience with this theoretical framework in the region, and in preparation to launch the Arab Memome Project, our research has uncovered some areas of exploration worthy of Memetic analysis and closer examination. Below is a starting platform envisioned to ignite the conversation about the future of the region. It is intended to give birth to a new paradigm in developmental thinking about the future of the Arab world.

Developing a Robust Middle Class

There is no higher calling for the future of the Middle East than the building of an indigenously-informed capitalist system with a socially and economically-empowered middle class. This is the ultimate goal of the Arab Memome Project. Third-Level capitalism can lead to societal collapse if its efforts are not balanced by a system of checks and balances to assure that it serves the greater good of the people.

As cultural economist and Chief Operating Officer of the CHE-Mideast, Said E. Dawlabani, points out in his book *Memenomics,* this is precisely what happened in the United States as a result of predatory Red capitalism that led to the Great Depression. The only way forward for the United States was for its leaders to redefine its cultural and economic values through the power of institutions.

After going through more than a decade of severe hardship the culture emerged into a Blue order-driven stage of economic development. The building of government guaranteed programs regulated predatory businesses while encouraging institutions like banks, universities, and large corporations to be responsible to the country's citizens. This is an example of the types of institutions necessary to building a middle class. It was visionary leaders like Franklin D. Roosevelt who created many of the U.S. institutions that empowered the common family. This forever changed the economic dynamics of the most resilient capitalist society in the history of humanity. Much like Roosevelt's New Deal plans, the Middle East must embark on its own new deal that creates its own independent and resilient economic institutions with fair opportunity for all who want to participate.

In light of where the global economy is today, visionary Middle Eastern leaders must look to empower innovation by funding research and development that adds value to the global economy. They must also look to empower a region-wide work ethic that builds capacities and skills within people. Empowering a robust manufacturing sector capable of processing all the petroleum byproducts today, will lead to many manufacturing innovations in the future. This sector played a major role in building the global middle class elsewhere, and it can do the same for the Middle East. More importantly, it can direct the Red energy of youth without formal education into productive pursuits and give them a new purpose away from destructive Red activities.

Leaders must also empower the educated Millennial Generation by providing it with the same institutional infrastructure that advanced countries have in place today. This will also involve the reformation of how business in the region gets done. The guidelines for business resilience outlined in the previous chapter must eventually be embraced region wide. There's no doubt that the knowledge economy is going to continue to grow. This is an economy empowered by Seventh-Level Yellow values. All stakeholders must participate in making sure the region embraces the knowledge economy, or be left behind. This is the new Arab Renaissance. The Arab Memome Project intends to address the building of an Arab middle class. It will require leadership, commitment, hard work and strategic planning capable of looking decades into the future.

Today, despite all the competition and threats the U.S. economy faces, its middle class remains the most powerful economic group in the world. This is due mostly to institutions that were put in place decades ago to guarantee economic security. Today, the wealth of this nation comes from human productive output that, unlike natural resources, is resilient, infinite and renewable.

Although many in the Middle East disagree with the United States' foreign policy, its domestic economic policies of the 1940s and 1950s are what is next for the Middle East. This is what made the United States an undisputed economic superpower for decades. While per capita wealth is much higher in smaller, richer countries in the Middle East like Qatar, Kuwait, and UAE, there is no other country in the world today that boasts a higher average income for a population as massive as that of the United States, the third most populous country behind China and India. The per capita GDP in China and India for 2012 was $6,072 and $1,492 respectively.[110] For the same year, per capita income for the United States was $49,922, more than eight times that of China and thirty-three times that of India.

No other system has distributed more wealth to its population than the capitalist system in the United States. This is due to a powerful middle class that was empowered socially and economically through institutions that were put in place by visionaries who built Blue Fourth-Level institutions. No culture in existence today has prospered long term without the prominent presence of a middle class and the purchasing power it creates in keeping local economies resilient and the population aligned with values of self-reliance.

It took decades for the United States to realign the values that embraced the spread of the middle class, and the Middle East will not be able to institutionalize change overnight. The region has received its share of criticism for having some of the worst economic data for a region so rich with natural resources. Based on the most recent available research, the value of economic output for all Arab countries in the Middle East and North Africa (MENA) region amounted to just 2.9 trillion USD for 2012, with oil and natural gas accounting for 73 percent of total exports and 78 percent of budget revenues.[111] Based on these figures and the population of the region, per capita income amounts to less than $650.

When compared to 2012 figures from the World Bank, this places the region in the 162nd place in per capita income, between Zimbabwe and Mozambique.[112] Importantly, should oil and natural gas revenues disappear without an economic emergence plan in place, based on income distribution today, the region will be tied in last place with Malawi and Congo for the world's poorest countries (based on 2012 income).

These income disparities have been the primary cause of the Arab Spring. In rural areas of Egypt, for example where people live on less than $2 a day, the removal of food subsidies that caused the price of sugar and bread to rise 300 percent pushed the poorest people to the breaking point. This is the Middle East's version of the French Revolution happening much faster in the age of information and knowledge. Despite that, it will still take several decades for the region to emerge into an order-driven Blue stage of development. Just like the accelerated speed of the revolution, the emergence into a region-wide robust middle class will happen much faster if it is approached properly.

As we look to the future, the CHE-Mideast has formulated strategies that The Arab Memome Project can undertake to assure that the transition is an evolutionary process rather than a revolutionary one. Seventh-Level Yellow leaders have to begin today to facilitate the growth and distribution of per capita income to rival that of first world countries. By aiming for this lofty goal, the Middle East may be forever transformed.

Spreading the Memes of Prosper and Let Prosper

The forward march of progress has become unstoppable. The Information Age has hollowed the manifesto of the Middle Eastern dictator. Social, cultural, political, and economic progress are all now informed by a global platform of transparency. The power is shifting to the people and the people want better lives than those brought about by war, repression, and enmity. Middle East development might parallel Dorothy's journey in the movie *The Wizard of Oz*. Policies of repression could be compared to the arduous road towards the Emerald City. Along the road, many joined forces in seeking answers to what ailed them. They risked their lives on this difficult journey, only to realize that the great and powerful Oz, who was supposed to have all the answers, was nothing more than a little man behind the curtain. They found that the true road to redemption was self-reliance, which was always within their reach.

The little men behind the Middle Eastern curtain are dictators, former military rulers, and implementers of repressive policies that keep their cultures behind the times. What is next for the region is a painful transition from PURPLE–Red cultural center of gravity to BLUE–Orange values that are in touch with a changing global village, but with a pragmatic awareness of the disappearing oil reserves. The finite oil commodity has been the primary source of wealth for the region for a major part of the last century.

Historically, Europe lingered in the dark ages of closed Blue during the era of the Spanish Inquisition until the Industrial Revolution—the enterprising Fifth-Level system—that acted as a superordinate pull out of the Dark Ages and through a socio-cultural transition to higher values. Dr. Beck's work in South Africa exemplified the powerful role that businesses can play in contributing to cultural transformation. Similarly, with our Build Palestine Initiative, we created an *optimistic, enterprising* super-ordinate goal for the Palestinians in order to give them hope about their future so they could go about building the needed institutions to support their vision. These are the values that informed the progressive Palestinian Prime Minister Fayyad to pursue the best future for his people.

The memes behind "prosper and let prosper" have acted as a primary catalyst for cultural progress for centuries. The pursuit of these values, if approached through the proper memetic channels, can render previous dynamics of conflict obsolete in time. Long-term prosperity has a way of moving many of the Zealots, Ideologues, and Flamethrowers toward moderate positions regardless of the issues in any culture. It is only through the Order-driven Blue and Enterprising Orange center positions on the Assimilation Contrast Effect graph of a society that a culture will have long-term prosperity and can shield itself from the destructive dynamics of closed Blue, complacent Purple, and feudal Red values.

Understanding the Memetic Implications of the Miracle of Dubai

In a region dominated by traditional values and oil wealth, Dubai represents what is possible for the future of the Middle East. This miracle in the desert has proven to the world that, given the right leadership, societal development can move through several stages of progress at what seems to be the speed of light. These are Arab values at their best: heroic Red leadership combined with a strategic Orange long-term vision for sustainable prosperity. Although much criticism has been leveled at the speed with which Dubai is being built, much of that progress speaks to the possibility of the region's diverse future. The values of commerce are deeply rooted in the region and in the history of Islam. As the Middle East emerges into Orange Fifth-Level values, many in the Muslim world want to adopt the enterprising virtues of the Prophet Mohammed. Historically oil and natural resources have only been the preferred mode of trade for the region for a short and temporary period of time. No one understands the implications of this better than the ruler of Dubai himself, who set out to build a diverse economy that sees beyond the limitations of oil:

> *Dubai's varied economic activities depend on a policy to decrease dependence on oil as the sole source of income. We promote the development of the trade sector, agricultural reform, national industry and national and international investment.*[113]
>
> His Highness Sheikh Mohammed bin Rashid Al Maktoum,
> the UAE Prime Minister, Vice President, and Ruler of Dubai

Understanding the importance of economic diversity for the whole region can act as a catalyst to propel the Middle East out of its current dysfunction and on the road to economic sustainability. The Middle East can learn from Dubai's heroic journey and adjust their visions and business practices to accommodate the most critical development stages for the future of the region. These are values that I often speak of at organizational and corporate leadership forums. They have given my clients a sustainable competitive edge. Now these values are being echoed by the visionary leadership in the region. Economic diversity not only leads to minimization of future risk, it enables entire cultures to engage in more complex interactions and trade that will eventually become a source of self-sufficiency. It informs the designers of institutions on their need to be more in tune with the future instead of just honoring the past. It rearranges values at the macro-memetic level to anticipate what the future will bring and inspires its leaders, like Sheikh Al Maktoum, to serve that future promise.

In the past, without visionary leadership, cultures lingered in tribalistic Purple and feudal Red value systems for centuries. The right leader, or a benevolent monarch as in Dubai, creates *life conditions* that propel a culture toward higher levels of complexity. With the immense wealth that is present in the Gulf region, Sheikh Al Maktoum viewed money differently than many other leaders. He envisioned it as an important agent for the development of Dubai's infrastructure and institutions, and not strictly as a facilitator of conspicuous consumption and personal wealth. This mature, long-term view of money and wealth will serve the region long after oil has disappeared. Economic diversity that is guided by leadership aimed at building human and institutional capacities has created a "pull" or a *superordinate goal* for Dubai that is redefining the current and future development of the Middle East. It is realigning the memetic stack of the tiny emirate and placing it in a position of regional leadership.

While this visionary development plan was designed to bring Dubai to a level of memetic complexity that rivals the West, *life conditions* in the region are integrating their own unique and indigenous expression, becoming the envy of the Middle East. This is the type of charismatic healthy leadership the rest of the region needs—leadership that sees common prosperity as the only way out of the current progressive stagnation and bloody stalemate.

What Dubai embarked on was a major systemic risk, but also one of the most ambitious development plans in modern human history. It is bringing individualistic values of personal success into a memetic mix rich with tribal generosity and tradition that is changing the Middle East and setting it up for advanced development. It is a unique and indigenous trail that is being blazed by risk, brave experimentation, and the ultimate desire to advance the culture. In the process, many of the memes that are unique to the Fifth-Level Orange system, including individual empowerment and scientific and strategic values, are taking root and will advance the future economies of the region.

As often is the case with initial stages of emergence into higher values, certain wild cards can derail a culture's efforts in its forward movement. Dubai was no exception. Between 2000 and 2008, without much free market Fifth-Level Orange complexity and with very little Blue commercial guidance in place, Dubai became an attraction to speculative investment and global predatory financial behavior. Buildings that touched the sky were being put up practically overnight. Global investors were buying properties off plans and selling them for many times the original price before they were even built. It was an unbridled RED–Orange feeding frenzy served by an endless stream of global capital, and it was impossible to identify the real levels of demand and market prices.

Red capitalism combined with Orange greed unconstrained by Blue triggered the meme codes that provided the region with its first lesson on modern Fifth-Level Orange emergence. As the rush to build this city-state came to an end in 2008, many of its private sector participants learned the lessons of risk-taking, the understanding of free market forces, and the need to engage in strategic planning. These are three memes of a healthy, well-regulated capitalist system, which have emerged over the centuries to make capitalist cultures so unique today.

As a result of this massive speculation and the bursting of the first modern day real-estate bubble in the Middle East, something very unique emerged from Dubai. As an open system since the financial crisis, it turned its focus to building unique Fourth-Level, Blue order-system institutions that guarantee investor protection and provide Dubai with a future with long-term stability. This didn't happen willingly, as entry into the Fifth-Level Orange system falsely views the Fourth-Level Blue system as an inconvenience (at best). Unhealthy Orange will fight healthy Blue every step of the way because it gets in the way of free trade. Skipping a cultural development stage almost always results in vulnerabilities and wild cards that can set back emergence. Dubai's focus on building modern day Fourth-Level Blue institutions came just in time.

Blue was institutionalized by His Highness Sheikh Khalifa bin Zayed Al Nahyan, the ruler of Abu Dhabi, who agreed to bail out Dubai World, the state-owned holdings company that was left with hundreds of billions in debt at the end of 2008. Because Dubai World was born into a culture of speculation, without much Blue accountability, it lacked strategic long-term planning. As global cash dried up in 2008, it was left with many speculative and unfinished projects worth billions of dollars. Abu Dhabi's conditions on its bailout injected the necessary Blue that is now building a stronger institutional foundation throughout the UAE.

The brief history of Dubai, as an experiment of an open system within the context of a global economic village has given the region an example of how careful and visionary planning can move cultures quickly and place them on the path towards global competitiveness. Although Dubai might have stumbled in its ambition, its progress represents the most advanced emergence of both the Fourth and Fifth Levels (BLUE–Orange) of value systems in the region in tune with the future, while at the same time honoring a storied and proud past.

Creating a Regional Superordinate Goal

Just as His Highness Sheikh Mohammed bin Rashid Al Maktoum, the UAE Prime Minister, Vice President and Ruler of Dubai, created a catalyst for change by seeking a diversified economy and changing the regional dynamics, so must an economic superordinate goal set it on a trajectory towards long-term prosperity. Also, just as we did in Palestine by declaring a superordinate goal to create the "Mumbai of the Middle East" the rest of the region must create a pull that makes it abandon its current dysfunction and align its future with the memes of prosperity. It seems that the Middle East today falls into two dominant camps of thought:

+ The first sees the solution for economic inequality as a return to traditional Islamic values.

+ The second wants to pursue prosperity but hasn't a strategy to implement economic policies that lead to long-term sustainability of their vision.

Importantly: Based on the foundational construct of a superordinate goal, the declaration of this goal must speak to these two competing camps equally. It must inspire them each in a way that challenges their leadership skills to the point where they are willing to override any threat to the achievement of this goal. If the goal speaks to all competing value systems along the values spectrum, it will seamlessly move culture away from its polarizing positions and elevate regional leadership to healthy positions on the values spectrum:

+ The first position is a healthy Ideologue Blue empowered by the enterprising traditions of Islam while being informed by the emerging global Blue values.

+ The second is a Pragmatic Orange that sees the culture in a modern light and chooses strategic compromises that result in a win-win situation for all.

+ The third is the Conciliator world-centric-Green that deepens the human bond and soothes the bumpy divide seen in women and globalized youth, and between sects, castes, and social classes.

While the ultimate goal of the Arab Memome Project is to bring Orange complexity to the region, that superordinate goal has to be identified from a Natural Design Perspective. Seventh-Level Yellow must see the need for current Enterprising Orange practices to evolve into more inclusive and sustainable forms that invite the scientific perspective, and create the ecosystems that encourages research and development. A Seventh-Level Yellow superordinate goal begins to design structures that speak the specific language of each level of the culture. It begins to align those values in a way that everyone can relate to and aspire after. If it speaks to the emergent values of the region, prosperity will inspire all to participate. A carefully crafted superordinate goal for the Arab world would have language similar to the following declaration:

To bring long-term prosperity to the region through sustainable business practices that offer opportunity for all beyond the age of oil.

Today, although much of the region seems to be occupied with the Arab Spring, the calling towards a superordinate goal, although thinly veiled, is beginning to appear. While *life conditions* in Egypt pointed to the election of an Islamist president, his had the behind-the-scenes support of Zealots and Flamethrowers within the Muslim Brotherhood. This caused him to be overthrown. These are becoming the natural lessons for Islamists, perhaps teaching them to moderate their views. Zealots who support frozen ideologies are proving to be out of touch with the needs of the people once they are elected to lead. What people need most is a governing system that lifts their lives out of poverty, gives them an optimistic view of the future, enables them to make a decent living, send their children to good schools, and improve their quality of life. These are all elements that must be included in a superordinate goal empowered by the "prosper and let prosper" values of the future.

Aligning the Future of Government to Meet the Superordinate Goal

The most pressing challenge, after creating a regional superordinate goal, is to design the form of governance that fits every country and be able to design a national system for governance that still aims to align institutions with the memes of prosperity. To design the form of governance that fits every country, a Seventh-Level Yellow leader would have to follow the MEMEtocracy principles that are outlined earlier in the book. For the region as a whole, its citizens should shift their thinking away from the belief that government knows best, although this might be true in the gulf region since governments there play a crucial role in developing the county's infrastructure.

Any regulatory structure of the Fourth-Level Blue system cannot be the guardian of innovation in a resilient society. It must design institutions that encourage the private sector to be free to explore every aspect of modern innovation in technology, medicine, alternative energy, manufacturing, and financial services. Moreover, it must fund the institutions that support all these endeavors. Governments designed from the Seventh-Level Yellow will align all their institutions to serve the superordinate goal.

As a part of the Middle East's emergence into Fifth-Level Orange values, leaders must evaluate the role of government and limit the extent of its involvement that is not aligned with the memes of prosperity. The function of government has to be liberated from its traditionally bureaucratic and domineering structures. It must also offer guarantees of private property rights and women's rights, the primary pillars behind the success of the capitalist system. As the region looks to establish goals toward a sustainable future, it must address the viability of a resilient private sector. It is the innovative nature of the memes of private enterprise that have historically brought culture into higher levels of expressions.

These are some of the many essential tenets of successful capitalism. In the case of Dubai, these realizations came to Sheikh Al Maktoum early on as he called for a very limited role of government. The result of those decisions opened up Dubai to global and regional investment like no other part of the Middle East had seen in its history.

In the Gulf Region, oil wealth has made welfare states out of many of the countries and monarchies. This is an entirely different level of "welfare" than the type that is seen in the West. The West's stage of development is Order Driven-Enterprise (BLUE–Orange) values (in places like the United States, Australia, and the UK), plus Egalitarian/Humanitarian Green values in Europe and just developing in the United States and elsewhere. Their welfare programs are designed as temporary measures that aid the disadvantaged while they search for employment, for example. The focus of these governments is on how to make individuals productive members of society in the quickest way possible.

While Millennials in the Middle East who acquire high levels of education in countries with Enterprising and Egalitarian values (ORANGE–Green) prepare themselves to assume responsibility for taking their culture to its next stage of development, they come back to a place where generational inequality dominates the landscape. These are the things that our technologies will bring to the forefront when addressing the future of the region. Our goal will be to create a balance between the traditional belief systems—such as those which are guided by the motto of *always respect the elders because they know best*—to values that appreciate meritocracy and the acquisition of new skills that are essential for survival in a globalized economy.

A government designed from the Seventh-Level Yellow system has to gradually wind down its welfare programs as it shifts its values from the *benevolent caretaker* state (Purple) to the *accommodator of prosperity* state (BLUE–Orange). This has to be done even if the region discovers more oil or natural resource reserves. Otherwise it will not emerge into the complex expression of the Enterprising Orange system with built-in sustainability. The great majority of revenues from oil, as in Norway, can go into a national wealth fund that augments the long-term prosperity of the culture, not one that defines it.

Through the Arab Memome Project, the CHE-Mideast will design each half-step at a time within a value system from the center of the gravity of the culture. We move with the healthy pace of emergence, not with the false expression of a higher value system that collapses due to misalignment with the needs of the people. We remove blockages in lower systems to make them healthy. These are the crucial design elements in our philosophy as new systems begin to replace old systems.

The road to advancement would change the functions in which government operates. A globally-competitive government must fill its key positions based on meritocracy. Government jobs go to the most qualified in the function they are looking to regulate, as governance requires technocrats, not bureaucrats or members of the extended family, to run its affairs. There will be no room in the future Middle East for nepotism and favoritism. These are the old passive values that eventually lead to perpetual obsolescence of the culture. They are the things that keep societies behind, especially when the rest of the world is moving forward at a much faster pace.

Based on some of the concepts discussed earlier in the book, parts of the region that are going through rebellion now would have to be memetically evaluated. Sadly, they might need to go through much more bloodshed and even prolonged civil wars to come to a place where they say "never again." That place of crisis is where the foundation of an Order-Driven Blue culture is reached. In passing through the fire, it can begin to build anew. For those nations, the memes of prosperity will act as a pull that will hasten the realignment of culture to the regional superordinate goal. However, a predictable scenario for the next stage of MEMEtocracy for these states will be an autocratic form of democracy that runs the trains on time and builds order and discipline as a permanent infrastructure.

Aligning the Future of Capitalism to Serve the Superordinate Goal

Looking to the future, the region faces many economic issues that need to be addressed in order to align them with a new superordinate goal. Many business practices that have become embedded in the culture as a result of oil wealth in the Gulf Cooperation Council (GCC) have to be re-examined. Other practices in non-Gulf Cooperation Council countries that are a result of Red capitalist exploitation must also be addressed in order to depress the dynamics that caused exploitation in the first place. What would many GCC leaders do if they were informed by the same business models of global corporations like those of General Electric, which has a one hundred fifty-year strategic plan, or the Department of Natural Resources of Washington State, which has a two hundred fifty-year strategic plan?

What does economic prosperity look like beyond the age of oil? A newspaper article published in 2011 by the British daily *The Guardian* claims that Saudi Arabia will reach peak oil by 2030.[114] If these claims are true, are there contingency plans being put in place to diversify the economy in such a short period of time? The premise that wealth from oil revenue can support the generous welfare programs that these states have is a fallacy that shouldn't even be entertained. Even the notion that revenues from sovereign wealth funds from oil will provide a substitute for economic diversity will be very short sighted. The fund managers at Dubai World should serve as a stark reminder that what seems to be safe and diversified one day, could become a catastrophic financial liability the next. Should the future of the region be placed in the hands of global investment bankers, the entire Middle East will be set back for centuries at the first post-peak oil financial crisis.

The less affluent parts of the Middle East, due to past repressive leadership, are even further behind in the global race for advancement. Countries like Libya, Egypt, Syria, and the rest of the Levant have to be reformed and modernized. Institutions that are geared for basic human development need to be built for the first time. In short, metrics that align the culture with Enterprising Orange values have to inform every institution in every country in the region if it wants to be considered a global player on the global economic stage in the next century.

The most resilient quality of a capitalist society is its human capital. It is human resilience and investment in science, research, and development that will create diverse and sustainable economies. This is the shape of economic power of the future and the Middle East is already decades behind. At the core of a viable and diverse economic sector is a resilient educational system that must be geared to educate the masses in skills and knowledge.

Aligning the Educational Systems to Serve the Superordinate Goal

The most important source of economic resilience is the pursuit of well-developed human capacities. Educational policies designed to serve the superordinate goal of the region will naturally move the leaders away from developing oil fields and make them focus on developing capacities of their people. Our Arab Memome Project calls especially on the Millennial Generation and women to be an integral part of this process. This is the only way that the more complex forms of global economic values can become a permanent part of the future of the region.

Seventh-Level Yellow leadership in education must be present at the ministerial level in every country in order for the region to meet its superordinate goal. A committee of Seventh-Level Yellow thinkers must have full authority, full CAPI, for setting educational policy. They must make education as the number one national priority and that declaration must be heard in every home and on every street. This committee must be void of any nepotism and corruption and must have an independent funding mechanism.

Seventh-Level Yellow leadership in education must be able to set specific advancement and performance measures that meet the needs of a competitive global economy. They must be able to align the educational aspirations of Arab youth with the best educational practices in the world. A Seventh-Level Yellow education requires the pursuit of partnerships with educational institutions and businesses to offer both STEM (Science, Technology, Engineering, Math) and broad-based scholarships based on merit or need for students of all ages. Scholarships should also support the arts and the trades and continuing education for adults. This will act as an insurance policy against the generational ill-effects of poverty. Leaders must be able to work effortlessly with regional economic centers of employment in order to determine future needs of the labor force, create a partnership with the private sector, and align with employers to provide internship opportunities and real-world work or research experiences.

An example is the newly created King Abdullah University for Science and Technology (KAUST) in the town of Thuwal along the shores of the Red Sea in Saudi Arabia. This is an institution like no other in the Middle East. In its short four years of existence, it is being dubbed as the MIT of the Arab World.[115] It is an oasis of research and development that attracts global scientific talent to its campus. This is indigenous, complex Orange in its earliest stages of existence in the region. It must be nurtured and made to grow. KAUST represents a self-sustaining ecosystem for scientific discoveries, a symbol of what is to come should the region make the serious commitment to move past the Age of Oil. An ecosystem made up of a multitude of KAUST-like institutions represents a resilient and organic emergence of a self-sustaining region grounded in the most advanced scientific practices. However, a university system alone cannot provide educational excellence for the entire culture. Early childhood education must be aligned with the region's superordinate goal.

The minds of future generations have to be shaped from an early age when a child enters grade school. Since the Arab Memome project calls for an Integral Design approach, parents will play a critical role in embedding the memes of self-reliance and the virtues of resilience as early as possible in a child's home life. The schools must place emphasis on the latest advancements in math and science as early as possible. While many elementary and secondary schools in the West tout the virtues of the Egalitarian-Humanitarian school systems, these models should not be copied in the Middle East. These schools will not be the proper memetic fit for the region. The educational system must go through several decades of teaching BLUE–Orange values that build the foundational stones of a culture while it attempts to compete on its own merits in a global economic marketplace.

Since this is a whole-systems approach, Seventh-Level Yellow leadership in education must address the qualifications of teachers and administrators and determine their alignment to the superordinate goal. Teaching as a career must be redefined as one of the most rewarding careers based on merit, and appropriately generous compensation should attract the most qualified teachers for the jobs. In addition to a focus on math and science, debate clubs must be fostered to encourage critical thinking and logical, rational and objective thought processes among students as early as possible.

Teachers recruited by a Seventh-Level Yellow educational system must be put through a prequalification process to insure their capacities and abilities to deliver on what's needed to meet the educational goals set to meet the superordinate goal. Administrators must also have awareness of the goals of the Seventh-Level Yellow leadership. They must always be searching for the newest teaching innovations that are adopted into the learning environment by the most successful schools around the globe.

These are some of the recommendations that the CHE-Mideast has identified as the economic, political, developmental, and educational issues that will inform the much larger Arab Memome Project. Final implementation plans would have to be adjusted as *life conditions* vary from one nation to the next as we're called upon to design for a specific country or part of the region. For now this will create a starting point for the debate on many of the reforms that await the Arab world. A more collective view on the future of the Arab child has to be debated in order for an organically designed system to emerge. Without addressing the kind of educational reforms the region needs to compete in a global economy, no economic reforms or superordinate goals of any kind would have a lasting effect.

A REGION ON A HERO'S JOURNEY

Building a modern-day Arab Renaissance starts with the goal of building a prosperous middle class that naturally turns the culture away from the ill effects of poverty and idle toil. This is an ambitious long-term project that requires the systemic involvement of all stakeholders in the region and in every nation, as that nation emerges at its own pace. The future survival of the wealthy and ruling class will depend greatly on their ability to be the visionaries of today. They have to believe that by adopting values of making wealth instead of taking wealth, they will increase the opportunities for all instead of continuing down the path of economics that create protectionist and destructive values. They have to be the ones who see with clear cognition that in absence of nationalistic programs for inclusion, the bloody Arab Spring will become the bloody Arab century.

The Arab Memome Project calls on these Seventh-Level Yellow leaders to take an active role in building the institutions that will transition the culture through one of its greatest historic challenges. Structural changes at all levels and sectors of society must begin today in order for the region to resume its glory from where it left off before the Industrial Revolution. As the title of this book implies, there is certain urgency for the region to *Emerge*. In order to do it right, the visionary leaders from within the culture have to rise and meet the challenges of joining an increasingly globalized world.

For me personally, although I live a comfortable life in the West, as a native of this land I feel the urgent calling of my ancestors to help. It is the historic duty that is embedded in the DNA of the Ghassanid Tribe and the entrepreneurial Phoenician spirit that runs in my veins. My ancestors were the nomadic people who originated from the Arab Peninsula and have never stopped caring about improving the lives of others for the better. They fought against the Persians and many other dynasties to preserve the Arab character of the region. Many have embraced the virtues of Islam while many remained Christians. Today, as Arab Nationals we have to redefine our values in terms of what the future looks like in the context of the global economic reality.

This is where a new journey for Arab heroism starts. The modern history of cultural emergence in the Middle East is filled with so many false starts. The region has suffered enough, from Nasserism and the fascist ideologies of the Baathists that were misaligned with the region's values, as well as from the military dictators who arrested the emergence of their people. Meanwhile, oil has done little to create economic values that add sustainable wealth and prosperity, and that must change.

My next-door neighbor in the West is a self-made Internet multi-millionaire, yet he takes joy in cleaning his own yard and trimming his own trees. These are the values that were created by the large middle class who emerged from the Industrial Age. It was the virtues of self-reliance that taught him and millions like him how to innovate and add value to a culture empowered by human capacities. By writing this book my hope is that my brother's children and their children in the future will live in a culture that champions the virtues of self-reliance and equal opportunity for all.

Today, the long-awaited journey for self-determination has begun. The Arab Spring is an organic movement that is led by a globalized Arab youth who can no longer accept the status quo. With unwavering bravery they have answered the call without being aware of the bloody consequences.

There will be setbacks and many false starts. There will even be temporary downshifts and a possible return to dictatorships and military rule. There will also be a need for the Muslim Brotherhood throughout the region to reevaluate what the movement stands for. Should it disappear into the underground or join the democratic process? Would it choose to be further polarized into the fringe of radicalism, or come to the middle position of their spectrum of values and push away their own radical elements? Their first chance at leadership in Egypt proved that zealots and flamethrowers can hijack the future of the region. Would they go back to the drawing table and try to formulate a strategy on how to evolve the movement into a more pragmatic position and participate in fruitful governance, or would the radicals continue to define what the movement stands for?

If the goal of MEMEtocracy is to make democracy functional, a post-Arab Spring in the Middle East points to many more decades of functional autocracy and benevolent, but functional monarchies. Those are the right forms of governance that will guide the region out of its current dysfunction. They have to be informed by the *Indigenous Intelligence* that directs the culture at its own pace, while empowering all its stakeholders for a more prosperous future for their children and grandchildren.

This is how the bravest heroes set out on a journey—often filled with pain and trepidation, but most of all with hope. Similar journeys in other parts of the world were just as painful and trying. What the region has in its favor today is that time has been accelerated considerably. Social networks, the knowledge economy, and the region's wealth reserves can substantially shorten the cycle of emergence. Global memes will continue to provide transparency until the developmental gaps between the region and the rest of the world narrow. Leaders who embrace the virtues of transparency, and recognize the invaluable power of institutions and the importance of a resilient private sector, will be the ones who will lead the Arab world to its 21st Century Renaissance. Let the journey begin.

FUNCTIONAL DEMOCRACY & THE EIGHT LEVELS OF HUMAN EXISTENCE

Copyright © Elza S. Maalouf and Dr. Don E. Beck 2014

ᵛMeme Levels	Meaning of Democracy	Political Form
8	• Global Governance • Macro management of all life forms • Seeking the common good in response to Global problems • Mix of holistic, cooperative, intuitive & cognitive systems	• Holonic Democracy • Whole-earth Networks • Interconnection of geo-consciousness • Self-organizing governance systems
7	• A process of integrating the majority of all the first tier political systems into a functional form of governance that works for all • People have the right to be who they are as long as they are not hurting anyone or the planet • Balance of government & private sector based on functionality	• Functional Democracy • Forms of governance that work based on value-system profiles and stages of development • Stratified systems designed with the input of the Indigenous Intelligence
6	• Everybody shares equally in reaching consensus • The purpose of the system is to care for "we the people" and the common good • Equal access to all resources by all people • The human bond has priority over political manipulation	• Social Democracy • Coalition governments • Highly successful in homogenous European societies • Taxes private enterprise to spread social services equally
5	• Pluralistic politics • Game of incentives within a system of checks and balances • Federal governance with full rights to states and provinces. • Relationship with losing party is to the strategic advantage of the winner • System turns politicians into corporate lobbyists after service	• Multi-party Democracy • Corporate states, Super PACs • Bill of Rights • Economic status sets power ratios resulting in wider gaps between the haves and have-nots
4	• Justice and Fairness for all • Everyone is equal under the law • Good people follow the law, rules and traditions • Disputes resolved through institutions and legal procedures • Duty to pay fair share to support the system • Autonomy and individuality is not encouraged. • The right to defend my country	• Authoritarian Democracy • Nation states • One Party Rule • Heavy hand of government • Winner takes all and rules all without input from the losing minority parties
3	• Whatever the Feudal Lord says it is • "Power to the People" is power to the clan leader and the chosen few • Feudal Distribution System • Institutions are vacuous—designed to enrich self and cronies. • Rich get richer, poor get poorer • All accept haves-have nots as reality	• Dictatorship • Feudal Empire • Domination • Corrupt autocracy • Strong-arm tactics • Patriarchy • No clear national political platform
2	• What our people decide to do. • Announced by the chief • Guided by the elders/mystical forces *This form of governance exists only in mixed systems with levels 3 and 4	• Tribes • Clans • Councils • Extended family • Lineage
1	• Survival-based groups • Genetic memory/instinct	• No concept of governance

^{V}Meme Levels	Perception of One Person, One Vote	Percent of Global Population in each Value System (^{V}GPS)
8	• Governance and voting decisions copy nature's movements, changes and patterns • Voting decisions are both a distinct and a blended part of the larger compassionate whole	• Won't appear until political systems are centered in the 7th level of values **0% ^{V}GPS**
7	• Recognizes that one person, one vote works for societies with dominant ^{V}MEMEs at the non-ideologue 4th Level or higher • Works with benevolent leaders within the 3rd and 4th level ^{V}MEMEs to establish institutions leading to one-person, one-vote systems in the future	• Germany (entering) • Northern Europe (entering) • Switzerland (entering) • Intelligent Cities in US and Canada (entering) **3% ^{V}GPS**
6	• Votes are important, but the loser still has an equal voice • Makes sure there is group consensus on a candidate before voting • Vote goes to the candidate who most supports the environment, social programs and gender equality	• Western Europe (mixed) • Northern Europe • Canada (mixed) • US (entering) **8% ^{V}GPS**
5	• Individual votes are highly valued and go to the candidate who shares voter's views • I vote for candidate who provides opportunity for personal success and financial achievement • The higher my net worth the higher the potential to steer political outcomes	• US, UK, Canada, Western Europe, Japan (mixed) • China (entering) • So. Korea, Singapore (entering) **24% ^{V}GPS**
4	• Votes matter to the one party that has all the right answers • Vote in line with family, church, and other civic groups who know the one true way • Candidate who shares my ethnicity and views on nationalism gets my vote	• Egypt (entering) • China (mixed) • So. Korea Singapore (mixed) • Russia, India (entering) • Eastern Europe • US, Japan (mixed) **27% ^{V}GPS**
3	• Votes go to feudal lords and Za'eems • Descending voters get eliminated from the political process. Opposition is thrown in jail, out of the country or killed. • Voting for winning candidate grants access to power • Power could be seized the next day	• Middle East, India (mixed) • Africa (mixed) • So. America (mixed) • Parts of S.E. Asia (mixed) • China (mixed) • Russia (mixed) **33% ^{V}GPS**
2	• Individual votes don't matter and are not encouraged by the group/tribe • Chief knows best • Full group allegiance to 3rd level leader, or 4th level ideology	• Middle East, India (mixed) • Africa (mixed) • China (mixed) • So. America (mixed) **5% ^{V}GPS**
1	• No concept of governance	**0% ^{V}GPS**

KEY: In the ^{V}GPS column, mixed system indicates more than one value system defines the country or region's political form. Entering means the values of the next system are emerging but don't define the country/region's institutions and electoral process yet. No designation indicates the corresponding system is the dominant form of governance.

Appendix A: Global Values Monitor: The Iceland Case Study

The Global Values Monitor by Dr. Don E. Beck
An Overview:

In 2005, Capacent Gallup in Iceland performed a pilot study using a research tool developed by Dr. Beck called the Global Values Monitor (GVM).[1] The purpose of the study was to detect the primary priority codes and worldviews, or the ᵛMemetic profile, of the Icelandic nation. A copy of the questionnaire follows.

In her dissertation paper, Marilyn Anne Hurlbut (1979) gave a detailed account of the development and test of the GVM questionnaire, with these additional goals:

1. Translate Graves' theoretical levels of existence into discrete components of attitude and behavior which could then be assessed with a written test instrument

2. Create such a written instrument

3. Test the instrument for reliability and validity (p. 1).

Hurlbut concluded that the new *Levels of Existence Test* "meets the standards of reliability and validity accepted within psychometrics, sufficiently to recommend that it be revised and further researched" (p. 205). Developers subsequently revised the test based on Hurlbut's recommendations.

Template for GVM questionnaire: Iceland

The 2005 and 2007 survey was constructed in four parts or vectors while in the 2009 survey, part 2 was excluded:

1. Values Survey

2. Country and Cultural

3. State of Change

4. Self Analysis

---

1 Information about the survey technique and products relating to Dr. Beck's tools can be found at http://www.onlinepeoplescanservices.com/info.asp

The Values Systems Part

Following is a description (in form of words or sentences) of seven different core values. Pls. provide your estimate on the importance of the values within the Icelandic culture and whether they are in the rise or decreasing in importance:

The questions related to both the perceived importance of the different core values or value systems and whether respondents felt they were on the increase or the decrease in importance. People were given statements they were supposed to rate "of critical importance" on a scale from 1–9, and on the rise on a scale from 1–9. The questions into each value system was divided in 3–4 sub-questions to make it easier to relate to the different traits described within each value system. Furthermore respondents were asked to prioritize the different values systems.

The results from the 2005 pilot and 2007 were quite dramatic in terms of the perception as to rising or decreasing strength of the value systems. The graph below shows clearly the polarities forming within the society:

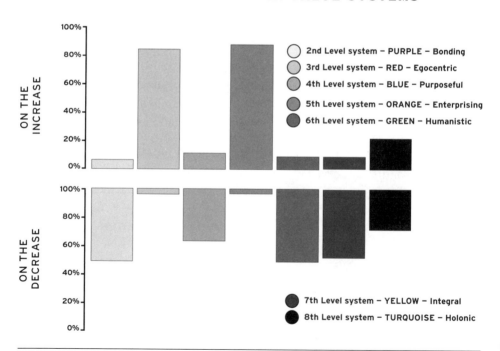

DIRECTION OF CHANGE IN VALUE SYSTEMS

These results from the 2007 survey, in which over 90% of respondents felt the egocentric and enterprising values system were on the rise, dominating the more sociocentric value systems. Looking at what happened a year later, with the financial crisis. The predictability of the results seem clear in hindsight, while no one really understood at the time the survey was done what it really meant.

Another example of the predictability of the values part is relating to the below results from the 2009 survey, where people were asked to prioritize the values system. A comparison is made with the 2007 survey (in black) to illustrate what was changing:

OVERAL RANKINGS OF VALUE SYSTEMS

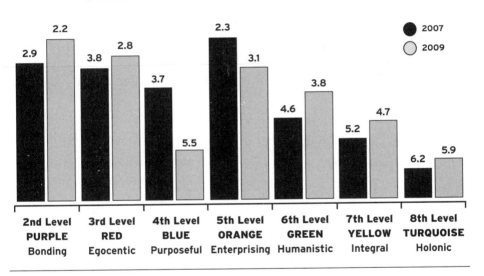

The 2009 survey was done just three months after the crisis. One of the most significant result of the survey is the fact that the Blue purposeful value system, relating to emphasis on law, order, discipline, sacrifice now for later rewards had dropped to having the lowest priorities. Everyone assumed that the crisis had resulted in the opposite, i.e. more emphasis on these attributes. A new government took over at this time and set out for major reforms in the social system. As it happened, there was little interest and the government had the biggest loss of votes in the history of the Icelandic republic. Contrary to assumptions, the general public has occupied with something quite different.

The State of Change

The 2007 and 2009 GVM surveys also employed the Change State Indicator; its phases are described as follows (Beck & Cowan, 1996, p. 85):

Alpha: stable and balanced. No change is needed.

Beta: uncertainty—there is something brewing, but I don't really know what it is.

Flex: in the process of change, confident in my ability to reach New Alpha stage without major difficulties.

Gamma: anger and confusion. Problems are piling up and I can't see any way around them. The situation is becoming overwhelming. If this condition persists, it will lead to a trapped state of mind, which blocks the ability to envision change.

Delta: inspired enthusiasm, out of the Gamma situation and on a surge upward to a new, healthy state of being.

New Alpha: stability in the next priority code in response to change in life conditions.

VECTOR THREE: STATE OF CHANGE

Questions were the following:

Different countries or cultures go through different Stages of Change. In this case, select the one statement below that best represents the overall state or condition in your country. You may pick only one.

Everything's OK and the world is basically stable.	O
Serious trouble is brewing beneath the surface.	O
Society is evolving gradually into a way of thinking that can solve the new problems and challenges.	O
Society is dangerously trapped behind barriers and is helpless and hopeless.	O
Society is revolting against the old order as it strives frantically to break free.	O
Society has overthrown the barriers and is now on a clear, steady course to a better future.	O

The results here also showed clearly how the wisdom of crowds operates in a social setting when analyzing the general situation. The results shown below are from the 2009 survey with the 2007 figures in solid black for comparison.

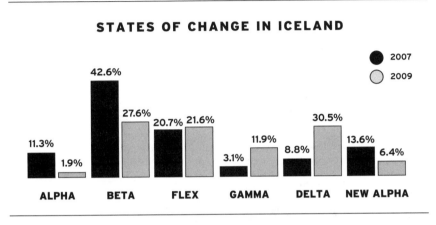

Figure 1. Comparison of Icelanders' perceptions 2007 and 2009

What is significant here is the high Beta value in 2007 as compared with the 2009 results, and the high Delta value in 2009 as compared with the 2007 analysis. In 2007 things were going better than any time before in Iceland's history, economically that is. No one should have had reason for concern. However almost half of the people were concerned and another 20% through there was a change going on. This supports the fact that the revolution or crisis happens way before it appears.

This analysis indicates that contrary to popular belief, Icelanders detected signs of decline already in 2007 in their life circumstances. A desire for change was evident in this period, indicating evolutionary pressures and readiness for system reformation.

Country and Culture

The third part of the study also included a predictive tool analyzing the traits of the people and culture. Referring to the same development during the last eight years, since the 2007 survey, the results showed clearly the reason why the people fared badly in the financial crisis, but also showed clearly as well, what traits would be crucial to recover quickly from the disaster. The results speak for themselves, but in the survey, people were asked to rate to extremes, as to where they felt the Icelandic nation was situated.

IMPRESSIONS OF THE ICELANDIC SOCIETY

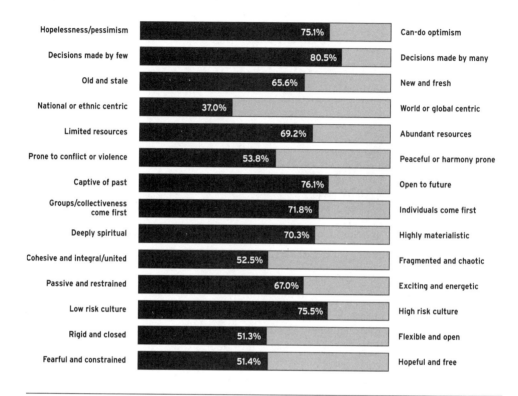

Hopelessness/pessimism	75.1%	Can-do optimism
Decisions made by few	80.5%	Decisions made by many
Old and stale	65.6%	New and fresh
National or ethnic centric	37.0%	World or global centric
Limited resources	69.2%	Abundant resources
Prone to conflict or violence	53.8%	Peaceful or harmony prone
Captive of past	76.1%	Open to future
Groups/collectiveness come first	71.8%	Individuals come first
Deeply spiritual	70.3%	Highly materialistic
Cohesive and integral/united	52.5%	Fragmented and chaotic
Passive and restrained	67.0%	Exciting and energetic
Low risk culture	75.5%	High risk culture
Rigid and closed	51.3%	Flexible and open
Fearful and constrained	51.4%	Hopeful and free

References

Beck, D. E. (n.d.). The many dimensions of change. Retrieved from http://www.spiraldynamics.net/the-many-dimensions-of-change.html

Beck, D. E., & Cowan, C. (1996). *Spiral dynamics: Mastering values, leadership, and change.* Cambridge, MA: Blackwell Business.

Beck, D., & Mackey, J. (2009). The upward flow of human development: Maps of the terrain. In M. Strong (Ed.), *Be the solution: How entrepreneurs and conscious capitalists can solve all the world's problems* (pp. 277-304). Hoboken, NJ: John Wiley & Sons.

Hurlbut, M. A. (1979). *Clare W. Graves' levels of psychological existence: A test design.* Retrieved from UMI Dissertation Express. (8000791).

Appendix B: The Global Values Monitor General Questionnaire

Template for GVM questionnaire—Your Country

First Part: Values Survey

Following is a description (in form of words or sentences) of seven different core values. Please provide your estimate on the importance of the values within your country and whether they are on the rise or decreasing in importance:

Q1
(Everyone)
Kinship Bonds–Mythical:

How important or unimportant do you think the following attributes are to your country?

	Critical Importance								Minimal Importance
Ethnic roots and respect for ancestors and older people	9	8	7	6	5	4	3	2	1
Folkways, lore, traditions and myths	9	8	7	6	5	4	3	2	1
Superstition	9	8	7	6	5	4	3	2	1
Close family ties providing safety and security against the outside world	9	8	7	6	5	4	3	2	1

Do you think the following attributes in your country are on the increase or the decrease?

	On the Increase								On the Decrease
Ethnic roots and respect for ancestors and older people	9	8	7	6	5	4	3	2	1
Folkways, lore, traditions and myths	9	8	7	6	5	4	3	2	1
Superstition	9	8	7	6	5	4	3	2	1
Close family ties providing safety and security against the outside world	9	8	7	6	5	4	3	2	1

Q2
(Everyone)
Egocentric–Imperial:

How important or unimportant do you think the following attributes are to your country?

	Critical Importance								Minimal Importance
Need to do things your own way	9	8	7	6	5	4	3	2	1
Living for the moment, no concerns about the future	9	8	7	6	5	4	3	2	1
Impatience, demands for quick results and rewards	9	8	7	6	5	4	3	2	1
Media is occupied with heroic leaders who command respect	9	8	7	6	5	4	3	2	1

Do you think the following attributes in your country are on the increase or the decrease?

	On the Increase								On the Decrease
Need to do things your own way	9	8	7	6	5	4	3	2	1
Living for the moment, no concerns about the future	9	8	7	6	5	4	3	2	1
Impatience, demands for quick results and rewards	9	8	7	6	5	4	3	2	1
Media is occupied with heroic leaders who command respect.	9	8	7	6	5	4	3	2	1

Q3
(Everyone)
Patriotic–Order Driven:

How important or unimportant do you think the following attributes are to your country?

	Critical Importance								Minimal Importance
Faith in superior power and the purpose of life	9	8	7	6	5	4	3	2	1
Forego impulsive acts through discipline to gain future rewards	9	8	7	6	5	4	3	2	1
Belief in a cause, system or ideology	9	8	7	6	5	4	3	2	1
Nationalism	9	8	7	6	5	4	3	2	1

Do you think the following attributes in your country are on the increase or the decrease?

	On the Increase								On the Decrease
Faith in superior power and the purpose of life	9	8	7	6	5	4	3	2	1
Forego impulsive acts through discipline to gain future rewards	9	8	7	6	5	4	3	2	1
Belief in a cause, system or ideology	9	8	7	6	5	4	3	2	1
Nationalism	9	8	7	6	5	4	3	2	1

Q4
(Everyone)
Progressive–Achievement

How important or unimportant do you think the following attributes are to your country?

	Critical Importance								Minimal Importance
Materialistic, strategic, pragmatic	9	8	7	6	5	4	3	2	1
Technology improves standard of living	9	8	7	6	5	4	3	2	1
You create your own fortune	9	8	7	6	5	4	3	2	1
Happiness is about personal achievement and tangible assets	9	8	7	6	5	4	3	2	1

Do you think the following attributes in your country are on the increase or the decrease?

	On the Increase								On the Decrease
Materialistic, strategic, pragmatic	9	8	7	6	5	4	3	2	1
Technology improves standard of living	9	8	7	6	5	4	3	2	1
You create your own fortune	9	8	7	6	5	4	3	2	1
Happiness is about personal achievement and tangible assets	9	8	7	6	5	4	3	2	1

Q5
(Everyone)
Sensitive–Sharing

How important or unimportant do you think the following attributes are to your country?

	Critical Importance								Minimal Importance
Warmth and concern for your fellow humans	9	8	7	6	5	4	3	2	1
Oppose racial, ethnic, gender and class divide	9	8	7	6	5	4	3	2	1
Equal rights for all	9	8	7	6	5	4	3	2	1
Humanitarian values are superior to materialism	9	8	7	6	5	4	3	2	1

Do you think the following attributes in your country are on the increase or the decrease?

	Critical Importance								Minimal Importance
Warmth and concern for your fellow humans	9	8	7	6	5	4	3	2	1
Oppose racial, ethnic, gender and class divide	9	8	7	6	5	4	3	2	1
Equal rights for all	9	8	7	6	5	4	3	2	1
Humanitarian values are superior to materialism	9	8	7	6	5	4	3	2	1

Q6
(Everyone)
Integral–Systemic:

How important or unimportant do you think the following attributes are to your country?

	Critical Importance								Minimal Importance
Balance between the individual and the whole	9	8	7	6	5	4	3	2	1
Emphasis on opportunity and prosperity for all	9	8	7	6	5	4	3	2	1
Individual responsibility is greater than collective mandates	9	8	7	6	5	4	3	2	1
High cognition of how everything is inter-connected	9	8	7	6	5	4	3	2	1

Do you think the following attributes in your country on the increase or the decrease?

	Critical Importance								Minimal Importance
Balance between the individual and the whole	9	8	7	6	5	4	3	2	1
Emphasis on opportunity and prosperity for all	9	8	7	6	5	4	3	2	1
Individual responsibility is greater than collective mandates	9	8	7	6	5	4	3	2	1
High cognition of how everything is interconnected	9	8	7	6	5	4	3	2	1

Q7
(Everyone)
Worldcentric–holistic:

How important or unimportant do you think the following attributes are to your country?

	Critical Importance								Minimal Importance
Emphasis on global common needs	9	8	7	6	5	4	3	2	1
Emphasis on "energy flow" and concern for life on Earth	9	8	7	6	5	4	3	2	1
The Earth regarded as one ecosystem	9	8	7	6	5	4	3	2	1
Worldview dominates institutions, individual thoughts and systems	9	8	7	6	5	4	3	2	1

Do you think the following attributes in your country on the increase or the decrease?

	Critical Importance								Minimal Importance
Emphasis on global common needs	9	8	7	6	5	4	3	2	1
Emphasis on "energy flow" and concern for life on Earth	9	8	7	6	5	4	3	2	1
The Earth regarded as one ecosystem	9	8	7	6	5	4	3	2	1
Worldview dominates institutions, individual thoughts and systems	9	8	7	6	5	4	3	2	1

Q8
(Everyone)
Priorities

Thinking about the above description of the seven core values, which do you think describes best your country? Prioritize the values where 1 is the best description, 2 the next etc. and finally 7 for the one you think is least descriptive.

Rank One through Seven in terms of priorities
where 1 is highest and 7 is lowest.

	Kinship Bonds – Mythical
	Egocentric – Imperial
	Patriotic – Order Driven
	Progressive – Achievement
	Sensitive – Sharing
	Integral – Systemic
	Worldcentric – Holistic

VECTOR TWO: COUNTRY AND CULTURAL

Indicate your impressions of your country based on these critical descriptions. You can only make one selection between the two end points

	High Intensity	Moderate Intensity	Mild Intensity	Mild Intensity	Moderate Intensity	High Intensity	
Can-Do Optimism	○ 5	○ 4 ○ 3	○ 2 ○ 1	○ 0	○ 1 ○ 2	○ 3 ○ 4	○ 5 Hopeless-Pessimism
Decisions made by a Few	○ 5	○ 4 ○ 3	○ 2 ○ 1	○ 0	○ 1 ○ 2	○ 3 ○ 4	○ 5 Decision made by the Many
New and Fresh	○ 5	○ 4 ○ 3	○ 2 ○ 1	○ 0	○ 1 ○ 2	○ 3 ○ 4	○ 5 Old and Stale
National or Ethnic Centric	○ 5	○ 4 ○ 3	○ 2 ○ 1	○ 0	○ 1 ○ 2	○ 3 ○ 4	○ 5 World or Global Centric
Abundant Resources	○ 5	○ 4 ○ 3	○ 2 ○ 1	○ 0	○ 1 ○ 2	○ 3 ○ 4	○ 5 Limited Resources
Conflict/ Violence Prone	○ 5	○ 4 ○ 3	○ 2 ○ 1	○ 0	○ 1 ○ 2	○ 3 ○ 4	○ 5 Peaceful/ Harmony Prone
Open to Future	○ 5	○ 4 ○ 3	○ 2 ○ 1	○ 0	○ 1 ○ 2	○ 3 ○ 4	○ 5 Captive of Past
Individuals Come First	○ 5	○ 4 ○ 3	○ 2 ○ 1	○ 0	○ 1 ○ 2	○ 3 ○ 4	○ 5 Groups/ Collective-ness Come First
Deeply Spiritual	○ 5	○ 4 ○ 3	○ 2 ○ 1	○ 0	○ 1 ○ 2	○ 3 ○ 4	○ 5 Highly Materialistic
Cohesive and United	○ 5	○ 4 ○ 3	○ 2 ○ 1	○ 0	○ 1 ○ 2	○ 3 ○ 4	○ 5 Fragmented and Chaotic
	High Intensity	Moderate Intensity	Mild Intensity	Mild Intensity	Moderate Intensity	High Intensity	

VECTOR THREE: STATE OF CHANGE

Different countries or cultures go through different Stages of Change. In this case, select the one statement below that best represents the overall state or condition in your country. You may pick only one.

Everything's OK and the world is basically stable.	○
Serious trouble is brewing beneath the surface.	○
Society is evolving gradually into a way of thinking that can solve the new problems and challenges.	○
Society is dangerously trapped behind barriers and is helpless and hopeless.	○
Society is revolting against the old order as it strives frantically to break free.	○
Society has overthrown the barriers and is now on a clear, steady course to a better future.	○

VECTOR FOUR: SELF ANALYSIS

Which of these groupings of words best describes you: (you may choose only one)

Spunky, risky, daring, often rebellious.	○
Self-reliant, autonomous, flexible with multiple interests.	○
Loyal, dependable, ordered with firm convictions and beliefs.	○
Ambitious, competitive, a "winner" with strong aspirations.	○
Society is revolting against the old order as it strives frantically to break free.	○
Warm, open, inclusive with focus on feelings and community.	○
Superstitious, tribal, with family/group/clan rituals.	○

Endnotes

1 Clare W. Graves, *The Never Ending Quest*, eds. Christopher Cowan and Natasha Todorovic (Santa Barbara, CA: ECLECT Publishing, 2005), 3-27.

2 Don Edward Beck and Christopher C. Cowan, *Spiral Dynamics: Mastering Values, Leadership and Change.* (Malden, MA Blackwell Publishing 1996, 2006), 29.

3 Svenja Caspers, Stepahn Heim, Mark G. Lucas, Egon Stephan, Lorenz Fischer, Katrin Amunts, and Karl Zilles, *Moral Concepts Set Decision Strategies to Abstract Values,* PLOS ONE Website, http://www.plosone.org/article/info%3Adoi%2F10.1371%2Fjournal. pone.0018451. Retrieved Jan 20, 2013.

4 Center for Human Emergence Middle East. http://www.humanemergencemiddleeast. org Retrieved January 20, 2013.

5 Egger, Vernon, *"A History of the Muslim World to 1405: The Making of a Civilization."* (New Jersey: Prentice Hall, 2009), p 33.

6 Adeeb Dawisha, *Arab Nationalism in the Twentieth Century, From Triumph to Despair* (Princeton, New Jersey: Princeton University Press, 2003), 39.

7 Dawisha, 3-4.

8 Robert Stephens, *Nasser: A Political Biography,* (New York: Simon and Schuster, 1971), 340.

9 Jeremy Jones, *Negotiating Change: The New Politics of the Middle East* (New York: I.B. Taurus & Co, 2009), 97.

10 Wikipedia: http://en.wikipedia.org/wiki/Palestine_refugee_camps. Retrieved January 14, 2014.

11 UNESCO, *Paper commissioned for the EFA Global Monitoring Report 2006,* Literacy for Life.

12 Elza S. Maalouf and Said E. Dawlabani "The Arab Spring; A Mythological Journey or a Myth?" *Kosmos Journal,* Fall-Winter 2011, 27-30.

13 Larry Persilly, "Norway's Different Approach to Oil and Gas Development," http:// www.arcticgas.gov. Retrieved Jan 31, 2013.

14 David D. Kirkpatrick and Mayy El-Sheikh, "Morsi Spurned Deals, Seeing Military as Tamed", *New York Times,* July 6, 2013.

15 Kareem Fahim and Mayy El-Sheikh, "Egypt, Dealing a Blow to the Muslim Brotherhood Deems it a Terrorist Group", *New York Times,* December 25, 2013.

16 Economy Watch, MENA Satistics and Indicators, http://www.economywatch.com/ economic-statistics/country/Middle-East/. Retrieved February 6, 2013.

17 Richard K. Vogler, *A World View of Criminal Justice* (Burlington, Vermont: Ashgate Publishing, 2005), 116.

18 "Erdogan: Democracy in the Middle East, Pluralism in Europe: Turkish view", *The Journal of Turkish Weekly,* http://www.turkishweekly.net/article/8/Erdo%3C011F%3Ean-democracy-in-the-middle-east-pluraliism-in-europe-turkish-view-.html. Retrieved January 18, 2013.

19 Beck and Cowan, 50.

20 Clare W. Graves, "Summary Statement: The Emergent Cyclical Double-Helix Model of the Adult Human Bio-psycho-social Systems," Boston May 20, 1981.

21 Don Beck and Graham Linscott, *The Crucible: Forging South Africa's Future,* Rev. ed. (Cheryl Beck representing the Center for Human Emergence, Denton, TX, 2011)

22 http://www.legis.state.tx.us/tlodocs/74R/billtext/html/SR00901F.htm. Retrieved January 20, 2013.

23 http://www.usb-ed.com/content/Pages/SA-hosts-key-global-gathering-on-sustainability-and-leadership.aspx#jFpuyOowYOueScli.99. Retrieved January 20, 2013.

24 http://www.grli.org Retrieved January 20, 2013.

25 Don Beck, Spiral Dynamics Integral, Large-Scale Psychology, *The Design and Trans-formation of Whole Societies,* http://www.spiraldynamics.net/2008/12/large-scale-psychology-the-design-and-transformation-of-whole-societies.html. Retrieved February 7, 2013.

26 Beck and Cowan 27-33.

27 Clare W. Graves, *The Never Ending Quest,* eds. Christopher Cowan and Natasha Todorovic (Santa Barbara, CA: ECLECT Publishing, 2005), 163.

28 Graves, 365.

29 From a discussion at the annual meeting of Evolutionary Leaders, San Francisco, CA, Nov, 2011.

30 Don Edward Beck, Spiral Dynamics Level 1 Course Manual (Denton, TX, Spiral Dynamics Group, 2006)

31 Beck and Cowan, 53,

32 Harm de Blij, *The Power of Place, Geography, Destiny and Globalization's Rough Land-scape* (New York: Oxford University Press, Inc. 2009), 256.

33 Beck and Cowan, 55.

34 Beck and Cowan, 63.

35 Beck and Cowan, 168.

36 Beck and Cowan, 42.

37 Beck and Cowan, 76-80.

38 Beck and Cowan 34-47.

39 Graves, 202.

40 Beck and Cowan, 202-215.

41 Beck and Cowan 215-228.

42 Roger Fisher, William Ury, Bruce Patten, *Getting to Yes: Negotiating Agreements Without Giving In* (New York: Houghton Mifflin Company, 1991) 33-35.

43 Beck and Cowan, 229-243.

44 Said E. Dawlabani, *Memenomics: The Next-Generation Economic System* (New York: SelectBooks 2013), 55-56.

45 Beck and Cowan, 245-259

46 Clare W. Graves, *The Never Ending Quest*, ed. Christopher Cowan and Natasha Todorovic (Santa Barbara, CA: ECLET Publishing, 2005) 315.

47 Times Higher Education World University Rankings http://www.timeshighereducation. co.uk/world-university-rankings/Retrieved February 18, 2014.

48 "Boardroom", Paddy Chayefsky, Network, DVD. Directed by Sidney Lumet, Los Angeles, CA: MGM, United Artists, 1976.

49 http://inventors.about.com/od/lstartinventions/a/Led.htm. Retrieved January 21, 2013.

50 Beck and Cowa, 260-265.

51 Graves, 339.

52 The Monroe Institute, http://www.monroeinstitute.org/. Retrieved Feb 20, 2013.

53 Graves designated levels of existence in alphabetical pairings with A through G representing existential problems, or Life Conditions and N through U representing the adaptive intelligences in the brain. G-T is the Seventh-Level Yellow system or the Yellow ᵛMEME in Spiral Dynamics.

54 Clare W. Graves, "Human Nature Prepares for a Momentous Leap," The Futurist, April 1974, 84.

55 Beck and Cowan, 279

56 Make it Right, Healthy Homes for Communities in Need, http://makeitright.org/. Retrieved 04-08-2013.

57 http://en.wikipedia.org/wiki/Allometry. Retrieved Feb 27, 2013.

58 Beck and Cowan, 286-289.

59 Teilhard de Chardin, *The Phenomenon of Man* (New York: Harper Collins Publishers, 1975), 259.

60 John Godolphin Bennett, *The Dramatic Universe, Volume 4* (London, Hodder & Stoughton Publishers, 1956), 130-131.

61 Beck and Cowan, 289.

62 Dawlabani, 67.

63 Winston Churchill, Churchill Speaks: Collected Speeches in Peace and War, 1897-1963, http://www.goodreads.com/quotes/tag/democracy. Retrieved 4-16-2013.

64 Elza S. Maalouf, *"South Africans Reinvent Themselves for the 21st Century"*, The Huffington Post, February 10, 2014. http://www.huffingtonpost.com/elza-s-maalouf/ south-africans-reinvent-themselves_b_4751851.html Retrieved March 11, 2014.

65 Alan Tonkin, *"Global Values Update; Evolving Values in the 21st Century, an Integrated View,"* Integral Leadership Review, January, 1 2009, (http://integralleadershipreview. com/4836-global-values-update-evolving-values-in-the-21st-century-an-integrated-view). Retrieved June 3, 2013.

66 Christopher Hellman, " *The World's Happiest (and Saddest) Countries, 2013,"* Forbes, October 29, 2013. http://www.forbes.com/sites/christopherhelman/2013/10/29/the-worlds-happiest-and-saddest-countries-2013/. Retrieved December 21, 2013.

67 Indigenous Intelligence, LLC. https://www.linkedin.com/company/indigenous-intelligence-llc. Retrieved 3/14/2013.

68 Theory of Multiple Intelligences, http://en.wikipedia.org/wiki/Theory_of_multiple_intelligences. Retrieved 3/19/2013.

69 L. Laubscher's PhD thesis is available as part of the permanent files of the Global Center for Human Emergence and is accessible to qualified researchers by contacting the center at http://www.humanemergence.org/

70 B. Jonsson's PhD thesis is available as part of the permanent files of the Global Center for Human Emergence and is accessible to qualified researchers by contacting the center at http://www.humanemergence.org/

71 Taken from a presentation made by Jonsson at the annual meeting of Spiral Dynamics practitioners' Confab in Dallas, Texas September 8, 2012 entitled "Searching for the True Blue: The Iceland Experience."

72 The Center for Human Emergence The Netherlands, http://www.humanemergence.nl/ Retrieved 3/3/2013.

73 Center for Human Emergence Canada, http://groupspaces.com/CHE-CAN/ Retrieved 3/3/2013.

74 Center for Responsible Politics, http://www.opensecrets.org/revolving/top.php?display=Z. Retrieved 4-24-2013.

75 http://en.wikipedia.org/wiki/United_States_presidential_election,_2008#Democratic_Party_nomination, and http://en.wikipedia.org/wiki/Results_of_the_2008_Democratic_Party_presidential_primaries. Retrieved February 20, 2014.

76 R. Buckminster Fuller. (n.d.). BrainyQuote.com. Retrieved May 20, 2013, from BrainyQuote.com. Web site: http://www.brainyquote.com/quotes/quotes/r/rbuckmins142431.html.

77 From a speech given by Beck at a Center for Human Emergence event in Austin, TX on March 9, 2013.

78 Whitley, B.E., & Kite, M.E. (2010). *The Psychology of Prejudice and Discrimination.* Belmont, CA: Wadsworth. pp. 325–330.

79 Sherif, M., Harvey, O.J., White, B.J., Hood, W., & Sherif, C.W. (1961). *Intergroup Conflict and Cooperation: The Robbers Cave Experiment.* Norman, OK: The University Book Exchange. pp. 155–184.

80 Sherif, C.W.; Sherif, M.S.; Nebergall, R.E. (1965). *Attitude and attitude change.* Philadelphia: W.B. Saunders Company

81 Beck, Don Edward (1966). *The Rhetoric of Conflict and Compromise: A Study in Civil War Causation.* University Microfilms, Inc., Ann Arbor, Michigan. p 226.

82 Jeff Poor, *Rachel Maddow compares Justice Antonin Scalia to a Racist Troll,* The Daily Caller, http://dailycaller.com/2013/03/01/rachel-maddow-compares-justice-antonin-scalia-to-racist-troll-video Retrieved May 23, 2013.

83 The Center for Human Emergence Middle East, UN position papers. http://www.humanemergencemiddleeast.org/. Retrieved June 12, 2013.

84 Beck and Cowan, 145.

85 The European Graduate School, Manuel De Landa. MeshWORKs, Hierarchies and Interfaces, http://www.egs.edu/faculty/manuel-de-landa/articles/MeshWORKs-hierarchies-and-interfaces. Retrieved April 23, 2013.

86 Taken from a speech given by Beck at a Center for Human Emergence Middle East event on May 3, 2003, in the West Bank. Video record available for examination at the CHE ME location in La Jolla, CA to qualified researchers.

87 Integral Israel http://www.integralisrael.org/english.htm. Retreived April 16, 2013.

88 Akiva Eldar, "The eight-stage spiral to peace in the Middle East," Harretz, February 12, 2006. http://www.haaretz.com/print-edition/features/the-eight-stage-spiral-to-peace-in-the-mideast-1.179848 Retrieved June 23, 2013.

89 "Excerpts of Olmert's speech pledging to resign." Reuters, July 30, 2008. http://www.reuters.com/article/2008/07/30/idUSL0225065 Retrieved June 25, 2013.

90 "Full text of speech "I regret my mistakes" Haaretz, July 31, 2008 http://www.haaretz.com/print-edition/news/full-text-of-speech-i-regret-my-mistakes-1.250899. Retrieved June 25, 2013.

91 Palestine Times, *Build Palestine Initiative; how to walk the talk,* January 26, 2007. http://www.humanemergencemiddleeast.org/docs/SDi_PalestineTimes. pdf?id=1459&arch=1&year=27&month=01&day=27. Retrieved July 5, 2013.

92 Don Beck and Graham Linscott, *The Crucible; Forging South Africa's Future* (Denton, Texas: Cherlynn Bec, Center for Human Emergence, 2011), 259.

93 Center for Human Emergence Middle East. http://www.humanemergencemiddleeast. org/build-palestine-blog/2008/02/palestine-emergence-in-the-words-of-one-of-its-enlightened-leaders. Retrieved July 8, 2013.

94 Center for Human Emergence Middle East, http://www.humanemergencemiddleeast. org/build-palestine-blog/2008/02/10-year-old-palestinian-girl-thinks-big-html. Retreived July 17, 2013.

95 Center for Human Emergence Middle East. http://www.humanemergencemiddleeast. org/build-palestine-blog/2008/02/palestinian-engineer-presents-ground-breaking-proposals. Retrieved July 9, 2013.

96 "Sixth Convention Fateh and the Building of a Nation," *Common Ground News Service,* August 20, 2009. http://www.commongroundnews.org/article.php?id=26127&lan= en&sp=0. Retrieved July 9. 2013.

97 What is a'MEME Barcode? http://spiraldynamics.net/barcode/ Retrieved July 9, 2013.

98 Tobias Buck, "Fayyad Boosts Palestinian Cause," *The Financial Times,* April 12, 2010.

99 Avi Yisasharof, "Palestinian Prime Minister Fayyad: A de facto state within two years," *Haaretz,* August 25, 2009.

100 Center for Research on Globalization, http://www.globalresearch.ca/what-kind-of-palestinian-state-in-2011-neoliberalism-and-world-bank-diktats/18638. Retrieved March 1, 2014.

101 Haaretz Digital Edition, http://www.haaretz.com/news/diplomacy-defense/full-transcript-of-abbas-speech-at-un-general-assembly-1.386385. Retrieved March 3, 2014.

102 United Nations Sixth-Seventh General Assembly, https://www.un.org/News/Press/ docs/2012/ga11317.doc.htm. Retrieved March 3, 2014.

103 The New York Times, (http://www.nytimes.com/2013/04/14/world/middleeast/ salam-fayyad-palestinian-prime-minister-resigns.html?_r=0) Retrieved June 20, 2013.

104 Wilber, Ken "Integral Business Practices." Training lecture, Integral Institute, Boulder, CO, October 2003.

105 Due to confidentiality agreements with this and other clients, I'm prevented from providing specific information other than the size of the client's company and the nature of the business. These cultural sensitivities are common throughout the Middle East and are in line with the values of the region.

106 Ken Wilber, *The Theory of Everything; An Integral Vision of Business, Politics, Science and Spirituality,* (Boston, MA: Shambhala Publications, Inc., 2000), 71.

107 Howard Gardner, *Frames of Mind; Theory of Multiple Intelligences,* (New York: Basic Books, 1983), 3-10.

108 Sheikh Mohammed bin Rashid Al Maktoum, "Our Ambitions for the Middle East," *The Wall Street Journal,* January 12, 2008, opinion pages.

109 The Human Genome Project (n.d.). In *Wikipedia.* http://en.wikipedia.org/wiki/Human_ Genome_Project Retrieved August 1, 2013.

110 The International Monetary Fund, *World Economic Outlook Database April 2013, Report for Selected Countries,* http://www.imf.org/external/data.htm. Retreived August 3, 2013.

111 Institute of International Finance, Economic research, the MENA countries, http:// www.iif.com/emr/mena/. Retrieved August 3, 2013.

112 The International Monetary Fund, *World Economic Outlook Database April 2013, Report for Selected Countries,* http://www.imf.org/external/data.htm. Retreived August 3, 2013.

113 Sheikh Mohammed bin Rashid Al Makhtoum, *Collection of Quotes,* http://sayingsearch. blogspot.com/2009/09/sheikh-mohammed-bin-rashid-al-maktoum_9184.html. Retrieved July 28, 2013.

114 John Vidal, "How much oil does Saudi Arabia actually have?" *The Guardian* [UK], August 8, 2011. http://www.theguardian.com/environment/blog/2011/feb/15/oil-saudi-arabia-reserves. Retrieved July 30, 2013.

115 King Abdullah University for Science and Technology, http://en.wikipedia.org/wiki/ King_Abdullah_University_of_Science_and_Technology. Retrieved July 31, 2013.

Acknowledgments

ON THE EASTERN PART OF THE SYRIAN DESERT, just east of the Jordan River, lies the town of Bosra Al Sham, an iconic symbol of the region's past civilizations. It was here during a moment of solitude on the steps of a Roman amphitheater in 2007 that the idea for this book came to me. The urgency to finish it came in February 2013, when the Syrian rebellion senselessly took away my friend and colleague Kassem Khalil, the mayor of the town. It is heroes around the world like Kassem who sacrifice their lives for a transcendent cause who should be acknowledged first.

So many people have made this book possible, that it would take a whole chapter to thank them all. First and foremost I owe a debt of gratitude to my mom, May Hayek, who contained me with her unbound love, taught me the values of individuality, and made me who I am today. I am equally indebted to the two Saids in my life for their unconditional love: My dad who defied tradition and nurtured my rebellious soul from a very young age; and my husband with his big heart, who understands me better than I understand myself, and who gave his invaluable contribution to this book. To my brothers who have the biggest hearts a little sister could ever want: Michel who carries the family's lineage as poet and philosopher, and who introduced me to my spiritual teacher; Ghassan, the hero, who always protected me and made me feel like a princess; and to Habib, who proved the Maaloufs can be successful business people as well as poets.

To my dear friend and colleague Don Beck, whose genius and courage to defy the status quo have inspired me for many years. Without his unconditional support and that of his wife Pat and daughter Belinda, this book would not have been possible. I also owe a depth of gratitude to my friend Jean Houston for her relentless inspiration to do the impossible and for the special moments of humor we continue to share. I would also like to acknowledge Deepak Chopra, the sage and the scientist for his encouragement and inspiration and to all the Evolutionary Leaders who work tirelessly on making our world a better place.

I am eternally grateful to my late Guru Sant Thakar Singh who set my soul on a journey of self-discovery and helped me deepen my consciousness. And to my spiritual sisters and brothers who live the simple life with enlightened souls. I am also thankful to Ken Wilber and the integral community for providing a prism that sees beyond the complexity of our modern lives. I am grateful to Dr. Ichak Adizes and Dr. Laura Frey Horn for the many opportunities they offered me to teach their graduate students. I also owe a debt of gratitude to my publisher Kenzi Sugihara at SelectBooks, Inc. for believing in the transformational nature of my work, and to my editor Nancy Sugihara for making my message clearer, and Kenichi Sugihara for expediting the entire process.

I owe a debt of gratitude to Joseph Farrah Maalouf, the legal scholar who took me under his wing and supported my activist spirit right out of law school. To my late friend Rose Farrah who provided me, at the age of fifteen an escape into a world of literature and art. And to Lynn Turner and Eva Johanesson for making me a part the first circle of conscious women that remains a cornerstone of my life today. I'm also thankful for my friend and colleague Kevin Kells whose service to humanity sets the example for what is important in life. For my childhood friend Lillian Ghantous, thank you for the precious childhood memories that have stayed with me for all the years. And to my dearest friend Rabih Ammoury for making me realize how urgently my work is needed in the Middle East.

Writing this book has been a labor of love and boundless joy for me. I am forever grateful for the support of my friend and colleague Fadwa al-Homaizi who embodies the quintessential Seventh-Level leader in Middle Eastern business. I am also profoundly thankful to my dear friend Sula Al Naqeeb who exemplifies the genius of the Millennial Generation that's changing the Arab world.

Finally, to my colleagues at the Global Centers for Human Emergence who make up our Turquoise tribe and work quietly behind the scenes to make the world a better place. Without your love, courage, and contribution, this book would not have been possible. For all that, I thank you.

Index

H

L

M